You Can Write A ROMANCE ... *and Get It Published!*

Never before has the opportunity to launch a writing career been so great! Thousands of romance novels are published every year. There are perhaps twenty different publishers of romances, and many have separate imprints to distinguish one type of romance from another. Why? Romances are **Big Money**. Harlequin Books alone sells nearly two hundred million romances a year, averaging a book a second!

If you've ever read romances and been a fan of the genre, you too can become a bestselling author. This complete handbook shows you how. It's a crash course on the publishing process, so you'll know what to expect and how to deal with it. You'll learn to become a professional writer—not only in the Romance genre—and you'll be amazed at how much you already know. You know simply because you've been reading and enjoying romance books—but didn't know how to analyze why some novels work and others don't. Yet it's easy to write a novel if you know the rules. Editors will welcome you with open arms if your work is done professionally.

Yvonne MacManus has written over 30 novels, 22 for Harlequin Books under pseudonyms. In various editorial capacities, she worked for major publishers such as Dell, Avon, Leisure, and Pocket Books, just to name a few. A former literary agent, she teaches university seminars and workshops on writing and editing. She's also a manuscript critiquer and, in her spare time, scripts videos.

"BUY THIS BOOK! READ THIS BOOK! LEARN FROM THIS BOOK!" As an agent I reject too many manuscripts because they do not follow the guidelines that romance publishers insist upon—and publishers' guidelines are no secret.

"You need to know the basics. All the basics. This book spells everything out. You have the tools at your fingertips. Use them! Go to it and much success to you."
— *Cherry Weiner*, Cherry Weiner Literary Agency

Author Yvonne MacManus

You Can Write A R❁MANCE...

and Get It Published!

Yvonne MacManus

Toad Hall
Press

Toad Hall Press

A division of:
TOAD HALL, Inc.
Rural Route 2, Box 16-B
Laceyville, PA 18623

Dedication

To all the writers with whom I've worked over
the years—whether I ultimately accepted your
manuscripts or not. I hope you learned as much
from me as I did from you . . . .

And to R.J.A.P., beloved Kubi, Taki, and
Haiku, and of course, Chiquita, Raisin, and Clancy.

TABLE OF CONTENTS

Preface from Kathryn Falk............................ i

Introduction to New Edition.......................... **vi**

CHAPTER ONE
You Can Write a Romance....................................... 1
> *Wherein we discuss the market in general, some*
> *history, and your prospects.*

CHAPTER TWO
The Manuscript: Your Calling Card...................................... 7
> *The importance of appearances and the necessity of*
> *providing a manuscript that's as professional*
> *as possible. Important to know; don't skip over*
> *(I'm watching!).*

CHAPTER THREE
The Blank Page before You...................................... 21
> *How to face the challenge of writing a book, from almost*
> *any perspective.*

CHAPTER FOUR
The Nitty-Gritty of Writing a Novel...................................... 29
> *Wherein you'd best know what good fiction techniques*
> *are from an editorial viewpoint. Vital to know.*

CHAPTER FIVE
The Worst Is Over ... or Is It?................................... 93
> *Understanding the practical side of the business.*
> *Do you need an agent, go the direct editorial route,*
> *or what? How to write a query letter and how*
> *submissions are handled.*

CHAPTER SIX

The Editor's Side of the Desk.. 109
Wherein the "other side of the story" is presented;
what an editor's day is like and how decisions are
reached. The perspective from the editor's viewpoint
and not the author's. The editorial process.

CHAPTER SEVEN

Details, Details.. 125
Understanding contractual terms and what they may
mean to the future of your work.

CHAPTER EIGHT

Fanfare and Hoopla.. 141
The decision-making process before your book is
published; publicity, promotion, advertising, etc.

CHAPTER NINE

The Denouement.. 151
A recap of fundamentals pertaining to writing a
romance.

APPENDIX

Glossary of Terms.. 154
A brief explanation of standard publishing terms.

Romance Publishers' Guidelines....................................... 165
What the major romance publishers are seeking.

Important Names and Addresses....................................... 205
Organizations and periodicals you should know about.

PREFACE

By *Kathryn Falk, Lady Barrow*
Founder and CEO of
Romantic Times Magazine

Since 1980-81, when sensual romances were demanded by female readers in response to the burgeoning women's sexual liberation movement, the American romance novel industry has doubled! Every American paperback publisher jumped on the bandwagon—created by Harlequin and Silhouette's short contemporaries and Avon's sensuous historicals. Various competitive romance lines followed to define and fulfill every woman's most sensuous fantasies. Some of the now-defunct lines had fascinating names: Ecstasy, To Have and To Hold, Second Chance at Love, Kismet, Circle of Love, and Velvet Glove.

This expansion led to a refining, a maturing, and a more sophisticated marketing of the genre. The result today is a rich variety of Historical, Contemporary, and Futuristic categories, reflective of modern women's tastes. By 1995, Romance sales grew to total 48% of total paperback sales.

In 1981, I started *Romantic Times* magazine, a monthly review publication geared to meet the needs of readers, booksellers, and published and unpublished writers. We review, rate and categorize approximately 120 new romances *each month*.

The average reader is a female over 30 years of age with some college education, who buys 20-40 books a month, spending more than $100 on her purchases and uses *RT* magazine as a shopping guide. She considers romance novels a hobby as well as a collectible, shops in speciality stores and friendly chain stores for her purchases, and probably receives some titles through a romance book club or as part of WaldenBooks Romance Reader program. Many of these bookstores are part of the *Romantic Times* network of 950 "Bookstores That Care," organized in the mid '80s. Many of these stores also carry second-hand books and service readers the way libraries used to do.

Unfortunately, romance novels have a very short shelf life (from three weeks to two months, in most cases). If a new reader wants an old title, these independent stores are usually the only available resource. When you're looking for a favorite author's backlist, or a friend's favorite "keepers," these stores are your only hope. "Keepers"—books readers keep on their shelves to re-read—are hard to find and many are worth quite a few dollars.

Anyone planning to write a romance first should read at least 100 of the "keepers." After studying them, choose to write the type of book you most enjoy reading. Obviously, if history is your forte, you'll study "keepers" in that category. If modern human relations and settings thrill you, long contemporaries are your direction. Break down your interests even more: romantic suspense; time travel, or the supernatural.

Doing extensive market research at a "Bookstore That Cares" is part of your training course. Open your eyes and heart to what readers want (arousal of emotions) and don't want (wimpy heroes or silly heroines). Remember, like fashion, romance novels are a culturally volatile, evolutionary, changing market. These books must reflect the readers' expectations and be a step ahead of their emotional awareness, which is why new writers are the life's blood that continues the genre. (Remember the duty of writers in the old days—to be the eyes of a reader's heart.)

Talk with knowledgeable booksellers. When a customer wants a new book (or a new dress), she wants something a little different each time, especially when she's buying so many! Fortunately, there are a wealth of sub-categories to choose from.

With **Historical Romances**—once termed by editors as "sex in hoop skirts"—you can choose various settings: **Viking, Medieval, American Civil War, American Revolutionary War, Regency**, along with **England, Scotland, Ireland**, particularly in the 15th to 19th centuries. Historical Romances can extend up to World War II.

Many authors favor the **Regency**, a rich historical niche set in England during the Napoleonic Wars. A special vernacular/slang flourishes in these witty novels. Read Georgette Heyer, Mary Balogh, and Jo Beverly; learn about *tweenies* and *rakehells*.

According to editors, **Swashbucklers** and **Indian/Western** romances are the most beloved sub-categories of the historicals. Look for books about pirates by Bertrice Small (Skye O'Malley) and Marsha Canham. Western and Indian heroes are found in titles by Roseanne Bittner, Georgina Gentry and Janis Reams Hudson.

The difference between a straight historical and an historical romance is the mix. There must be at least 75% romance in the plot to qualify as an Historical Romance—and that means more sensual tension than history.

When reviewing Historical Romances, the *Romantic Times* staff always notes if there is extreme violence in any of the historical scenes or if the heroine is overpowered by force bordering on rape, scenes that certainly stimulate fantasies in some readers and offend others.

Some of the hottest historical romance names are Nan Ryan, Susan Johnson, Thea Devine and Virginia Henley. Readers should look for an old classic, *Sweet, Savage Love* by Rosemary Rogers, in which one heroine took on entire continents and kept the bedroom door open while it happened! Bertrice Small, known as "Lust's Leading Lady," is also a "hot" writer.

The skills and techniques required to write a good Historical Romance have a rich history that still stands today. *Katherine* by Anya Seton, *Angelique* by Serganne Golon, *Kadin* by Bertrice Small, and *The Rosylynde Chronicles* by Roberta Gellis are classics written more than twenty years ago—and should be on every new writer's list! Judith McNaught, Catherine Coulter, Linda Howard, Jude Deveraux, Julie Garwood, Linda Lael Miller, Mary Lyle Rogers, and newcomers Catherine Anderson, Jill Barnett, Pamela Morsi, Diana Gabaldon, Kristen Hannah, Christina Sky, Andrea Kane, Judith O'Brien and Rebecca

Paisley are among the second wave of writers who are creating some of the classics of today. Saving the best for the last, Johanna Lindsey is the longest-running and most successful historical romance writer of all time and still writes two books a year.

A good romance sweeps the reader away from her reality . . . a relief all women need. Writers can place the reader in the heroine's shoes, allowing the reader's imagination to live in another world with new emotional experiences. And yes, the reader does fall in love and have an affair with a different man every night—if she's a fast reader! That's why romance readers have healthier sex lives. Women's deepest fantasies and emotions are the mainstay of romance novels. According to that *grand dame* of the genre, Barbara Cartland, still writing at the age of 93, "A woman of any age likes to feel loved by the man of her dreams, and in my books two souls meet."

Since love has no boundaries, neither does age. Romances can be shared (and written) by any female at any age and in any language. (A book on evolutionary psychology would help you understand what every woman craves, if you still aren't sure.) If you can stir *everywoman's* fantasies and emotions, you're on your way to becoming a successful romance writer. It may be a cliché, but you've got to "make them laugh and make them cry!"

One tip on writing a romance: be certain you know intimately a particular period of history or are very familiar with a particular modern setting (or are willing to master one)! Stick to that period or setting for several books. And consider if you're comfortable with *less* or *more* sexuality.

Romantic Times Magazine has a helpful rating on Historical Romances. If slightly sensual, the books are rated "Sweet"—i.e. the story leaves the sexual scenes to the reader's imagination. The majority of readers, however, go for Spicy books and especially Sexy ones—the more explicit and graphic, the better. Will this help? You can be like Judith McNaught, who writes her sex scenes *after* the manuscript is finished and—as the saying goes—inserts them carefully!

Short, contemporary romances are particularly sought after because they can be read in one sitting, or before falling asleep. "Better than Valium," claims Dame Barbara, who also favors the short page length. Her virgins usually kiss on page 152, in every language.

Harlequin (which also owns Silhouette) is the world's largest romance publisher, with editors/translators in all the major countries. This company specializes in short contemporary romances, sometimes 60 books a month, broken down into different lines such as Special Edition, Temptation, Desire, Shadows and Intrigue. Their leading authors (and there are many) include Nora Roberts, Linda Howard, Stella Cameron, Cathie Linz, Mary Kirk, Mary Kay McComas and Cheryl Reavis. (Recently they launched single-title, longer contemporaries by authors such as Heather Graham and Barbara Bretton.) The only other publishing house with a continuing program of short contemporaries is Bantam with its Loveswept line.

Every writer should pay attention to Harlequin/Silhouette's marketing skills. They use focus groups to keep their finger on the pulse of romance readers around the world. Editors—and special writers—are encouraged to plan innovatively. Harlequin's mail-order membership, rumored to be 700,000, is highly profitable. Recently the company produced four 90-minute romance films based on their own titles, which debuted in the Fall of 1994 on CBS's "Sunday Matinee."

You may wonder if Danielle Steel is a romance author. Steel insists steadfastly that she's *not* a romance writer. But stop five women in a bookstore and ask about their favorite romance authors and invariably they'll mention Danielle Steel. She has her own formula: Woman meets man, man dies, woman meets another man and he dies too. Or, Man meets woman, woman dies, man meets another woman and *she* dies too. Sounds like an easy formula, but can you write a book in 16 days like Ms. Steel? Prolificness can't be learned; it's an inbred talent.

By reading the reviews and articles in *Romantic Times*, you'll soon be an expert on differentiating between the sub-categories. As a budding writer, always note which publishers are producing what kinds of romances. You might as well start learning the "biz" words as you learn the "buzz" words.

This is the start of the 21st Century. Along with learning the techniques and skills of romance writing, I also advise you to visualize how your book will translate into a movie. Keep up the action—we are now a visual society, with shorter reading spans. Opportunities to translate your book into film or to write directly for TV/movie projects are beckoning. Get accustomed to thinking "movie" as you outline your plot.

There is a documented male-female communications gap. So much so that the American Greetings card company has created "Love Talk," the first and only major card line to address the different communication styles between the sexes. They point out that: men need to feel important and tend to communicate non-verbally; women want to hear they are loved and communicate very verbally.

I feel that romance novels are more easily executed by women than men. Most men don't know what a woman craves (communication and great sex) or what it means for a woman to be made love to. So my advice to any writing man is to find a female writing partner to advise you on sensual tension and explicit scenes! Men are usually strong at logical strategy, being left-brained creatures that they are, so ladies—recruit your domestic partner if you want help in plotting your first manuscript. Who knows, you two could be the next "Judith Michael" team, one of the best-selling authors of mainstream women's fiction. You did know they were a married couple with opulent homes in Chicago and Aspen? It could be you!

Once you know the elements that please readers, once you learn the techniques and format for writing in a particular sub-category, when you've finished studying how to write the better book, there's the final important step: outline it, write it and finish it! Don't expect your first attempt to be the one that makes it. I predict you'll need several finished manuscripts under your belt to learn the craft sufficiently.

On your way, pay attention to how the successful writers manage their career. Nobody makes it in any business, particularly the book biz, if they don't understand the marketing of the product. If you dare say, in a whiny voice, "Isn't promotion up to the publisher or agent?" I'll fly right over like Wonder Woman and wash out your mouth with scented soap. Don't fall into that silly female trap of thinking you don't have to learn the biz. It's also up to you know which month is best for your book's, release, which agent gets the high advances, which covers are most effective, which direction to take when promoting your book, and how to make alliances amongst your peers. Stick with the winners and business heads in the pack. Leave the complainers and sadists to sharpen their claws together.

Judith McNaught says without hesitation, ***"I'm a business woman first and a writer second."***

One more word. Don't sign over your foreign rights like a lamb at slaughter. If you wish to keep them with your publisher rather than your agent, try for a "mutual marketing" clause in the contract. I even recommend a non-exclusive arrangement with your agent! Global publishing, audio rights, film rights—these are part of your future as a romance author. Keep flexible. I'm a foreign agent myself, with imprints around the world; I'd love to bid on your book.

Romantic Times provides information on agents, publishers, reference and how-to-write books, and holds an annual convention, where workshops in writing and promoting books are a mainstay. (For more information and how to contact us, see the section **Important Names and Addresses**.)

In the summer of 1995, the *Romantic Times* Book Catalog introduced new women's sensual fiction. Sexually explicit love scenes were being demanded by readers wanting fantasies written by and for women. We sold 2000 books almost immediately. This phenomenon led to my own imprint, which launches in 1996. Our guidelines are included in this book!

I hope you make your dream come true and write a bestselling romance. Let me know when it happens or if you need any help on the way.

Kathryn Falk, Lady Barrow
Brooklyn, NY 1995

INTRODUCTION

When this book was originally published in 1983, it sold very well. Very well indeed, for a trade paperback written by—to all intents and purposes—an "unknown" author (i.e., not Danielle Steel or Kathryn Falk) . . . .

Then, the publisher and I agreed that its shelf life was probably over, and that the category of romance fiction had in all likelihood run its course. So in June 1987 the rights were reverted to me.

We were both in error. Grossly in error. Today, KMart (the largest paperback book retailer in America) states that over 40% of all its book sales are in the romance genre. And according to *Publisher's Weekly* (the "bible" of the book industry), romances account for 48.6% of total mass-market paperback sales nationally, via all retail sources that stock them. Romance sales amount to approximately 900 million dollars. One fifth of the books that sell over a million copies are romances. And if you include reissues, there are roughly 150 romances published every month!

So even though more than a decade has passed since the first edition of this book went out of print, the demand for it is just as great—if not greater—than ever!

And romances have grown up. Gone are the simpering, helpless heroines of the past; they're full-blooded, competent, intelligent women to meet today's readers' expectations. Solid, well-plotted romances are being turned into TV movies; there are romance competitions, and there are occult romances, science-fiction romances, traditional romances, non-traditional, romantic-suspense (though that's been with us for decades), and any variation on a theme you can come up with. And there are romance writers' clubs and conferences, local and national.

In short, the market is bigger than ever. And if romances account for nearly 50% of all paperbacks sold, no one's making fun at us anymore. *Uh-uh*. And with that huge a chunk of the market in our camp, one wonders if romances should even be properly considered as "category" fiction anymore. Wouldn't it seem evident that it's become mainstream by virtue of market share?

And if you want to tap into it, to write your own romance, the best advice to you is *read* what's already available . . . read, read, and read some more. Decide which category of romance you're most comfortable with before tackling one of your own. Maybe you've already done this, but your homework doesn't end there.

Go back to some of your favorite romances and reread them. While you're reading, take notes. Read a book first for its overall content; i.e., the plot and tone of the book (style, mood, pace, etc.). Pretend you're a detective or analyst. Are there any flaws in the plot? If so, what are they? How could this have been avoided? For instance, could a simple phone call have straightened out the problem facing the heroine? Could antagonisms be overcome with relative ease if some common sense had been brought to them? Readers are far more sophisticated today; they don't buy the contrived oversights that writers used to be able to get away with. Yes, they want to read a romance, but they want to read a well-written one . . . not just anything.

Are details correct throughout the book? An example of this would be if the author states there's a floral print armchair in the master bedroom, but later in the book it becomes a plaid print. Consistency with details can make or break a novel. And it's *your* job, not your editor's, to keep track of them.

One of the biggest mistakes novices make is to believe that their sole obligation is to write an interesting romance. Spelling, grammar, punctuation, they believe, are up to the editor to correct. Wrong.

In today's publishing world, your manuscript should be as close to ready for press as you're capable of making it. Should you happen to live in a community with a college or university (or within driving distance), ask an English teacher to go over your work to check for errors. Not style (such as beginning a sentence with "and," incomplete sentences, contractions, and so forth), but just for spelling, grammar, and punctuation. If need be, offer to pay the teacher for the task.

If an editor sees too many misspellings or errors, or that the author hasn't gone to the bother to learn how to properly format a manuscript, it will be rejected. Why? Time. And yes, the old saw was never truer: time is money. A couple of decades ago, when most publishing companies were independently owned, editors had the freedom to decide if an author's manuscript was good enough to deserve the time needed to work with the author for revisions, to restructure it, if necessary. That seldom happens today. There are very, very few independent publishers left; almost all major publishing companies are owned by huge conglomerates.

> **It's your job, not your editor's, to keep track of details. For an editor, time is money.**

Pocket Books used to be a division of Simon & Schuster. Then Simon & Schuster was purchased by the Gulf & Western Corporation. G&W subsequently sold the whole ball of wax to Paramount Communications. Since Paramount was acquired by Viacom recently, the "bean-counters" will be carefully monitoring profits from the book division. None of those huge organizations is interested in "working with authors"; they're interested in the bottom line on the Profit & Loss statement. Spending a lot of time having to edit or correct a manuscript directly affects the company's profits. Yes, of course, there are exceptions. However, you'll find that usually these exceptions are reserved for authors whose novels have done well in the past—not for newcomers. Even first-rate, professional writers are subject to their ups and downs with literary output.

At the public library, ask to see *Literary Market Place*. It's a huge annual directory of every company connected with the book publishing world. It not only lists editors, publicists, et al., but who the parent companies are. It's also an excellent directory to be familiar with. Editors change jobs frequently (usually for better pay—or more autonomy, maybe with better pay and maybe not). If you had some previous correspondence with an editor at, say, Harlequin, a couple of years ago . . . and you wish to contact that person again, make sure the editor's still there. She or he may have changed jobs in the interim.

Similarly, romance editorial guidelines (or poopsheets) will change. What Silhouette was looking for a year ago may not be what the company seeks now, and may change a year hence. So while I will be enclosing the guidelines from the major romance publishers, double-check that they still apply. (In fact, just before we went to press, Kensington, whose guidelines are included in the book, decided to abandon the guidelines and encourage writers to experiment.) Too, it's not unusual for publishers to become over-inventoried with manuscripts too similar in basic underlying plot. It's a good way of not wasting your time on a book no one's going to want. If your backdrop is the wine business, with a divorced woman seeking a new relationship, and a publisher already has two other romances with the wine business as the background, there's no point to writing it.

> **Books are products; they are manufactured and sold.**

But don't throw the baby out with the bath water, for Pete's sake. If you have special information about a particular kind of business or industry (or have thoroughly researched it), don't just dump the idea of writing a book. Instead, dump the notion of it for a romance—use the background for a mystery, or a family saga.

Don't forget that publishing is a business—just like any other business. Books are products; they are manufactured and sold. So keep in mind that you will be expected to be businesslike.

The fact that it's a fun business does not diminish the need for a professional manner, from your initial contact straight through to the end of your writing career—should that day ever come. It does for some people. Burnout can happen in any career. Or, for some, they move on to other types of fiction. If you happen to have a book publisher in your area, ask an editorial employee what good business etiquette involves.

This book is for you, the novice. It is designed to provide you with good fiction techniques (that can be applied to any genre in addition to romances), and to give you a crash course on the publishing process so you'll know what to expect. If you understand what editors must go through on any given day, you will, one hopes, develop some patience with how long it takes to see a manuscript through to publication . . . and beyond.

So read on . . . and good luck! The opportunity is there; you need only make that opportunity yours . . . .

CHAPTER ONE

You Can Write A Romance!

Perhaps in the entire history of book publishing, there has never been such a phenomenon as the apparently limitless success of "romances."

The quotation marks are used simply because the romance category book is far from anything new; it dates farther back than Charlotte Bronte's *Jane Eyre*. And its popularity has been singularly enduring, unlike other types of category fiction. Westerns, for instance, will be popular for maybe a decade then fade away; the same is true of mysteries; and to a lesser degree, science-fiction. Brisk sales of certain categories seem to come in waves; what's really selling today may not be tomorrow—like fads, they come and go.

But this hasn't proven true for romances. Perhaps, at least in part, due to publishers paying more attention to what fans have to say; to insider tips gleaned from *Romantic Times*, an important periodical published by Kathryn Falk; and in some cases, test marketing a book. The point, however, is that there hasn't been any significant slack in the sales of romance novels.

The history of the romance marketplace can be traced to the popularity of gothic romance novels (contemporary or historical). In the mid- to late-1960s, Paperback Library (now known as Warner Books) can be pretty much credited with the successful launching of gothic novels. My use of the word "gothic" shouldn't be confused with the classics that usually involved the supernatural, often set in medieval times, and usually involving horror.

By the sixties, gothics often contained mystery, danger, or intrigue. But few, if any, involved the occult and were generally set in a time-frame closer to our own—such as the 1800s—or even in our own era. Your mother probably read them. Regardless of who was publishing them, they all had basic dark blue backgrounds, with a young heroine in the foreground, fleeing from some unseen danger; in the background, of course, was a mansion with a single window lighted. After a few years, all of them with such similar covers, Paperback Library began to be concerned that women could no longer distinguish if they'd read the book or not, so management decided to run a book with the same elements on the cover (i.e., mansion, woman-in-distress, etc.), but with green as the dominant color. The novel's lift-off fizzled. It was a sales disaster.

Undaunted and determined, Paperback Library then reprinted exactly the same novel with precisely the same cover, but with blue instead of green as the dominant color and sales soared. The moral? Women *can* tell a book by its cover! However, that was in the old days, before massive marketing and research—and before (hard as it may be to believe today) publishers did any television advertising, and daytime talk shows hadn't come into serious play. Estimates from different sources may vary, but it's generally agreed that one appearance on the "Oprah" show to plug your book will result in at least 40,000 copies sold. However, don't get your hopes up too high. It's highly unlikely you'll be invited to a national TV talk show with your first romance. In fact, to be blunt, your chances are slim and none.

However, by the late sixties, I had already had eight novels of my own published, and had worked as an editor with three New York City publishing firms. Seeing how hugely successful gothics were, I telephoned my now-deceased friend, Peggy Roth; Peggy was then editor-in-chief at Paperback Library.

"Peggy," I said hesitantly, "what is the formula for writing a gothic?"

"Simple," she replied. "Put an innocent young woman in an isolated mansion. There is a brooding young man, and a sinister older woman. For the first thirty pages, set your scene, mood, and characters. On page thirty-one, the hero will say 'Good morning,' as he passes by the heroine. For the next ten pages, the heroine will wonder what he meant by that."

Although it seems laughable now, back then it was a good formula and made a lot of money for those involved. But indeed, we've come a long way, baby!

You may also be interested to know that though Harlequin Books was founded in 1949, few Americans had ever heard of them until the early 1960s. Back then, editors in New York City were snickering and chortling over Harlequin's romances. "They're going to lose their shirts," was a common-place remark. (Oh, yeah?)

At that time, Viña Del Mar was already pretty much a forgotten author, though Frances Parkinson Keyes was still doing quite well (the Barbara Cartland of her era, though not nearly so successful in a monetary sense). Nurse/doctor novels were still somewhat popular, but losing out to gothics. That trend took over and lasted for approximately ten years.

By the early 1970s, romantic-suspense began to squeeze out gothics . . . not because gothics weren't any good, but because the public was no longer buying them.

Throughout all this time, American publishers were still waiting for the ignoble demise of Harlequin Books. "It *can't* last much longer," was to be heard at many a luncheon in chic New York City restaurants. (The Energizer bunny hadn't been born yet or maybe they would have known better.)

Historical romances loomed on the horizon, and for the success of these, most of the credit has to go to Avon Books. As the publisher of Kathleen Woodiwiss and Rosemary Rogers, Avon pumped a fortune into advertising, special displays for book retailers, and so forth. General fiction editors couldn't believe the success these books had. "But they're nothing more than 'bodice rippers'!" was heard in the quiet halls of editorial departments. (*Uh-huh.* Yeah, right.)

However, what all of these categories had in common was the element of romance: Would the heroine find true love? She might be standing with her back to the cliff, accusing the villain of dastardly deeds. Or never know what the hero is thinking and therefore fear she will not be noticed by him. Or even a series of misunderstandings between hero and heroine could serve to maintain the suspense of the main question: Would the heroine find true love?

All during this time, Harlequin Books spent more and more money on marketing research and test marketing; something rarely, if ever, done by American publishers in the past. However, as Harlequin's profits rose and its endurance was enhanced with ever-increasing sales, American publishers finally had to concede that there was, indeed, a solid market for romances.

Reluctantly, perhaps even with crossed fingers, they decided to enter the romance market. Why should they let a Canadian-based company make all the profits? They would supply the American reader with American heroines; flesh-and-blood women who live just like the average citizen in the USA. Tentatively, they put their romance toes into retail's water.

Now? There are at least sixteen American publishers of romances, both in mass-market and trade paperback formats, and many of them have separate imprints to distinguish one type of romance from another. <u>Ro-</u>

Writing is a craft, like cooking or carpentry.

<u>mances Are Big Money</u>. Naysayers may complain, whine, or protest, but publishers of romances are laughing all the way to the bank. And so are the authors who write them. And just between us (don't let on to your editor), selling romances to publishers can make the difference between your ability to buy Essence of Aardvark or Elizabeth Taylor's latest fragrance, a five-year-old Toyota sedan or a new Mazda convertible, or spending your retirement years in a trailer camp outside Pittsburgh or living the good life of utter luxury in Spain. Honest. If you're lucky and your book takes off, you're on your way to a very, very lucrative career.

Even back in 1981, romance novels totaled up to forty percent of all paperbacks sold. Harlequin Books alone was selling nearly two hundred million romances, averaging a book per second or 3,600 books per hour—twenty-four hours a day, every day of the year!

Since there are considerably more publishers of romances today than there used to be, your chances of making a sale are vastly increased. Professional writers can only write so many in a year—which leaves gaps in publishers' schedules. Who's going to fill those gaps? You are. That's the whole purpose behind this how-to book.

Writing is a craft, like cooking or carpentry. How *well* you write may elevate it to art, but first you must learn the craft of it. And, like any craft, there are basic rules. If the recipe calls for oregano, and you use cinnamon, don't be surprised if your dinner guests beg off from a return engagement. Editors are, to all intents and purposes, your dinner guests. They are also highly trained "chefs" who can tell good cuisine from a can of tuna with some mushroom soup ladled over it. Similarly, if the construction kit says to use common nails, and you use finishing nails, that coffee table will be firewood in the very near future.

Not only can you learn how to become a solid, professional writer . . . but you'll be amazed at how much you already know subliminally. You know because you've been reading and enjoying romances for years; you simply hadn't made the time to analyze just why some novels work, or why you're disappointed in others. It's a lot easier to write a novel if you know what the rules are; editors will be far more receptive to your work if it is done professionally (i.e., up to the expected standards within the publishing industry); and your book will have a better chance for success in the marketplace if it measures up to what the professionals turn out.

Before the first edition of this book was published, *The New York Times* found out that I was writing it. A reporter telephoned me and among the first questions was: "Aren't you worried about the competition? If you give away all your secrets, what's to say these new writers won't shove you out of the picture?"

My reply was and remains quite simple: (1) If, after more than twenty-five years as a professional novelist and book editor, I can't stay one jump ahead of beginners, then I ought to step down; (2) No two people will ever bring precisely the same ingredients to a novel; while it may look like a tomato to you, it looks like a red apple to me. In brief, we all respond differently from one situation to another; e.g., our perspectives aren't the same. And (3) I do not write *only* romances anyway. Perhaps of foremost importance, though, is that there is plenty of room for everyone. The need for good romances is increasing, not diminishing.

> **Trees must die somewhere before books can be published. If not for yourself, if not for your editior, then for the sake of the trees . . . do your very best.**

And there's also the matter of responsibility in maintaining quality within the profession, both editorially and at the writing level. Most of you already know that the romance genre has been the butt of a lot of humor, from harmless teasing to disgusted derision. Sometimes it's warranted, sometimes not. In one romance I read, the author wrote that the heroine pulled her vehicle "between two officious looking cars." Officious? Clearly she meant *official*. And I don't totally blame the author for that. Writers are immersed in getting the story down, deep in concentration. I blame the editor and copyeditor for that error. It's part of their job to catch that kind of mistake. Although, fair is fair, if the author had waited a month or so, then reread her novel, she might have caught it herself.

But to those dissenters who claim romance writers are just churning out potboilers for money, I say: So was Shakespeare. He lived from the income generated by his writing. No one in his epoch could have predicted that

Shakespeare's work would become the milestone against which others were measured. That his work has endured over the centuries is a tribute to his genius—yes. Yet the fact remains that he wrote for money. And if "Romeo and Juliet" isn't a romance (albeit with a tragic ending), what is? Shakespeare's writing was to entertain—pure and simple. And that's what today's romances do. They're not everyone's preferred reading nor are they intended to be. However, an intelligent heroine, in a believable situation, can be every bit as interesting as in any other kind of novel.

I honestly and sincerely believe that it is in the best interests of professional writers to help amateurs as much as possible. To date, there's been a not-too-concealed condescension among professionals toward beginners— and that's silly. First, most professional writers received help from someone along the line of their own apprenticeships. It's only fair to do the same for others. Second, if we're ever going to make romances a respected category for fiction, the better the quality of writing, the faster romances will be credited as worthwhile contributions . . . not just pap for the masses. There's no reason in the world why a well-written romance couldn't appeal every bit as much to ardent feminists as to less politically involved women; or men, for that matter. The basis of romances is the pursuit of a lasting, fulfilling love—who among us isn't interested in that?

However, if your heroine is *only* interested in sexual fulfillment, or in "landing her man," then this is not only trite, but a disservice to the millions of people who read these books. Would you advise your daughter or son that the only thing that's important in life is to "be married"? No. There should be common interests and goals, tenderness and respect. There is ample opportunity for any writer of romances to provide a genuine reason for the attraction—beyond the physical. Observing a thoughtful deed, noticing a compassionate act...being aware of a man's character—or, for that matter, a woman's—as a loving and caring person is far more important than his appearance. Writers need only give it a bit of thought, with a desire to create positive, rewarding relationships as opposed to headstrong antagonisms rooted in nothing more than unexpected physical attraction.

Not just "anything" should be published simply because it falls into a particular category. Or, to be candid, keep in mind that trees must die somewhere before books can be published. If not for yourself, if not for your editor, then for the sake of the trees...do your very best. You, the editors, and publishers at large have a responsibility. It's not heavier than the earth, nor as beyond your grasp as the next galaxy. Learning the techniques of good writing in romance writing will take a little time and a bit of effort; but once down pat, it's like riding a bicycle—you'll never forget the rules, and they will overlap into other types of fiction as well.

You made an investment of money when you bought this book. That investment is for you to learn, to grow, to improve, and to profit. Much as I dislike old adages—not because they're repeated so frequently, but because they are so infuriatingly, consistently true—one bears repeating here: If it's worth doing at all, it's worth doing it right. Your name will go on that book. If you want to take pride in its publication, give it your best shot. You've nothing to lose, and everything to gain (to coin a phrase).

Anyone can write a book, but only you can write one you'll be proud of. Most of the rules are so simple you'll find yourself laughing at not having noticed them before. However, the best news is that you're way ahead of the game without even realizing it: You can already speak, read, and write in the English language. After that, the rest is a cinch!

And in case you're worrying about not having a formal education—forget it. Sure, it would help. The more you know, the more you can bring to a novel. But it is not essential. Some of the best American writers (not to mention Abraham Lincoln) never went to college; some of them didn't even finish high school.

Writing, like parenting, is frequently far more instinctual than formally taught. You learn by trial and error. This book, though, intends to spare you as many common mistakes as possible to give you an edge over those who simply forge ahead, oblivious to a few easy pointers that could spell the difference between acceptance and rejection.

CHAPTER TWO

The Manuscript: Your Calling Card

Contrary to popular thinking, most writers do not live in New York City. They live all over the USA; in cities, small towns, farms, and wee hamlets. Some live in retirement communities, both in this country and in Baja California. Writers come in all sizes and shapes, ethnic, religious, and racial backgrounds. The nice part about being a writer is that no one sees you at work (outside of family, of course). So you don't have to don pantyhose and heels. Grace Metalious, the author of *Peyton Place*, used to refer to her "writer's outfit"; this consisted of sneakers, jeans, and a baggy old sweatshirt. In *Romancing The Stone*, Joan Wilder wrote in her bathrobe.

The truth is that access to editors is rarely important, or even desirable. If every editor received one phone call per day, from every writer he or she is working with, there would be no time left for any editorial work to be done.

As it is, most editors perform the bulk of their editorial duties at home—without overtime pay. There are so many interruptions in an editor's day that sustained concentration is seldom possible. This is one reason why many editors prefer that authors write to them with their questions as opposed to telephone calls. A letter can be read when there is time or a break in the day, but a phone call is nothing more than an intrusive, disruptive interruption that breaks concentration.

So whatever thoughts you may have been entertaining about being "too far away" to attempt to write or sell a romance novel, erase them from your mind. What is important is how you "introduce" yourself to the prospective editor—your manuscript, and the cover letter that accompanies it, is the editor's first impression of you and your work. And as the old saw goes, you'll never get a second chance to make a good first impression. If you wouldn't dream of going on a job interview in a housecoat, with your hair up in rollers, take the time to be every bit as professional in appearance with your manuscript.

As is true with just about everything, there are rules and guidelines. These are not recommended arbitrarily but for very solid reasons.

Appearance

Try to leave a one and one-half inch margin all the way around each page of your manuscript. Be sure you double-space every single line of it. Even if you want to quote a few lines, such as a poem, that too must be double-spaced. It would be wise, though, to indent quoted material (such as a letter or text from another source) at both right and left margins so the editor can tell that this is not part of the text, but a quote.

Be sure that you use a good, relatively new ribbon in either your typewriter or computer. If you have a dot matrix printer, get it to print "letter quality" type. Editors read for a living; they're not going to punish their eyes with a faded ribbon's printout.

Okay, so why are these things important? you ask. When a manuscript is accepted for publication, and is being edited, there are numerous times when editors make marginal notes about the story that they intend to question the author about. Therefore, each page needs sufficient space in the margins. The reason for double-spacing is to have space for corrections to be made: typographical errors, misspellings, improper syntax, or any number of other changes that will be required during the editing and copyediting procedures.

Clean type and a good ribbon are important both to the editor *and* to the typesetter. The volume of books most editors work with is impressive. When you stop to think of the number of manuscripts they must read over the years, be sympathetic about their tired eyes! It is not rare—though hardly commonplace—for a submission to be so difficult to read that an editor sends it right back to the author—unread!

> ## Sometimes a submission is so difficult to read that an editor sends it right back to the author— unread!

If you're using a typewriter, not a computer, there may be strikeovers; an "i" typed directly over an "e," for instance. Typesetters won't know which is correct. If one can't tell if the letter's an *i* or an *e*, errors—which are time-consuming to correct and therefore costly—will be made. Bear in mind that typesetters have nothing to do with editorial decisions. They receive a manuscript and simply set what they read into type for subsequent delivery to the printer. In fact, it isn't in the least unusual for typesetters to be rather poor in English (they're often foreigners). Typesetters are not permitted to change a single letter or comma; they must follow the copyedited manuscript as it is given to them, errors and all. So it is to *your* advantage to submit as clean and professional a manuscript as it is in your power to provide. And today, with relatively inexpensive computer clones, or word processors, it's worth the investment to buy one. Or, as I did some years ago, find a dealer who leases the equipment on a monthly basis—try out different models to see which one suits you best.

However, this demands a word of caution. Do not, repeat, not, rely on the spell-check many computers have. The spell-check simply verifies that the word exists and is spelled correctly. As an example, take the words they're, there, and their. They are all spelled correctly. But if you inadvertently typed the wrong one ("There over their," she said), the spell-check can't differentiate in context. So proofread your display before you print it out; and then proofread the printout. And if you're working with a series of drafts you need to print out, turn the paper over and type on the other side. Why waste paper? (Since I didn't grow up with the electronic marvels of today, I still need to see hard copy to be sure the text is error-free.)

Okay, those admonitions aside, there's the other side of the coin. Do not allow yourself to become so overwhelmed with the possibility of error that you can't be creative. You will make mistakes; there has never been a totally error-free manuscript, and there probably never will be. This does not, though, give any writer the license to be sloppy or inconsiderate. Now that you know why it's important to present as clean a manuscript as you can, it will soon become automatic that you'll catch yourself in a spelling or grammatical error at the moment it's committed.

Yes, pencilled-in (not ink) corrections are acceptable: If they are clearly printed, and if there aren't too many of them on a page. Again, by the time you make your corrections, the editors add theirs, and then the manuscript is copyedited, what's left could be an unreadable mess. As a rule of thumb, if you have one or two pencilled corrections on a page, that is quite acceptable. However, if the corrections run for line after line, then retype the material.

Should that become necessary, very often the changes will run longer than the original material. This isn't a major problem with a computer or word processor; you simply have to page-down or -up to correct the pagination. On a typewriter, though, it is handled differently. Say the changes occur on page 159. The "spillover" material should not be numbered page 160, but 159-A (continuing on with the alphabet as required *unless* you intend to repaginate the entire balance of the manuscript).

If you only wish to insert a sentence or two to what you've already written, turn the paper sideways in your typewriter, write them out, then pencil in where this material is to be inserted. Again, with a computer or word processor, changes become a breeze. However, I've learned not to paginate on the display until I'm absolutely certain I've written exactly what I want. It saves a lot of time.

All book manuscripts should be numbered beginning with page one right on through to the very end; i.e., sequentially. Magazine and newspaper writers frequently use a different numbering system such as 4/125. This would refer to Chapter 4, page 125. That's because magazines and newspapers are often typeset in whole, individual sections such as the sports section, or business section; books are not. Instead, books are often broken up into chunks and sections of it handed to a variety of typesetters; it's much faster, therefore more economical, to put the pages in order if no one has to think about where this page or that one is from.

By the way, some writers—a sure tip-off about insecurity—put their name and address on every page. If you really must do that, then do so on the back of the page.

Chapters
Oddly enough, many novice writers worry about how far down the page to

place the chapter heading. The truth of it is that it really doesn't matter as long as it's easily identified. If you want your manuscript to be "pretty," then the more "air" it has, the better it will look. If you want to be absolutely certain that there can be no confusion, then start each new chapter halfway down the page.

Editors are frequently asked how long a chapter should be. An anecdote about Abraham Lincoln may serve us well here. A reporter, poking fun at his great height, once asked him: "Mr. Lincoln, how long should a man's legs be?" "Long enough," Mr. Lincoln replied, "to reach from his hips to the ground." And this is basically true about the length of chapters: Long enough to move the story forward and leave the reader eager to turn the page to read more.

However, with category fiction, readers are accustomed to some degree of standardization. A one- or two-page chapter is entirely too cute and gimmicky. Strive for about ten pages minimum per chapter; nine, if you must, or twelve if you wish. Few people read a novel at one sitting, so it is best to give them places to break—like a commercial on television—where they can do something else before resuming with the novel. It doesn't have to be with a new chapter, either.

You've often read novels where there is a space between the paragraphs, yet within the same chapter. Sometimes there are asterisks (***) or insignias (###) inside the space. This is called a one-line break. To point this out to the typesetter, the copyeditor will write it out as: —1#—. Within your manuscript, however, you can indicate this simply by double-double-spacing, with or without asterisks.

And the one-line break can be very useful. You've just written a four-page scene that is setting up your heroine for a terrible disapppointment. You know it, the reader knows it; but the heroine doesn't. Rather than milking the scene to fill up ten pages to make a chapter, using the one-line break alerts the reader that we're jumping ahead in time (thus eliminating the tedium of the heroine's every waking moment) to advance the story more dramatically. Or it can be to indicate a flashback. It can be used to go directly to the scene wherein the heroine learns of her disappointment, or even to sustain the suspense for the reader by sidetracking to a subplot.

> In good fiction, it should be possible to read the dialogue aloud, without identifying who's speaking, and yet the listeners will know which character it is.

In general fiction, the one-line break is also used to prepare the reader for a switch in narrative viewpoint (usually referred to as "multiple viewpoint"). If we're to get "inside the head" of several characters, the one-line break prepares us for a switch to another character's point of view. Since romances are almost always written strictly from the heroine's viewpoint, this wouldn't apply.

Dialogue

Dialogue must be conversational. No one in real life would say, for instance: "I am going to the market now, George. Good-bye." Of course not! It's far more likely we'd say: "I'm off to the market, George. 'Bye." Although, the first version could be highly effective if you want to indicate a terse, even angry response. Most of us tend to get a bit more formal when we're upset.

Let's take that example again to show you what I mean as if it were a real scene.

```
    "I'm off to the market, George. 'Bye." The screen door
slammed slightly and moments later she was in the car,
switching on the ignition.
```

All very blithe and upbeat. Right? Now see how it changes.

```
    "I am going to the market now, George. Good-bye." Her
words hung on the air with tight-lipped disapproval as the
screen door slammed shut.
```

See the difference? You can almost feel the tension with the second version. Dialogue is a superb way to convey what tone you want, what mood, without having to stop the storyline. You don't need to say that she was furious or happy—the dialogue does it for you by the way you phrase it.

Let's borrow from the Bard for another example. Everyone is familiar with Hamlet's line, "To be or not to be, that is the question." Shakespeare could have written that as, "The question is whether or not I should kill myself." The first version is literature with a poetic bent; the second is simply making a statement. Same message, different word choices.

Play around with dialogue till you feel comfortable with it. No two people speak precisely the same. Decide what speech patterns each of your characters will have. Some people talk in a faltering manner, some speak very quickly, some use a lot of slang, some use none at all, and so forth. Naturally, you mustn't overdo these patterns or they'll become repetitive and boring. If you decide one character, let's say a teenager, says "uh" a lot...use "uh" sparingly. The reader will keep it in mind whenever that teenager appears on the page. (Note that "uh" is in italics because it's not really a word but a sound.)

In good fiction, it "should" be possible to read the dialogue aloud, without identifying who's speaking, and yet the listener will know which character it is. I put "should" in quotes because it's very difficult to accomplish. But strive for it. In time, you'll master the technique.

Then there's the matter of how to type it for clarity in the reader's mind. For this to happen, don't run in several characters' dialogue all in the same paragraph. For each exchange or reply, begin a new paragraph. It also helps to eliminate repetitive "she said," and so forth.

Here's the wrong way:

```
"Hello," she said, hoping it was Dick returning her call.
"Miss Laird? It's me, Mona, the switchboard operator."
She smiled to herself. Even though it was not Dick, at least
she was being kind enough to check back with me. "Hi, Mona."
"Did you get your party all right?" she asked. "No," she
said, "but he should be calling any minute now."
```

Okay. Who's saying what? Which one smiled to herself? Confusing, isn't it? Here's the right way:

```
"Hello," she said, hoping it was Dick returning her call.
"Miss Laird? It's me, Mona, the switchboard operator."
She smiled to herself. Even though it was not Dick, at
least she was being kind enough to check back with me. "Hi,
Mona."
"Did you get your party all right?"
"No," she said, "but he should be calling any minute now."
```

Yes, I could have used people's names throughout, but that can wear thin quickly. By keeping each speaker's dialogue separate, with a new paragraph, you really can follow who's saying what rather easily.

When you're writing dialogue, read it aloud to yourself...or ask someone else to speak the lines so you can listen carefully. Also note that I deliberately gave Mona an ungrammatical line. To be correct, she would have said, "It's I, Mona," and not "It's me." However, in today's common usage, it would be extremely formal to say "It's I" and not in keeping with Mona's occupational status.

Notice that any accompanying text is placed <u>with the speaker's actions,</u> not separately or with a new paragraph. Example:

```
Sylvia paused briefly, then with a sigh, opened the door.
"Hello, Dan."
"Am I forgiven?" he asked, taking her in his arms.
```

By keeping the action with the speaker, readers will know who's doing what as well as whose line it is. This is especially important in scenes where the dialogue involves three or more people; or if only two characters are in the scene but are of the same sex. If there are, say, three female characters having lunch at a restaurant, it becomes very easy for the reader to lose track of which woman is saying what unless you use the character's name for every line—and that can become tedious.

One way to avoid the problem is to be clear in your own mind what characters look like, and what gestures or habits are common to each. Let's say Sylvia and her mother, Jan, are joined for lunch by Sylvia's sister, Olga. Sylvia, you've decided, is a redhead; Jan, being older may perhaps be a bit on the plump side and is very tactile; and Olga is a blonde, given to nervousness.

12

Their individual descriptions occurred early in the novel, so readers already know what each character looks like. Let's give it a go.

```
     Sylvia and her mother were already seated at the round
table in the garden room of the restaurant. Smoothing the
mauve tablecloth, Jan smiled as the waiter brought their
drinks. "I wonder what's keeping Olga," she said idly.
     "There she is now," Sylvia remarked, waving to her sister.
     Seconds later, Olga had joined them. Her car keys fell
to the carpet and she retrieved them like a bird plucking
a worm. Like her sister, she ordered a glass  of white
wine. "The traffic's terrible today," she commented with
a little smile of apology.
     "Is that why you're late?" her mother asked.
     Brushing back a stubborn lock of red hair, her sister said,
"You should have allowed more time."
     "Now don't start nagging," she said, her plump fingers
cupping the frozen margarita.
```

Did you have any difficulty recognizing which character was speaking? By referring to physical characteristics, or gestures — in this example, brushing back the stubborn lock of hair, and the plump fingers—you can get away from having to name each of them every time someone speaks.

Note too that only double quotation marks are used. In this country, book publishers use the single quotation mark *only* for a quote within a quote. Magazines and newspapers do not necessarily adhere to this rule, but book publishers do. In the United Kingdom, usage is reversed; they put the double quotation marks inside the single quotation marks. However, you are probably writing your romance for publication in this country (before it sells to England for British publication, of course), so stick to American rules.

Punctuation and common usage

Don't Panic! Very few writers—even professional ones—are any good at punctuation. Let common sense and your ears be your guide. "My ears?" you ask. Yes. Read a sentence aloud and listen to yourself. If you pause, put a comma in the written line where the pause occurs. If it's a whole new thought, put a period. However, over the last few years, both writers and editors are getting away from the overuse of commas. The attitude is that the "old-fashioned" rules for commas just make reading too stilted. As long as the meaning of the sentence is clear without the comma, then leave it out. An example might be: Over the years it's become traditional to omit commas unless they're absolutely necessary.

Before, we would have placed a comma after "over the years" and before "unless they're absolutely necessary." That's because it was to set off prepositional phrases. But the sentence is quite clear without the commas. Now, just for the fun of it, reread the opening sentence of this paragraph without the comma: Before we would have placed a comma after "over the years . . . ." Without the comma, the meaning of "before" is changed. With it you know that I'm referring to "previously" in the sense of an era or time; without it, though, it becomes restrictive in the sense of "prior to," or condition to be met, as in: Before I'll let you drive my car, you'll need to get a license . So the correct use of commas is quite important if you want your message to be clear.

Dashes and ellipses — that's what three periods in a row are called — can also be useful to the novelist. Few category novels are written with parentheses: they're unexpected and therefore jarring to the eye. Instead, to set off an independent yet related thought, dashes are used. (On your typewriter/ computer, a dash is indicated by two consecutive hyphens: --. Make note, too, that there is no space between the preceding word, and the last word, before you continue. Just flip through the pages of this book wherever dashes have been used and you'll see what I mean.)

However, dashes can also be used in written dialogue to indicate an abrupt termination of a spoken thought or an interruption:

"I'd planned to propose to her," he said, "but now I'm not so sure—"

(Or)

"This entire situation is getting out af hand, and—"
"Listen to me darling! Please!"

The first example shows a sense of dangling uncertainty; the second indicates that the speaker's comment was interrupted. Take note, please, that if a dash occurs at the end of the sentence, no further punctuation is needed. Ellipses are also used in this manner in contemporary fiction. You can let a sentence hang midair, lead into a sentence with them to indicate lack of conviction or hesitancy, or use them to show that something was left unspoken.

"When Mark said that to me, I didn't feel anger so much as, well...shame. "
"Shame! After all he's done to you?"
"I know, I know...." She shrugged.

Ellipses are also used to indicate that information has been omitted, particularly in nonfiction—articles, books, reports, quotations, etc. Paperback copywriters are especially fond of using them to the publisher's advantage. Let's say a book has been reviewed, and the review states: "A splendid example of a really trite romance." To a copywriter, that translates to: "A splendid example of a . . . romance." It may not be above-board or moral, but it's legal and it sells books. That's what makes Show Biz.

Many writers put so many periods down between words that one would think they were being paid extra for them. The rule is simple. Ellipses are three periods, followed by the correct punctuation (it's a little more compli-cated than that, but for purposes of preparing a manuscript, that's good enough). Senior citizens who are purists about punctuation will recall that the sequence used to be the reverse; that the correct punctuation came first, followed by the ellipsis. Today, though, especially with the advent of the computer, it's the other way around.

```
"Speaking of the devil...."
"How can you ask that...?"
"I wish I knew...," she said.
```

And so on. However, don't let such things worry you excessively. The story is the main thing; correct punctuation merely simplifies an editor's working life and makes you appear more professional. Just keep in mind that if an editor spots *too* many errors, you will be diminishing your chances for acceptance—if you're unsure about such things, ask someone else to read it for you before submitting. But in the long run, just do the best you can and avoid becoming a slave to detail. Or, follow the example of many professional writers who use either a computer or word processor. First you write the novel, or chapter. When it's complete, *then* go back and reread it for errors in punctuation, spelling, etc. That way you don't have to think about it at all during the creative process. If you're using a typewriter, it's not so easy to do; you'll just have to type those pages containing errors over again.

For my own part, I find dashes to be subtly harsher than el-lipses. . .more abrupt. For that reason, I often use dashes for male

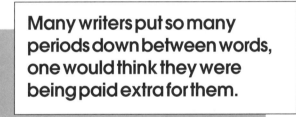

Many writers put so many periods down between words, one would think they were being paid extra for them.

characters, and ellipses for females. Just an idiosyncracy. . . .

For those of you who are interested in the preservation of the English language, you may wish to buy a copy of the *Manual of Style,* published by the Chicago University Press. It is the most commonly used reference work in the book publishing industry though some publishers have their own house styles. Dictionaries also vary, and again, the most commonly used one is the Merriam-Webster Dictionary. (Beware: Not all dictionaries called Webster are *the* Merriam-Webster.) However, between these two works, virtually any question you may have on punctuation, usage, and so forth, will be answered.

Try to get the latest editions you can afford insofar as English is a living language, still changing, and ever expanding . Fifteen years ago, it was recommended to hyphenate "teen-ager"; now it's one word. We used to hyphenate "health-care giver" because it was a compound adjective; today it's more likely to be combined as "healthcare giver" and doesn't require a hyphen. In the 1920s, the word "today" was hyphenated as "to-day." So usage does change. And of course, new words come into our lexicon and how words may be used will change. "Laser" didn't exist in 1925, nor did "computer"—though "compute, "computable," and "computation" did. "Access" and "impact" could only be used as nouns prior to the arrival of the computer; today they're both used as verbs.

How to figure out the word count.

Publishers merrily tell writers that they want manuscripts of 55,000 or 60,000 or 90,000 words and expect authors to know what that translates to in number of pages. I have met authors who have literally counted *every* single word in their manuscripts only because they didn't know how to "strike an average."

Your word count will vary depending on whether you are using a pica or elite typeface, your margins, and how many write-ins you have.

There are highly complex ways to estimate a word count, and some easy ways that are not quite as accurate . . . but close enough. Writers are not generally mathematical geniuses and they shouldn't be expected to whip out ye olde slide ruler (or pocket calculator) to do the production editor's job. A good approximate count should suffice.

It is important to use the same type size for the entire manuscript; i.e., don't start the novel with a pica typeface, then switch to an elite, then back to pica, and so on. This can *really* louse up the word count. And if you begin new chapters at one-quarter down the page, then *all* chapters should begin at the same place to make your life easier when it's time to estimate the length of your novel.

Obviously, it would be simpler to wait till the book is finished and provide a more accurate word count. However, to get at least a hint of how many words will be on how many pages, let's say you've written the first chapter—ten double-spaced pages. Ignore the chapter page and go directly to full pages. What you're going to do, starting with the top line (unless it's dialogue—ignore brief dialogue lines), is count how many words there are on it; then drop down about four lines (again, skip short dialogue) and count how many words that line has.

Let's say you average twenty-four lines per typewritten page. You'll have counted how many words there are on each of six lines. Let's say: 10, 13, 9, 12, 14, and 11. Now you're going to "strike an average." Add up those six sums, then *divide* them by six . The answer (11.3 words) is how many words per line you are averaging . To find out how many words per *page*, multiply 11.3 times your average of 24 lines. This gives you an average of 271.2 words per page. You can knock off the .2, if you wish; but if it goes up to a .5 or higher, then round it off as an additional word.

And, of course, your chapter pages will have fewer words depending on how far down you start each chapter. But let's say nine pages times 271 words (2,439 words), *plus* the number of words on your chapter page maybe another 136 words. That gives you a total of 2,575 words (approximately) for the opening ten pages of manuscript. From this you can pretty well estimate how many pages will be required to meet the publisher's needs.

Since you now know that you're averaging 271 words per manuscript page, and the publisher wants, let's say, 90,000 words, simply divide 90,000 by 2,575. Your completed manuscript should be about 332 pages. If you want to double-check yourself, multiply 332 times 271 and you'll get 89,972 word—which is pretty darned close.

Among the benefits of doing a word count early on, is that it can aid you to determine the plot and subplots, twists and turns. If you compute the word count at the end of the first chapter, and you see that you'll be falling short of what's expected, that's your opportunity to improve or expand the plot and actions. Conversely, if you learn that you're going to go way over the desired word count, you can trim sail before it's too late.

Once you've finished the novel, count out and average as many pages as you have the patience for (at least ten at random). The more you count out, the more accurate your estimate will be. Take the total number of pages of your manuscript and multiply that by 271 words (unless your new average is altered, then use the new figure). Then deduct the number of words per chapter heading . . . and how many lines are missing at the end of each chapter. There's no way to predict that every chapter ending will be a full page of manuscript; sometimes it'll be half a line, or half a page. So this must be taken under consideration too, and subtracted from the word count.

A few final remarks regarding the preparation of the manuscript: MAKE A COPY before submitting it! If you don't have access to a duplicating machine at the office, then check your Yellow Pages. Just about any community in this country has a business that provides duplicating services. Comparison shop, though, prices will vary.

In the ol' days, when an editor received a manuscript that was an obvious copy, it was assumed that the author was committing that heinous sin of multiple submission. Fortunately, that's no longer the instant reaction. Today, the only thing you must do is mention in your cover letter that you're keeping the original at home.

Why is it better to submit a copy than the original? Manuscripts get lost in the mail, they fall behind file cabinets, coffee is inadvertently spilled on them, or an editor's lunch, etc., etc. If you keep the copy and send the original, and something happens to it, then all you'll be able to do is make a copy of a copy—and lose the sharpness of the original. Even if you've written your novel on a computer, and it's no big deal to make another printout . . . still that costs time and money. It's tying up your printer, and putting more stress on it than necessary; then there's the cost of the paper itself, ribbon replacement . . . . No. It's still better if you keep the original. Just don't forget to mention in your cover letter that you're not making a multiple submission.

Also, don't indicate that the work has been copyrighted—especially if you haven't formally copyrighted it with the Library of Congress. For openers, under the revised copyright laws (around 1975 or so), a work is automatically copyrighted at the time of its creation. Next, showing that it's been copyrighted alerts the editor that you mistrust him or her (or worse, that you may be a "problem" author given to unjustified lawsuits). It's exceedingly rare that an editor will swipe your story. In publishing, an editor's reputation is extremely important and word gets around very, very quickly. If an editor steals your work, that editor will never be salaried in publishing again. The truth of the matter is that it's more likely that another writer will steal it than would an editor. It's called plagiarism and it happens. Not often, but it does occur. Editors are on salary; dirt-poor writers have little or no income. I was plagiarized once, in the early sixties. At that, I would never have known except that an irate fan wrote to me blasting me for stooping so low as to change the title, character's names and locale, but leave everything else the same—word for word. Whoa! What's going on here? Further sleuthing turned up a small, struggling paperback publisher who bought the manuscript from a guy in Texas for a mere $500.00. Yes, I could've sued. But I would have had to establish residence in Texas first . . . and I had no desire to do that. All I was able to accomplish was to prevent the publisher from further distribution of the book.

Another thing you should know is not to bind the manuscript in any way. It's traditional, and preferred, to just put a couple of rubberbands going in each direction, with a cardboard stiffener. Even if your manuscript is accepted, the typesetter will have to guillotine the spine and you'll have wasted your money for a binding that is neither wanted nor necessary.

Due to the computer and laser printing, some writers make the mistake of trying to make the manuscript look as much like a published book as possible; i.e., they print on both sides of the page. Don't. It will still have to be typeset.

And all submissions must have a title page. Without one, how can the editor know how to contact you? A typical title page will look like the sample on page 19.

With regard to your cover letter, do not make the mistake so many beginners fall heir to. Do not suggest what the cover illustration should be, what the jacket copy should be, or anything else pertaining to the book's overall appearance and format. It alerts the editor to the fact that you're an amateur. All of this will be handled by either in-house or freelance professionals who know what they're doing.

Your responsibility ends with the writing of the book—unless you're agenting it yourself. Period.

If your submission is as a result of having been invited to send in your work, on the strength of a query letter and synopsis, then keep the cover letter brief. If you're sending the manuscript without an invitation, be sure you enclose a self-addressed stamped envelope suitable for its return. Your cover letter should be brief; not more than one page. Your synopsis (and you must enclose one) may run five or six pages, as much as you require. The synopsis should also be a soft-sell of the book's potential. This might be because you've used, say, a background of industrial safety within your plot. This means, then, that beyond those who are interested in romances, the publisher may find an added market to those people who are involved with industrial safety. Anything that will help sell your book should be told to the prospective editor. So the synopsis will first tell the editor what the story's about, and what the

Jane Doe
Romance Lane
Love City, World
Telephone: 213/555-1234

PASSION'S BRIGHT GLEAMING

A romance novel
by Jane Doe
(or your pseudonym or d/b/a)

Projected length: 65,000 words (or whatever)

Agented by: (provide name, address, and phone number, if
this applies)

market is. And if you have a résumé or précis, enclose that too.

And if you want to be advised if your manuscript arrived at its destination, you should enclose a self-addressed postcard. On the blank side of it, type in:

```
(Date)
Your manuscript, (title), was received on _____, 1995.
Please allow_____ weeks for our decision. Comments
(if any ): (leave some space)_____
_____


At the bottom, type in the name of the editor you're
sending it to, and the publisher's name.
```

That way there can be no confusion as to which manuscript, and which publisher, the postcard is referring to. Especially if you have more than one novel "doing the rounds." Which, by the way, is a very smart thing to do. The more manuscripts you have "out there," the better your chances that one of them will sell.

Or, if you wish, spend the money for mailing it with a return-receipt requested from the post office. Naturally, a postcard is less expensive but there's no guarantee the receiving editor will remember to fill it out and send it to you. I've often received the postcard weeks and weeks after my manuscript had already been rejected or accepted. With a return receipt, you know it reached its destination and when.

And even though I've said it before, it's worth repeating. As author, you can't submit a copy of your manuscript to more than one editor or agent at a time. Yes, it's a time-consuming and frustrating situation; while rare, I've had to wait as much as a year to get a decision on a manuscript. The waiting is grim. But those are the rules. Why? It's simple. The editor/agent *finally* gets to your manuscript and reads it . . . and likes it. The editor/agent then contacts you about your book only to learn that it's been bought by a different publisher or that you've gone with a different agent. You have just alienated the editor/agent who is quite likely to bad-mouth you as a rank amateur who doesn't bother to learn the amenities of the publishing business. And you'd better give up any hopes of ever submitting to that editor/agent in the future.

Agents, however, at their own discretion may submit as many copies of the manuscript as they wish. It's called an auction. The agent will announce that the manuscript is being auctioned off and, in some cases, even put a base-price on the bidding. This rarely (if ever) happens with romances, but there's no harm in you knowing about it in case you write something that's non-category. Auctioning is generally reserved for books with enormous sales potential, e.g. a prospective bestseller.

CHAPTER THREE

The Blank Page Before You

If there's anything that will drive a writer to religious comfort, or a stiff drink, faster than that first blank page, I can't imagine what it might be. There it is, glaringly white, blankly smug, defying you to come up with a good opening sentence . . . much less a paragraph or chapter. To the beginning novelist, that first blank page can only be compared to coming from the wrong side of the tracks and being commanded to be presented to the Royal couple at the reception. It can be scary. All the things you know about yourself, the confidence you've built up in any number of areas of life, are now about to be put to the test. Will you make a social gaffe ("Hi, Princey-poo! Read any good books lately? *Ha, ha*."), use the wrong fork, spill the soup down your bodice, trip on the grass, etc., etc.? In your daily routine at home, none of these things is particularly important to you. Perhaps royal or diplomatic protocol and superior social graces have no bearing on your world. (They don't for most people.)

But if you've never written a novel before, the feeling can be analogous. Happily, as a writer, you don't have to appear in person—it's the novel that counts, not who you are. Editors don't care if you have runs in your pantyhose, are three feet tall, or weigh four hundred pounds. It's the manuscript that matters—what you have to say, and how well you've said it.

Most how-to books on creative writing spend a considerable amount of time on what should go into the plot of a novel. In this particular situation, however, most of you will already be fans of romances and have an excellent idea of what should be included. But if you're one of those rare people who has never read a romance (not even out of sheer curiosity), your homework will soon fill you in on all the necessary elements. (And don't forget to get the publisher's latest guidelines before you begin!)

Obviously, you'll want to avoid any truly downbeat situations for your story. Your heroine will not find herself hooked on drugs, or among the homeless, nor will your hero be an alcoholic. And certainly no one will be a child abuser—though it's conceivable a character might intervene to save a victim of abuse. (Admittedly, some of the newer lines of romances are getting more realistic; let each publisher's set of guidelines direct you with regard to that.)

Frankly, in all my years of editorial experience, I find that novices have the least amount of difficulty coming up with a plot. Where they bog down and sometimes fail miserably is in the actual writing of the novel. For this reason,

I'm not going to spend all that much time on how to plot a book so much as how to write it.

There are as many different approaches to writing a novel as there are people who write them. There is no One Truth or Right Way. I tend to prefer to think of a title first; that more or less sets the tone for me. But if I can't think of one immediately, forget it. Just sit down and start writing; the title will evolve ultimately.

> **The simplest way to tackle a novel is to write an outline first.**

Other writers wait till the book is completed, or frequently submit a manuscript with the disavowing "Untitled Manuscript" on the title page. That's okay. Editors are very good at coming up with suitable titles; in fact, they are generally much better at it than authors. And paperback editors will generally change your title anyway; it may be too close to another book's title.

For a while (a very short while!), I played around with referring to *The Oxford Dictionary of Quotations* as a source for titles. You know, something lofty sounding that I could then provide the full quote for in the front matter of the book. To show you just how stupid even an old pro can be, I was going to write a romance with suspense elements, so I figured something about "fate" might be interesting. In consulting the *Oxford*, I found the following:

Ah Love! could thou and I with Fate conspire
To grasp this sorry Scheme of Things entire,
Would not we shatter it to bits — and then
Re-mold it nearer to the Heart's Desire!

A little quatrain from Omar Khayyam's *Rubaiyat*. Did I choose "Heart's Desire" for the title? Of course not. Instead, I used *With Fate Conspire*. Know what everyone else remembered the title to be? "With Mate Perspire." I am not joking.

As if that weren't bad enough, I later wrote a novel (same *Oxford* sourcebook . . . I should throw it away!) of the same genre and gleaned from George Meredith's *The Empty Purse*:

"Keep the young generations in hail,
And bequeath them no tumbled house!"

So I titled the novel *Bequeath Them No Tumbled House*. Result? Any erroneous variation you can come up with. "No Tumbled House" might have been okay, but can you imagine any denture wearer trying to ask for that book? It sold quite well, though I think it was on the basis of the illustration. Fortunately, when the paperback rights were sold, the editor had the smarts to change the title to *Deadly Legacy*. Why didn't I think of that!

However, to this day, I still tend to want a title before facing the blank page. That way, I can write my name and address up at the top, drop down and center the title and repeat my name (or pseudonym), and then toward the bottom of the page, my projected word length. In this self-deceiving manner, I figure I've licked the blank-page syndrome. It's not blank; all I need now is what to do as a follow-up. A self-serving delusion, yet it seems to work.

Some writers stare out the window, others pace with glazed eyes, and some can only write while standing up while others can only write while stretched out. However, a word of caution may be appropriate here. If you're working with a typewriter, the source of light should come from behind you. But if you're working with a computer's display, the source of light should be in front of you. And you should take a break every two hours. Stretch, walk around the block, but get away from the display for at least ten minutes every two hours. You should never *ever* work with a display screen in a room with no windows. (Even if your job requires you to use a computer in a windowless room, buy a cheap tungsten lamp to offset overhead glare and the display's toll on your eyes.)

Some few lucky writers just plunge in with a what-the-heck attitude—it can always be rewritten if it isn't any good. When I first started writing, I would laboriously agonize over three, four, or more rewrites (on cheapest possible paper) before sending my work to an editor. Today? My first draft is my last. I've learned the craft, and developed a writing muscle; only if an editor requests changes—which hasn't occurred in more than a decade—do I rewrite anything. Note, however, that I will do rewrites if asked.

The simplest way to tackle a novel is to write an outline first. I, of course, am incapable of doing that. My outlines bear as much relevance to the finished product as the blueprint for the space shuttle applies to the manu-facturing of lipsticks. My characters evolve in the writing; so does the story. It is a *rotten way* to write a book. It's far more work, and leads to many excuses to run senseless errands, and it's a definite means of insuring insomnia. I could go on and on about how awful it is not to be able to write an outline; instead, let me urge you to acquire good writing habits from the onset. You won't regret it, believe me.

With an outline, you *know* what you're going to write next; without one, every day is yet another blank page. For some, it comes easily; how I envy them. If it doesn't happen that way for you, let me suggest that you block off some time with your family or friends...make writing the outline a fun project with everyone's input. Even if you don't use their suggestions, more often than not, you'll get fresh ideas *because* something else was brought up. In the motion picture business, this is known as "winging it." A germ of an idea is kicked around by any number of people; it might involve screenwriters and the director or producer, but they all come up with "Maybe this happens," or "Maybe that . . . ." The suggestion itself may not be appropriate but it may spark a spin-off idea for furthering the story that's a really good twist or hook. So encourage a round-table for fresh input on how the plot will evolve.

Get a lot of ruled pads and sharpened pencils. Play "chairman of the board," if you wish, calling upon your "key executives" for feedback prior to launching an "advertising campaign."

Because of the variety of romances on the market today, you will do your homework first: Decide what *type* of romance you want to write (which should be based on the type of romance you most enjoy reading). Virgin heroine, no smoking or drinking; a heroine on the rebound, or a widow; a setting that's exotic . . . and so forth. How far should the love scenes go? That depends on which publisher you're aiming at. Before you can determine that, you should read at least five or six novels from each publisher; as you read, make a breakdown of what happens in every single chapter. For instance:

```
Chapter 1: Heroine loses job; meets ultimate hero by end
of chapter. Instant attraction, but resents his condescen-
sion.
    Chapter 2: Heroine has no luck finding a job; sees ad in
paper that sounds too good to be true. Applies for job only
to learn the boss is the ultimate hero. He makes a derisive
remark and she's offended—can she afford to let pride
prevent her from making a living?
```

And so on. What you're doing is "blocking out" the complete action of the novel before you sit down to write a word of your own. Your family and friends can help; in fact, you will find them very involved, caring about the day's output, coming up with new ideas, and it can be a great deal of fun.

When you get to love scenes in a published book, pay very careful attention. How many pages are devoted to the love scene in comparision to the rest of the chapter? How many love scenes are there throughout the book? How explicit are they?

The love scenes, as you already know, are what the readers want, what they paid good money for. The extent of these scenes will differ from publisher to publisher depending upon its marketing objectives. Think about what *you* remember about a romance two weeks after you've read it: Do you remember the heroine's career direction? Probably not. You remember the romance. That's what these books are all about. So when you are working on your plot— having dissected what the editorial requirements are—be sure to provide at least as much romance as other books in that publisher's line.

Naturally, all romance and nothing else can become dull reading. You'll need to have complications, setbacks, hopes, and so forth, to break up the principal story line. Some romances are very simple: Girl meets boy, girl falls in love with boy, he falls in love with her, circumstances (parents or whatever) prevent them from getting together (chastely?), but all is wonderful in the end. "Love conquers all" is as good a one-line summary as any.

The majority of romance publishers today are seeking more mature heroines (in IQ or experience, not necessarily an older woman). She's capable of tying her own shoelaces, able to make a living or run her own business, and the only thing that's missing is True Love. Again, you'll have to research each publisher's preference before you start to block out your own novel. Your only reliable source of reference will be to break down the plot lines of novels they have recently published, weld this to their guidelines, and come up with an interesting variation on the theme. Remember that these are formula books—tried and proved to be popular and successful. Do not bring in that your heroine's great-aunt was the first registered nurse in the Territory of Arizona unless it is essential to the story itself! And at that, play it down. It could interfere with the action of the novel and will certainly take space away from romantic tension.

The general rule of thumb for any plot in commercial fiction (be it high drama, tragedy, or romance) is:

> Introduce your protagonist and give her a set of problems to overcome: job, family, health, or whatever. In addition to the love interest, much of the novel will deal with her efforts to overcome these problems. She will think she's going to succeed, only to fail (in a romance, preferably through someone else's intervention instead of her own mistake). She will make numerous efforts, have modest gains and some setbacks. The ending of the book is the resolution: If successful, it's a happy ending; if unsuccessful (which never happens in romances), it's a sad ending.

Although the love interest must be integral to the plot, there must be subplots as well. No one lives on a single plateau; there are layers to our lives, things that may vary in importance, but still requiring our attention. A best friend who's in dire financial straits and the heroine is helpless to lend money; a dying relative whom the heroine cherishes; she's behind in the mortgage and is about to lose her home . . . . <u>Anything that adds conflict to the story, in addition to the love interest, is a subplot.</u> Note the prefix: *sub*. These situations are not as important as the romance itself, but lend color and pique interest. They're also very useful to reveal the heroine in different settings; how she handles people or problems can only serve to help us understand the heroine better.

And depending on the publisher's word-count requirements, you might only need one subplot or you may need three or four. The longer the novel, the more subplots you'll need—or make them so complex you can get away with fewer. For instance, if your heroine is trying to run a medical clinic in Borneo and is having problems with (1) the natives who are skeptical, (2) with the local government (mistrustful of a female physician), and (3) with getting medical supplies, your hands will be full weaving these elements into the primary purpose of the novel: romance.

A good subplot is a smaller story within your overall one, and as such should be given less attention. <u>In fact, a good subplot should be easily lifted right out of the novel and never be missed.</u> Here's another example based on the earlier premise. The heroine has just lost her job. Problem #1. Is she an orphan, the sole support of her kid sister? If so, then kid sister could become Problem #2. The kid sister may need open-heart surgery, or is up for the Olympics team, or somesuch. How can our heroine provide for the kid? Now it's not only her own survival and well-being, but her sister's future as well. Like soap operas, the more questions your plot provokes, the better—word-count permitting.

As for heroes, well, double-check what your publisher is looking for. It used to be that he was extremely handsome, brooding, but overbearing and pompous (he wasn't really, he just made a poor first impression). Many publishers have gotten away from stereotyping heroes and heroines. When the two meet, there can be instant attraction but something intervenes shortly thereafter. Maybe the hero is in the Army Reserves and is called to duty; maybe the company he works for is transferring him to an out-of-state branch; or any other means of causing a significant separation. Again, publishers today are seeking more believable characters and situations.

> **Anything that adds conflict to the story, in addition to the love interest, is a subplot.**

But let's go back to the premise mentioned before. The heroine, Midge, meets the hero, Jerry, socially. Though she thinks he's attractive, they don't hit it off, so she turns to join a different group of guests. Midge figures it was only a casual encounter and she'll never see Jerry again. Then Midge applies for that super job only to be floored by the fact that Jerry will be her boss if she accepts it.

Enter Jerry's fiancée, Ellen. She's a shallow yet cunning person, and perhaps fearing the competition Midge might present, she makes derogatory remarks about Midge—which we learn about from another source since Ellen wouldn't have been present during Midge's interview. Is Ellen going to be around much? Does she work there too? Just how much trouble can Ellen make for Midge? And will Jerry let her get away with it? (Be sure you read the publisher's guidelines very carefully before having Midge's competitor for Jerry's affections set up as the designing, conniving type. As romances flood the marketplace, some publishers are complaining that this type of secondary character is being overworked. But for now, let's just proceed.)

In the meantime, we still have the sister with a torn ligament two weeks before the finals, unable to pay entry fees (if such exist). So poor Midge has to make a decision. She didn't like Jerry on a how-do-you-do, and his fiancée is a troublemaker. On the other hand, even heroines have to put bread on the table. So, against her better judgment, Midge accepts the job...confident that she'll find another one in the near future, resign, and be done with Jerry and hovering Ellen. Naturally, finding another job becomes impossible (recession, layoffs in her field) or too impractical (too far for an old car to commute, less salary).

However, what we've set up is that the heroine is making a mini-sacrifice for her sister (Midge is a decent sort); is accepting a job she might not have taken otherwise; is in conflict/attraction with Jerry; possible hostilities with

Ellen; and has to worry about her sister's future. Main plot: Midge and Jerry. Subplot: Sister's welfare. Possible added subplot: Conflict/antagonism with Ellen, or better yet, a coworker.

We all know that Midge and Jerry will fall in love and be happy forevermore—but *how* does it come to pass? With all those obstacles between them, the thing that keeps your reader turning pages is to find out what happens to make them realize they're meant for each other. Then, to add spice and variety, we have the subplot(s). If you wouldn't make a soup with only one herb, why would you write a novel with only one storyline?

Of course, Jerry is really a wonderful, intelligent, passionate man. It used to be that a series of misunderstandings (generally negative) is what kept hero and heroine apart. Romance publishers have been getting away from that. It's too pat, too contrived. I personally prefer romances where the conflicts arise from outside sources; not simply because Jerry is an arrogant male chauvinist. Stories are far more convincing, and the heroines more easily identified with, if the problems between hero and heroine are not superficial snarlings and stamping of a petite foot.

What if, for instance, Jerry was about to make a takeover bid for a smaller company. Midge could meet other characters who defame Jerry, coloring her thinking about him. Then if she happens to overhear (not eavesdrop) Jerry in an argument with the competitor and he really sounds like he doesn't give a damn who gets hurt by the takeover, well, at least in that way she's going on something relatively tangible for disliking him. Of course, none of what she's been told is true; but if Midge, at an early-on point, tells him what she's heard . . . he'd have hurt feelings, probably think her an industrial spy, and he too would be "justified" in treating her unchivalrously—no matter how attracted to her, which he certainly is!

However, as you can readily see, this permits our Midge to have an IQ that's higher than plant life. And because the hero has been put on the defensive, his actions are also acceptable. The reader knows they're both really wonderful people,

> **Publishers today are seeking more believable characters and situations.**

meant for each other . . . so it's up to you, the author, to keep that element of suspense going. They can have good moments together, showing tenderness and caring; or share a special experience (finding a lost puppy) and let their guards down for a while. Let's face it: They're aching to be in each other's arms . . . but you've got to keep the reader wondering how it'll all come to pass till the end of the novel. By reading the romances of others, you'll quickly see how that is accomplished: Diversions, either through subplots or by separation, or a variety of other ways.

Here's a puzzler for you: What if Midge is holding a full-time job and is going to night school for her degree? When would she have time to date? How would you work that out? A simple, easy way would be to make Jerry her professor or a fellow student. Put yourself to the test; how else could it be written? C'mon, get those creative juices flowing!

I said earlier that I can't plot a novel before it's written. This is not quite true. I'm lazy. I can, though, so dazzle you with complications that you'll *think* there's a plot. To repeat, this is not the best way to go. Wrong. Do not do as I do but as I say. <u>Learning to block out your book beforehand can save you—and the editor—a lot of grief later on.</u> It's a habit to be ingrained early, like brushing your teeth or locking the doors before bedtime. The habits you develop (or fail to) right now are the habits you'll be stuck with for the rest of your writing career. Even as good posture will help protect the organs in your body, good writing habits can save you from writer's block, wasted time, or wishing you'd taken up plumbing as a career.

However, you should be apprised of the fact that once you're into the novel itself, some characters will become more prominent than you'd anticipated when blocking out the novel; or that some of the situations don't work quite as well as you had expected. This is only natural and part of the creative process. You're not writing directions to your home, but inventing a story. You should not veer radically from your outline; yet, should that become necessary—and it will from time to time—then let your editor know at once (presupposing you've been given a contract on the basis of a partial manuscript). It could change her or his mind about your book, so get an okay first. You may be the creator, but your editor has the last word.

And once you know what will be contained in the story (whether chapter by chapter, or overall sequence of events), then every day's work becomes as simple as a coloring book. The ingredients are all there; you only have to fill in the blank space with the color, imagination, descriptives, dialogue, and pace of a darned good novel. Let the error of my ways be your guiding light to a safe harbor!

CHAPTER FOUR
The Nitty-Gritty of Writing a Novel

One of the reasons there aren't more novelists around is because writing takes a great deal of discipline; your own, and that of others around you. It's not easy. In fact, in some ways, it's quite similar to trying to live within your budget . . . only in this scenario, time equates with money. You need to budget your time. Another reason so many "wannabes" give up is because writing a novel is probably one of the loneliest of all the creative endeavors.

Yes, yes, there will be someone out there who will argue this, but let's face it. Once a painter has finished, s/he can place the painting on display (at home or in a gallery) and get instant feedback. People will show whether they like it or not. Musicians and playwrights have their worked performed, and the degree of applause indicates how well the work is received; similarly actors are dependent upon applause to indicate how well they did.

But a novelist? No. You write it all alone. You might ask your spouse or a neighbor to read it, but you're keenly aware that this isn't a "professional" opinion. So you send the manuscript to some faceless editor or agent, and await a decision—all alone. Loved ones may empathize with the strain of waiting and waiting . . . but you birthed it and it's your baby. Even once it's accepted, awaiting its publication, you're still all alone. Not until a novel is published, and you're lucky enough to have it reviewed, do you have an inkling of its acceptance. Or if not reviewed, at least your royalty report will indicate how well it's doing. It could take months and even years to see how well your "baby" has done. In this business, you've got to have a strong stomach and a superior sense of humor . . . .

All right, so you've now read six romances by your favorite authors and have decided what type of romance you would like to write. You've already sent for the publisher's most recent guidelines and know what type of heroine and hero their editors are seeking. You know, let's say, that they expect at least one subplot, and that the preferred length of the novel is between 60,000 and a shade under 75,000 words. (This is just for purposes of an example; each romance line will have different requirements.)

The guidelines have given you all the basic elements they want to see in their romances. And you have now worked out your complete plot. You have covered your bases (type of romance), your foundation is secure (which publisher to submit to), and you have your blueprint (outline) at the ready. It's time to erect the building itself. Or more accurately, let's make a movie.

29

Movie? Yes. That's basically what you are doing with a novel. You are the casting director, script consultant, cameraman/woman, director, set designer, costume designer, wardrobe mistress, and last but not least, you are the "god" to the characters you will be creating. In the movies, because it is visual, you see that the heroine is wearing a low-cut clinging gown and looks gorgeous in it. The hero crosses the immense living room in the opulent Tudor mansion and pours himself a brandy. You don't need "words" because you can see it. The heroine might smile, the hero may frown, and because it's visual we don't need a word of dialogue to have a good idea of what each is thinking—depending, of course, on the scenes that precede this one.

You must create the same "picture" in the reader's mind without benefit of camera—just typewritten words on pieces of white paper. A novel can be as boring as the annual report to the stockholders *even though* it has a fascinating premise. To make it come alive, to create a living mural, is what separates novelists from textbook writers (no offense, but textbooks aren't usually very exciting reading).

All professional writers have their tricks for breathing life into blank pages. Yet seemingly idiotic things can ruin an author's intent—the most common one being interruptions. You will soon learn that because you're working at home, friends or relatives consider you to be idle, doing absolutely nothing. Especially if they see you stretched out staring at the ceiling or standing by the window, seemingly daydreaming. It's very difficult for others to realize that you are working! You're thinking through a scene, or deciding what some of the characters need to do next, of how one character is going to respond to another or to a situation. <u>You're thinking, and that's work.</u> Interruptions can totally destroy your concentration.

An answering machine will solve intrusive telephone calls. If you're expecting an important call (maybe you're simultaneously looking for a job, or a relative is ill), and you can afford it, get the kind of telephone that shows you the calling number. Then you'll know if you need to pick up the receiver or wait till later to return a call.

What isn't so easily solved, though, are interruptions from family members—especially children. You'll have to train them. It's as simple as that—but easier said than done. Young children, in particular, aren't going to understand "Mommy's working, dear." If children need your attention during the day, then plan to write while they're napping or after they've gone to bed for the evening. If you don't plan *around* the needs of your children, either they or your book will be shortchanged and no one wants that. Of course, if your children are already of school age, that helps a great deal.

One writer/mother I once knew hired a babysitter for the mornings, and she rented a one-room office to work in, sharing it with someone else who only needed office space in the afternoons. Not everyone can afford this "escape route," however. So it may be best to have a family discussion on how to handle the situation; what's fair to everyone involved.

Part of that discussion, by the way, will involve delegating housework—if your children are old enough for the responsibility. If they're too young, then take a long, hard look at your home. What *has* to be done daily (keeping kitchen and bathrooms clean); what can be done once a week (dusting, vacuuming); what about marketing, keeping food and essentials on hand (how about evenings instead of daytime shopping?). If your kid is in the Little League, is it feasible to ask another parent to pick up the child and return him or her after practice? Can you time-share other duties?

These and other decisions need to be made to ensure you have sufficient time to (1) reread what you've already written to make sure you're not duplicating the information, (2) to try to regain the mood you were in when you left off—or, as per your outline, come up with a total change of pace/mood—and (3) to set about the writing itself. If you had accepted a salaried job, the hours would be set and that's that.

Writing isn't all that different. You must set your own schedule and, short of emergencies, never swerve from it. This means, of course, that the family must understand and cooperate. They must accept that writing is a job—except that you can't guarantee you'll ever be paid for it. Similar to a lawyer accepting a case on a contingency basis, everyone must agree that you've got a good shot at success, but no promises can be made. Even if you've already sold five or six novels in the past, there are no guarantees you'll sell the next one. It happens. Believe me. So never become complacent about your work. Treat each new novel as if you'd never written one before; give it everything you've got—and don't worry, you'll be amazed to learn there's more where that came from (i.e., everything you've got).

> Let's make a movie. Movie? Yes. That's basically what you are doing with a novel. You are the casting director, script consultant, cameraman/woman, director, set designer, costume designer, wardrobe mistress, and last but not least, you are the "god" to the characters you will be creating.

You should have a comfortable typing chair with good back support, and a table or desk that is the right height for the keyboard and to place your hands and wrists at a comfortable position. Note that the key word here is "should." If you can't have those things, don't use them as an excuse. I've written novels sitting cross-legged on my bed, or arching like a willow tree from couch to coffee table. It's hell on the back, but it certainly can be done. The only time I've ever been totally unable to write (for no apparent reason) was when I was living in England. I didn't know *why* I was unable to write for a very long time. But then I figured it out. I lived in a basement flat, and there was no window where I had set up the typewriter. And if I can't stare out a window, I'm in deep trouble.

On the other hand, I've known writers who prefer windowless rooms because there are no distractions. Suit yourself.

Another "little" item. When I was struggling to get a particular scene just right, I was bogging. I'd always turned on my stereo to a classical music station before sitting down to work; it was automatic, like checking my paper supply. On this occasion, however, I wanted a lighthearted, frothy scene of ebullient optimism—and it just wasn't working. It read as if the heroine was fighting tears and putting on a brave front—not at all what I wanted! Disgusted with myself, I went to pour myself a cup of coffee. Only then did I realize that the radio station was broadcasting Strauss's "Death and Transfiguration"! My mood was being altered, subliminally by the music in the background. I've since switched to using the turntable of my stereo; or more likely, the audiocassette since it has a "kickover" to a second cassette, reducing trips to turn the record over.

Before sitting down to write, I decide what mood I'll need and preselect music to get me into the right frame of mind. However, I know writers who must work in total silence lest their concentration be shattered. You're going to have to work out what's best for you; not to the point of pampering yourself, or being just too precious, but discovering just how you work most efficiently.

And, to repeat, if you're using a computer, be sure your source of light is in front of you; with a typewriter, behind you. With either, take a break every couple of hours or so. Do a different task. Not only will this aid you collect your thoughts, but it can help prevent carpal tunnel syndrome (a disease that afflicts people who perform the same manual tasks repeatedly, for protracted periods of time, without any change in basic movement).

Display screens bring their own set of possible problems, such as eye disease due to overexposure to the rays similarly emitted by TV sets (only worse because you're much closer to the display than you're likely to be with the TV). If

> **Put yourself into your heroine's shoes. If you don't, your readers won't.**

you're up for it, do some exercises. This will help get the blood to your brain, refresh you both physically and mentally, and one hopes, aid in the avoidance of a double chin from lack of exercise. Naturally, don't take a break when you're in the middle of a scene and on a roll . . . . But if you're between scenes or hitting a snag, that's a perfect time.

And this leads me to probably one of the most important aspects of being a novelist. <u>While you are writing a scene, you must believe every word of it!</u> It doesn't matter if it has nothing to do with what you may have experienced in your own life—you must put yourself in your heroine's shoes and feel every emotion she endures. You must see the world around your character as she does, not as you would. If everything in your own world is going along nicely, but your character is having a rough time of it . . . see the world through her eyes, not yours. To you the glass is half full; to your character (at that moment), the glass is half empty. A sunny room, when everything is going well, is bright and cheerful; but if your heroine's just lost her job, the glare is blinding and she'll let down the shades or close the draperies.

I can't overly stress the importance of putting yourself into your heroine's shoes. If you don't, your readers won't. Just like an actor, you must "prepare" for your scene; especially if it's one that takes you outside your own personal experience. Novels should evoke emotions from their readers; if they don't, they'll fail.

Don't think about precisely the right words or punctuation in emotion-charged scenes (happy or sad); get your feelings in tune with your heroine's and give it everything you've got. You can make corrections later, when you're going over the material to be sure you've conveyed the mood/attitude you want. Even if it means retyping the pages, establishing the mood or action is infinitely more important. You are in charge, like a master puppeteer, and you must imbue your characters with depth and sincerity. And whatever the situation your heroine may find herself in, it must be believable or it won't work.

To make it believable, think about the characters' backgrounds. Are they college educated? From another country? High school dropouts? Do they have regional differences? For example, someone born and reared in Brooklyn will have different speech patterns, and quite possibly, attitudes, from someone who was born and reared in Montana. A character from Brooklyn might say: "He should only live so long!" But someone from Montana might say: "Fat chance!" Generally, someone from a community with strong European (particularly Eastern Europe) influences is wordier—and often more colorfully so—than someone who is not. Your characters' dialogue must conform to his or her background and upbringing.

The same is true of descriptives. Too often, budding novelists fail to give enough thought to descriptions. If we're in a diner, for instance, the seat or booth coverings won't be genuine leather. They might be Naugahyde, or plastic imitations, but they won't be leather. If your heroine's in a good mood, she probably won't pay much attention to the decor. In a bad mood, though, she might notice that there's a tear in the fabric, the utensils aren't as clean as she'd like—in short, when we're on a bummer, we're more likely to find fault than virtue.

In a diner, you'll get paper napkins and dimestore flatware; your coffee will probably be brought to you in a cheap white mug or cup and saucer. Is the mug chipped? Is your heroine the type of person who worries about germs and requests a different mug? Or let's say her order is being prepared by a short-order cook and it isn't prepared to her liking. Does she send it back? Does she simply shrug and let it go? Her decision will tell the reader a great deal about your heroine: she's fussy, she's amenable, she's up tight, she's easygoing (etc.). Or it can simply show what her mood is at that moment in time. If she's normally even-tempered but right now is out of sorts, you won't have to say she's upset—her behavior will indicate it.

But in a four-star restaurant, what changes? The "booth" becomes a "banquette" that is upholstered in genuine leather or costly fabric; expensive brass candelabra dot the richly textured walls; linen tablecloths and napkins are used; tableware will include fine china and crystal; a lighted candle is likely to be present; and your menu selection (note, not "order" but "selection") is prepared by a chef (not a cook—who, if not from Europe, is probably a graduate of the CIA [Culinary Institute of America, not the spy network]). Such details must conform to the situation you are providing. If they don't, they won't be plausible. Remember, you're also the set director. What your heroine observes about her ambience will tell us what kind of person she is; or at least, one facet of her personality.

> **Memorize this: Emotion is not a dirty word. Abuse of it could be. Learn to lead the reader to the brink; but always give your reader credit for imagining the rest.**

If you have never been in a four-star restaurant, or at a formal dinner, do your homework before you place your heroine in that type of situation. If you can afford it, buy a good book on etiquette. Failing that, go to the public library. There are "rules" to follow and even if your heroine doesn't know what they are, you should so you can explain her discomfort or hesitancy. If your heroine is naive, she may think it strange that her wine glass is poured only halfway up with a red wine and is served at room temperature—after being allowed to "breathe" for at least 40-45 minutes.

If she's sophisticated, she would be appalled that the red wine is poured to the rim and that it's chilled. You'll need to know what foods are compatible with what kinds of wine. That too you can find out at the public library; there are numerous books about wines and what foods are compatible and which are not. Carrots, for instance, are not compatible with most red wines. With leafy salads, no wine is served (and the salad is a separate course of the meal, not served with the entree). Little things can trip you up if you don't double-check first. Things like a formal dinner has no fewer than twelve guests. The guest of honor, if female, is seated to the host's right; if a male, to the right of the hostess.

Hey, look! I didn't invent these rules, so don't blame me. If you don't want to go to the bother of learning correct etiquette and all that stuff, then don't put your heroine in that kind of situation.

Obviously in romances, nothing too grim or depressing is going to happen to our heroines. However, they should be capable of sufficient depth to be able to do more than merely smile, frown, stamp a foot (does any woman still "stamp her pretty little foot"?), or be reduced to putty because the hero said, "Good morning."

You have days when you awaken filled with a wonderful feeling that something marvelous is going to happen; and other days when you're dragged out, not quite yourself, and all you can think about is how to get through the day till bedtime. So should your heroine. A salesclerk's courtesy and a smile can bring you out of a low mood; the sun breaking through the clouds on a rainy day; that old photograph of you as a kid (when your dog was taller than you were) . . . all sorts of things can change your outlook. So can the reverse of these situations: A rude salesclerk; a lovely day turned gray; or the snapshot of your mother three weeks before she died. *Use* these elements for your heroine; they are common to most of us, we understand why she's being affected . . . make the readers believe they actually know this young woman, care for her and are rooting for her to find happiness.

Too often, beginning writers create static people. These people are happy, sad, passionately aroused, or angry. They are also flat, uninteresting, shallow, and unbelievable. If you don't set the mood and circumstances, gently leading the reader to understand why a character reacts the way s/he does, then you're not involving the reader. You're merely stating the facts, with no intellectual or emotional depth the reader can clearly perceive.

A novel I recently read stated that the heroine and a female character became close friends (Note: "became" best friends, they weren't already friends from the beginning of the novel). It was never indicated how this came to pass, we were never involved in a revelatory scene—so it wasn't believable that they were so close. In this same novel, an incidental character dies and the heroine is utterly bereft. Why? She hardly knew that person. It didn't make sense so the heroine's reaction wasn't believable.

I've written scenes where I have literally cried while at my typewriter. Five hours later, I've gone out to dinner and forgotten the entire day's work—but it's there, every emotion-charged word of it, waiting for me to come back the next day. It is unimportant that this is fiction, that the character doesn't really exist. What's important is that you believe she exists while you are writing about her. (No, I'm not talking about "possession." I'm talking about throwing yourself into the role. Later, when you reread what you've written, you then become the director and film editor. If it became too maudlin or melodramatic, change it! You can always tone down what you've written . . . but recapturing an emotion-charged scene is almost impossible.)

My own way of working is to write by the scene, not by the chapter. If I complete an entire chapter in one sitting (with suitable breaks, of course), that's wonderful. But I am far more concerned with credibility, with "reader identification" (an editorial term to indicate the average reader will be able to "identify" with the hero or heroine). So how many pages I write per day is not as significant to me as the quality of each scene. I also do not reread what I've written on the same day; I'm too close to it (unless I'm just proofreading for typos). I wait till the next day when I've a clearer perspective on it. And when deadlines permit, I'll wait for several weeks to reread my work; it's amazing how much objectivity some distance in time will provide.

Memorize this: Emotion is not a dirty word. Abuse of it could be. Learn to lead the reader to the brink; but always give your reader credit for imagining the rest.

Then there's the matter of an author's responsibility. Yes, you are responsible for what you write. Short of libel, you won't be fined or jailed, but you still have a responsibility to your readers. Remember that people tend to believe what they see in print. "Well, it was in the newspaper yesterday, so it has to be true." What about poor reportage, slanted editorials, and so on? And when people read novels, if the characters have no depth to them, most readers will think that whatever happened isn't all that bad (or all that wonderful).

If your heroine has any prejudices, you're telling the reader that it's all right to be prejudiced. If your hero is deceitful and is never brought up short for it, you're telling readers it's okay to lie. (While one hopes your editor will catch such things, you can't always rely on someone else. The buck stops with you.) Similarly, if your heroine's only objective is to find Mr. Right, then you're telling your readers that "love" is more important than integrity, loyalty, mutual interests, and so forth.

I've read historical romances where the heroine is raped and her reaction to this is: "How dare he!" Good grief! Talk about lack of responsibility as a novelist! As you may have gathered, I am strongly against rape as part of romance. It only glamorizes an act of violence in an era when most women are scared silly to leave their homes after dark—or even worse, terrified of what will happen when their spouses come home.

You are responsible for the illusions you create, the reactions of your characters. Remember, you are "god" in fiction and as "god," you must accept the trust given to you by your readers.

Viewpoint
There is the first-person narrative (told as if the reader were hearing the story firsthand by use of "I"). There is the third-person narrative (using "she"). Then there is the multiple viewpoint, and the omniscient.

In multiple viewpoint, the author chooses two or three, or even four, characters from whom we will learn what is happening. For this to be properly done, there must be a one-line break (see **Glossary**) for every switch in viewpoint, or a new chapter begun. Each character can only know what he or she learns by witnessing something, or being told, has read or is reading, or overhearing. (This is also true of first- and third-person narrative.)

With the omniscient, the author creates a godlike situation wherein the reader is privy to what each of the main characters is thinking or feeling; and sometimes the author will interject him- or herself by tipping the reader off that there's more to the matter than any of the characters realize. When you, as author, place yourself in a position where you know what everyone is thinking, what's going on hither and yonder (regardless of whether or not your primary characters are present), you are writing from the omniscient viewpoint. Only experts or fools attempt it.

It is very seldom that either the first person or the omniscient can be handled with any real degree of effectiveness or success. It should not be attempted until you are really secure in your grasp of fiction techniques. Repeat: Until you're confident that you can master either first person or the omniscient—don't attempt them. Although I've had over 30 books published . . . . I've never attempted to write from the omniscient viewpoint. First-person, yes (and only after six of my novels had been published), but not the omniscient. Does that tell you anything . . .?

However, some romance writers will try for the first person, so we may as well cover it and put it to rest. The wrong way:

```
I stood by the window. I looked out and I thought: Gosh,
won't it ever stop raining? Then I sighed and I went back
to my desk. But it was no use. I couldn't work.
```

That's a very short paragraph, but count how many times the word "I" is used. That's part of the problem with first-person narrative; authors trip over themselves with needless repetition. It ceases to become a good novel and instead could be entitled *The Big I*. If you're not a master of first-person, then "I" becomes more important than the reader; it comes across as if you're writing this for your own ego's benefit and not for the reader's entertainment. (You may wish to note that the same problem exists with nonfiction. Any article or work of nonfiction that is written from the first-person perspective easily becomes boring, or stilted and self-conscious.)

So let's try it another way to illustrate writing in the first person that is less tedious. The right way:

```
Standing by the window, my spirits as damp as the rain
that pelted the roof and trees, it seemed to me that the sun
would never shine again. Sighing, I returned to my desk.
But it was no use; the weather and recent events made work
impossible.
```

Count how many times the word "I" is used. Not only has it been used but once . . . but the writing itself is far more effective, more mood provoking.

If you insist on writing in the first person, remember that you must capture your reader's imagination and make her feel as if *she* is the heroine—as if every time she sees the word "I" she identifies with the character as herself, not the author. (Remember too, that if the reader is 5'2" and weighs 200 pounds, and your heroine is 5'8" and weighs 130 pounds,

What you must adhere to (with all but the omniscient viewpoint) is the basic fact that your heroine (first-person or third-person narrative) can not know anything other than her own thoughts, what she witnesses, reads, is told, or in some indirect manner becomes aware of.

it's going to be rough convincing the reader that she's anything like the heroine.)

If it's *I-I-I*, you're alienating the reader. I've read books (both fiction and nonfiction) where the word "I" is used as often as twenty-two times on a single page. What does that telegraph to the reader: I'm more important, or you're more important? <u>I means me; you means you.</u>

And even the one time "I" appears in that second example, it too could be eradicated. What if:

```
Standing by the window, my spirits as damp as the rain
that pelted the roof and trees, it seemed to me that the sun
would never shine again. Returning to my desk with a heavy
sigh, attempting to work, it was soon evident that work was
impossible; the weather and recent events made concentra-
tion too elusive.
```

Now "I" doesn't appear at all—and so much the better. Why is "me/my" better than "I"? Think about it. The reader's eye can easily identify with me/my because it could equally apply to the reader. They're more subjective and personal. But once you've said "I," that's totally altered.

For this reason, many publishers of romances prefer the third-person narrative. Without benefit of a degree in psychology, it's been my observation that readers can more readily identify with a "her" (or a "him") than a "me." Moreover, the problem of eye-stopping repetition is avoided. The eye glances over the words "she" and "her" with far greater ease than with "I" and "me." It is also much easier to write in the third person, and less self-conscious.

Whenever possible, I always urge beginning writers to stick to the third person until they are truly ready to try something new. Simplistically, one has to learn to walk before one can run. Which is not to imply that the use of the third-person narrative is an easy way out. Some of the most complex and valuable contributions to the world of literature were written in the third person. However, it is the easiest to master quickly. Spanish and Esperanto, for instance, are the easiest languages to learn; that does not mean they are devoid of nuance or eloquence.

You have numerous latitudes with the third-person narrative that you might not have with other forms. For instance, when the heroine is standing before her mirror. If you say: "I looked at myself and wondered if he thought me pretty," the heroine sounds vain and self-centered. However, if you say: "She looked at herself in the mirror and wondered if he thought she was pretty," suddenly it becomes a very real, plausible question that any young woman might ask—and it's easier for the reader to identify with the character.

Omniscient and multiple viewpoints are rarely used—if ever—in today's romances. Again, to do so is to risk losing reader identification. Romance readers want to believe that they, too, are young and thin, intelligent, lithe and beautiful, and that the world lies ahead of them. That's half the fun of reading romances in the first place. They transport us outside ourselves, giving us a whole new image of what we're like (or could be), and provide a whole new world to live in and explore. There's no dirty linen in the hamper and your husband or significant other isn't *really* watching a game on television, but planning where to take you out to dinner the next evening.

Escape. That's where it's at. We all need to break away from our everyday routines once in awhile; it's healthy. Whether you're reading science fiction, mysteries, a western, or any other invented story . . . it's escape. If you can learn something at the same time (such as the fact that gold can't be picked up with a magnet, or that the origin of the word "panic" comes from the Greek god, Pan—it is said that Pan delighted in hiding behind bushes in order to ambush passersby and scare them), that's all to the better. However, it isn't the main thrust.

<u>What you must adhere to (with all but the omniscient viewpoint) is the basic fact that your heroine (first-person or third-person narrative) can not know anything other than her own thoughts, what she witnesses, reads, is told, or in some indirect manner becomes aware of.</u>

You can't, for instance, have the bulk of the story from the heroine's viewpoint and suddenly switch to the men's club where the hero is lunching with an old chum. Or more accurately, you "can" do so, but it's not good fiction writing—unless you're writing the novel from a multiple viewpoint, which has its own set of rules.

Let's use Midge and Jerry again. If Midge isn't present, or doesn't learn what happened at that luncheon by some other means (a friend tells her, the hero lets it slip, whatever), then Midge can't possibly know what was taking place. She wasn't there.

The only way you can know that your mother and father had dinner out last night is either because they told you, someone else saw them at the restaurant and tells you, or you went along. The same is true for first-person narratives, third-person narratives, and multiple viewpoint.

It is no different from what happens in real life. You have had a best friend for fifteen years and believe you know her very well. However, you can't look at her and be absolutely certain that you *know* what she's thinking. You can surmise, guess, predict, base your response from her facial expression, assess by nervous habit, and so on. But you can't *know*.

If every time Jerry becomes agitated he suddenly starts playing with his left earlobe, then it's pretty safe to assume that such an action indicates his attitude. On the other hand, you could have your heroine, Midge, believing she is aware of his thoughts . . . only to learn that Jerry's ear was itching.

Similarly, when someone frowns; is it from anger, worry, concern, or poor eyesight? Now, you as the author can provide a lot of information for the reader's interpretation . . . or the heroine's. Example:

```
    Midge gazed at Jerry, torn between what she knew she must
do and what she wished were possible.  She longed to touch
him, but was afraid.  "I have no choice, Jerry," she said
softly.  "I must leave here."
    For a  torturously long moment, he said nothing.  Then,
```

```
gently taking her chin in his hand, Jerry smiled sadly. "I
know.  I wish it weren't true, but—"  A frown creased his
brow.
```

Okay. We know that Midge wants to stay, and it's quite clear that Jerry
wants her to also. Midge understands his sad smile . . . but what does his
frown indicate? We don't know. But let's do it in another way.

```
    Midge gazed at Jerry, torn between what she knew she
must do and what she wished were possible.  The words she
longed to say simply wouldn't come out; he had hurt her
too deeply.
    "I'm leaving, Jerry.  There's nothing you can to do stop
me!"  Her words hung on the air like a dark, ominous mist.
She hadn't intended a threatening tone, yet the words
seemed to have a life of their own.
    A frown creased his brow.
```

Now with this version, we've got quite a different situation—despite the
fact that little was really changed. We now know that much as Midge would
like to bridge their rift, she can't. Hurt, maybe defensive, she blurts out her
intent to Jerry far more harshly than even she had intended.

By not giving Jerry any lines or mitigating gestures, neither Midge nor the
reader knows what's on his mind. The frown could mean almost anything
from pained heartbreak to mere annoyance.

How was this accomplished? By the words and actions chosen to convey the
tone of the scene. The next line might have Midge wondering what his
thoughts are; or turning on her heel, leaving him behind, never knowing what
he was thinking at that moment.

As you plan each upcoming scene, first decide what you want the reader to
know, or not know but be kept guessing. If you want the reader to understand
that at least a temporary resolution has been reached, then go ahead and fill
in the blanks. But if you want the reader to be on tenterhooks, eager to find
out more (also known as a "cliff-hanger"), then provide as little information
as possible so the reader will have to turn pages to learn more.

Here's another example:

```
    Midge turned to face Jerry, her heart bursting to let him
know that she knew he had been instrumental in getting her
the job.  Yet he stood with his back to her, mutely staring
out the window. Would her admission make him defensive? She
didn't know.
    Quietly, almost inaudibly, she said, "Thank you, Jerry."
    He turned to face her, a frown creasing his brow.  "You
know?"  His words were more of a statement than a question.
    "Yes," she replied simply.
    He seemed about to speak, then with a shrug of his
```

shoulders he retreated to some private world, again gazing out the window.

Midge hesitated, hoping he might say something more, something to indicate his true feelings. Did Jerry really care so little about her that her feelings were of little consequence to him? And if so, why had he gone to the trouble to intervene on her behalf? Why had he tried to keep it a secret?

After what seemed an eternity, Midge sighed softly and left his office.

Okay, what have we set up here? Midge is holding back as much as she can without actually denying Jerry information. He, on the other hand, seems to have more knowledge than he wishes to admit. Is this a cliff-hanger or what? It's a great way to end a chapter or a one-line break leading to another scene or jump in time . . . forward or backward.

Let's explore the one-line break a bit more just to be sure you've got its purpose. For instance, you've set up a scene where Jerry and Midge's friends have just shared a pizza, having a great time talking, laughing, and just being relaxed. Except, Jerry wasn't quite as congenial as Midge would have hoped. Instead of milking the scene for pages and pages, you can use the one-line break to indicate a passage of time. You can completely change the locale and the mood because the reader, having seen the one-line break, is expecting it.

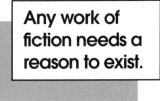

Any work of fiction needs a reason to exist.

Again, a one-line break is a double double-space, sometimes with asterisks or other insignia. It tells the reader that we're jumping ahead or back, or (with multiple viewpoint) switching to another character's point of view. We're still bound by the same rules if another character's point of view is introduced. We can only know what that character knows and nothing else. But, like the story of the blind men and the elephant, we're seeing the same story from a different perspective. Or, perhaps, getting additional information that the heroine wouldn't know about. That can be a huge help, or an enormous hindrance. It's up to you, the author, to know if it's beneficial or not. However, make sure you understand the editorial guidelines before taking on the multiple viewpoint; again, it's rarely done in romances.

Another area where beginners often err is to say entirely too much when the same "message" can be conveyed subliminally. You don't have to put every detail down on paper; in fact, it's better and tighter writing if you don't. And this is especially true with secondary or incidental characters, who shouldn't get as much time devoted to them in the first place.

The waitress sauntered leisurely to their table, chewing gum as if it were an act of protest.

"Yeah? What's yours?" she drawled out, her eyes never

meeting theirs.

This waitress will not get a tip. Moreover, you don't have to say what she's thinking. It's in her very attitude and manner. She doesn't walk; she saunters. You can almost hear and see her shuffling along, the sounds of her shoes on the floor. She's chewing gum and drawls. Does she snap her gum? Is her drawl a Southern accent or simply indifference? And she avoids eye contact—a trait often associated with shiftiness, or insecurity. Moreover, her dialogue is far from polite or congenial. You can practically see her removing the pencil stub from behind her ear—without saying so. Compare the above to:

> The waitress, a pretty young woman with a freshly scrubbed
> look to her, rushed to the table with an aura of apology.
> "I'm sorry it took me so long to get here. May I take your
> order now?"

We get an entirely different person with very few words. She's rushing, she has an air of apology, she says she's sorry, and she's polite. We get a full picture without having to stop the flow of the story with descriptives. Being a forgiving and compassionate hero, Jerry will leave her no less than fifteen percent of the tab. (The size of the tip will vary depending on locale; in major cities, twenty percent is generally recommended.) However, the reader can instantly dislike the first waitress, but feel immediately sympathetic toward the second. All because of the way it was phrased. And your main characters, depending on their own frames of mind, will react accordingly.

If you want us to be uncertain just how nice a guy Jerry really is (maybe that merger fell through), he could be incensed by Waitress #1, or mildly annoyed with Waitress #2. If you want us to see another side of Jerry, let his reaction be a humorous one. What you direct your characters to do and say is all we have to go on as readers.

Unless you have an infallible memory, buy a three-ring notebook and keep it as a log.

Should you want Midge to be short-tempered, you'd better provide a very valid reason for it; and ideally, she should regret taking out her problems on an innocent second or third party. Otherwise Midge will come across as a snappish, self-centered nit.

Note too that each paragraph begins with a different word from the one before, or even two or three paragraphs before. This aids the flow of the story. If you have a series of paragraphs all beginning with the same word, it becomes monotonous. I have read manuscripts where an entire page's worth of paragraphs all began with the character's name—BOR-ing! So when it's time to review what you've written, check that you haven't made the same mistake.

And while we're at it, there's something else you should know. Any work of fiction needs a reason to exist. Harking back to the responsibility of authors, there should be an underlying, unspoken question: When the reader finishes this book, s/he will know _____ (fill in the blanks). A novel should have the capability of answering the reason for its existence with a one-line moral or statement: Crime doesn't pay, love conquers all—whatever. Just because you've written five hundred pages of manuscript doesn't make it worthwhile. What will the reader learn from it? If you don't have a reason (besides monetary) for writing the book . . . why are you writing it?

Yes, lots of books are published that have no reason to exist (no basis for the attraction other than physical, for example, and neither hero nor heroine learn anything from their experiences).

> **What you name your characters can convey a *sense*, or picture, of who they are.**

However, that doesn't mean they *should* have been published— only that they were. A good editor seeking a good romance to publish will also be looking for that underlying *raison d'être*. Before you begin to write, ask yourself what moral will be learned from the romance.

If you're stumped for an answer, think of the Ten Commandments as a source: Thou shalt not commit adultery, thou shall honor thy father and mother, and so forth. You might consider a situation where your heroine sees her parents as stiff-backed prudes and the heroine—asserting her independence—doesn't get along with them very well. As one of your subplots, her problems with her parents might become more complex (especially if she's attracted to someone they disapprove of). Does the heroine make any effort to overcome their objections? To win them over? Or does she simply decide that it's her life and she'll lead it any way she wishes—thank you very much! It may well be a matter of miscommunication; she's not taken the time, or made the effort, to understand where her parents stand and why. While the reader may realize she's being close-minded and stubborn, it's not at all clear to the heroine herself. Then perhaps her parents are in a serious auto accident, verging on death. Does this open new vistas for the heroine? Does she see another side of them that she'd not seen before?

Such a situation not only helps us to understand the heroine better, but offers numerous opportunities for you, as author, to explore her character in greater depth. What does she learn from the experience? Well, it might be: Judge not lest ye be judged.

Maybe Jerry turns out to be a shallow guy who doesn't even bother to be supportive of Midge, or to visit her parents. What has she learned from this development? That parents aren't always wrong, that they do have your best interests at heart, and just because you disagree doesn't obviate the validity of their advice. Or, put more succinctly: Honor thy father and mother.

Okay. Midge now knows Jerry's a fink. Is there another romance in the wings? Someone she really likes but doesn't think of in a romantic way (yet)? Does she dump Jerry, or foolishly continue the relationship? What she decides gives the reader plenty of insight into her character and ability to apply reason.

But this example should trigger all sorts of ideas for your heroine to grow and mature. Does she have any siblings? Do they get along? Note, however, that this is a subplot. Don't dwell on it any more than is necessary to get your heroine involved, and to grow from it.

> **The people you introduce in the opening two or three chapters must appear throughout the novel; that's the rule. They are your primary characters.**

One more thing that may prove helpful, and something I rely upon. Unless you have an infallible memory, buy a three-ring notebook and keep it as a log. Use a separate page (at least) for every major character. This will include physical descriptions, background (inclusive of parents and education), and anything else that is essential to the character's persona. If she or he grew up in a trailer camp or a two-story brick house, log this information in. If your main character is living elsewhere, with an apartment or home of his or her own, draw a floorplan. My own are quite crude, but they suffice to know if the kitchen is off of this room or that, where the laundry area is (if there is one), and so forth. Think about what kind of decor would appeal to each of your characters, and log that in too. Some people prefer an eclectic ambience, mixing antiques with other period pieces, and even a few modern pieces. Others are strictly into Early American, or French Provincial. The types of furniture, wall hangings, or other items of decor should reflect the character's personal tastes—and, possibly, financial status.

For example, since I can't afford "fine art" (Van Gogh, Turner, Rembrandt, et al.), I would still prefer to have an original oil painting than a lithograph. Perhaps the original oil painting is by a total unknown—but it's something I like and it pleases me to see it whenever I pass by. I haven't purchased it as an investment, but for my own pleasure. Other people might decorate with prints of famous paintings and be just as happy as I am with originals. Many people will have a recliner chair or two in front of the TV; I'd die first! So keep in mind that the things your characters choose to live with are reflections upon their tastes and personalities. Just for fun, you might want to have your heroine's apartment decorated with an American Indian motif, but smack-dab, bigger-than-life is an Art Deco floor lamp. It's in total contrast to her chosen lifestyle. It could be that her favorite aunt left it to her in her will. So your heroine might explain, "I know it's awful," she said, laughing. "I just can't bear to part with it . . . and I can't figure out where to hide it either."

If you keep a thorough log, you will never have to flip back through the pages, or the display, to remember what you've set up. If you have access to "Windows" with your computer, that's your reference log. If you, even as I, are of the generation that has to see it as hard copy, a written log is probably better. The point is to have a ready-reference of all the details with regard to your characters and their environs. It's enormously helpful.

Character Names and Descriptions

Most of us have favorite men's and women's names; and names that we tend to associate (no matter how illogically) with people we've known before whom we did or didn't like. It's purely happenstance, and foolish, of course. I've known four Phils in my life and disliked them all. So if I were to meet a man named Phil tomorrow, I'd be wary. Maybe he's a terrific fellow, but with a name that carries that stigma, I'm going to be on my guard.

Aside from such subjective approaches, what you name your characters can convey a sense, or a picture, of who they are. Ronald and Stephen, for instance, have a gentler, more refined "feel" to them than Brad or Burt. That doesn't mean that Brad and Burt aren't refined...only that we're more apt to be surprised if they are. Think in terms of how names sound. Soft vowels convey softer impressions; hard vowels are abrupt, curt. If you want to hit a middle ground, a hero who can be imposing yet genteel underneath, strive for names that straddle their sounds: Derek, Alex, Robert, Peter, etc.

The same is even more important for your heroine and other female characters. By way of example, if I were writing a romance, I would never give the heroine the name of Midge (as I've done here). It's a "nowhere" name, conveys very little, and is far from melodious or soft. I might give it to her best friend, but not to the heroine. Imagine, if you will, your heroine in her lover's arms, and he says, "I love you, Midge." *Midge? Uh-uh.* Stephanie, Julia, Sophia, Lisa—maybe. But Midge? *Aarrggh!* Or, for that matter, can you conceive of a woman named Erika as anything other than tall, willowy, blonde (maybe a redhead), and probably headstrong? But if she's named Bibi, or Connie, the whole image changes.

Try to select names that will convey to the reader what a character's personality is like, or bearing, or attitude. What does an unusual name, or combination of names, suggest? For openers, I'll give you a personal example. People will remember that I have an unusual (though far from rare) first name. They will call me LaVonne, Yavonne, Avon, Yolanda, Inez, or Zelda— they know it's not commonplace, but can't remember what it is. The same is true of my last name. I get: McMalice, McManners, or my all-time favorite, McAnus. And of course, no one ever remembers that I'm a *Mac* and not a *Mc*.

Guess what? I've had to fight (well, not literally, but at least insist) for the correct pronunciation and spelling of both my names for my entire life. This, in turn, has led to my developing into something of a scrapper in real life, more inclined to righteous indignation than to a submissive "Oh well." It also means it takes me forever to sign a check or receipt—and there's never enough space. How much space do you need to write Jane Doe? Which also means, of course, that I'm sensitive to people's names and I'm quick to verify that I have the name(s) correctly.

However, if your characters are named Sue Green and Dick Smith . . . there are no surface identity realities to grapple with. All signature lines are amply long enough to write their names, everyone remembers what each's name is, and so forth. If you wouldn't give your first born just any old name—merely for the sake of having a name—then be as thoughtful about what you name your characters. Names conjure images in the reader's mind. For instance: close your eyes for a moment and say aloud "Pete." What do you see? Probably an easy-going guy, nice looking without being overly handsome, and in all likelihood, the kind of fellow you'd really like as a pal. He's the kind of guy who'll happily give your battery a jump-start.

Now close your eyes again, and say aloud "Peter." Whoa! What happens here? Slim, erudite and sophisticated, perhaps a tennis player, something of a snob, maybe, or even a tad arrogant—and he's not likely to get his hands dirty. Do this same exercise with other names: Joe/Joseph, Madeline/Maddy, Frederick/Fred, Jennifer/Jenny, and so on. If you didn't realize it before, this should aid you to understand the importance of names for your characters (or children, for that matter).

Another aspect of assigned names that beginning writers seldom think about is the avoidance of similarity either in sound or beginning letters. If Jim is your hero, don't have Jack as a secondary character—or Jane and Jill, respectively. The same is true for last names. Not only should you vary how many syllables there are, and be sure that the same letters don't begin each name (although if one character's last name is Swift, you could conceivably get away with another's surname being Salisbury or Santiago), but also try to avoid surnames that are too foreign to the American ear—unless your character is a foreigner, of course. While Roget and Colbert are originally French names, Americans are quite accustomed to hearing them and they are easily read and assimilated.

The importance of breaking up the sound (syllables and first letter) is increased proportionately to how many characters you are introducing at the beginning of your novel. Try not to have more than four or five main/secondary characters. <u>The people you introduce in the opening two or three chapters must appear throughout the novel; that's the rule. They are your primary characters.</u> Think about how the mind "reads" names. If your heroine is Judith, a secondary female character should have a name that's one syllable or three—Kate or Alicia or Mary Beth.

Incidental characters may be introduced (waitress, bellboy, secretary, CEO, etc.) whenever they're necessary to further the plot; but as incidental characters, they get very, very little space. Just remember that you can't introduce any instrumental or primary characters halfway, or later, through the novel. It's poor form. So it's essential that you determine who's primary and who isn't before you start to write.

How do you decide who's primary and who isn't? Well, you know your heroine and hero are primary. You couldn't have a romance without them. So other primary characters are those who are instrumental in their effect upon the hero and heroine; characters who influence, or bring about insight or changes within the hero and heroine. This could be a best friend, one's boss, parents, siblings, a rival or others. But they must have a strong influence (good or bad) in the story. They may also be part of a subplot.

Let's say that the heroine has a boss who's never heard of sexual harassment on the job. Subplot? You bet! Perhaps even more importantly, it's a chance to explain how verbal innuendo can be construed as sexual harassment for those who still haven't figured it out.

By way of illustrating how you can make a contribution with your novel, many male authors have asked me to define sexual harassment so their heroes won't be guilty of it. These male authors sincerely want to do the right thing, but—like so many people, male or female—they're not exactly sure what it is. Although it's overly simplistic, my response pretty much covers the bases: If you wouldn't want it done or said to your mother, wife, daughter, or sister, aunt, grandmother (etc., etc.), then don't do it yourself. Lewd remarks or gestures are lewd; there's no mitigating circumstance such as, "Dammit, I was just kidding." Yeah? Would you feel the same way if it were said (done) to your mother or wife? Figure it out.

And before we get too carried away with male-bashing, keep in mind that women are also guilty of sexual harassment. You may want to explore that aspect of this serious issue in your novel. What if your heroine works for a female boss who's always coming on to a muscle-

> **I assign each major character an astrological sign.**

building junior executive? What complications will arise? Will the head of the personnel department believe his complaint? Will the matter be treated seriously? Probably not. Today's society tends to belittle a man's discomfort in such a situation. A "stud" will take the female boss up on her suggestiveness; so there really isn't a problem (unless he's a kiss-and-tell and she fires him). Yet a decent, sensitive guy (maybe he has four older sisters) will probably just have to seek employment elsewhere. Sexual harassment can be just as uncomfortable for a man as it is for a woman. The principal difference is that men aren't usually raped . . . .

Then there's the matter of "can" she fire him? Large corporations usually have someone within the personnel department who's an expert in labor relations (not just union employees). Bosses are no longer free to simply fire someone—justly or unjustly—unless there's a violation of the employment agreement: stealing, cheating, lying, etc. And in many companies, the employee must receive three written warnings about his/her conduct which are on file with the personnel department.

Nowadays there are strict rules. If you telephone a former employer to get a reference, that employer can't (by law) tell you anything more than the dates that s/he worked there, and confirm that a salary was in the four- or five- or six-figure bracket—but not the exact salary. Personnel isn't permitted to say anything good or bad without the former employee's written permission. So if you're using the office as a major part of your novel's setting, brush up on fair labor laws.

But I digress, so I'll un-digress. Every bit as important as the names of characters, descriptions should vary too. If all your females are blonde and blue-eyed, not only is it going to confuse the reader, but you are also doing yourself a disservice. Let's say that for the dialogue of the preceding two lines, you've written: "she said." You want to break it up. It's a scene between two women—right? If one of them is a brunette, you can get away from yet another "she said" by substituting "the brunette replied."

If you really have to have similar appearances (mother and daughter, for instance), at least you can then use "the older woman said" or "the younger woman answered." If you opt for identical twins, you're on your own!

Moreover, how you choose to describe your characters—especially the heroine and hero—should be carefully considered. For some reason (no one really knows why), redheaded heroes rarely work as a suitable love object for heroines (though TV may be changing this); however, the reverse works beautifully. Redheaded heroines offer cliché opportunities: hot temper, proud, sexy, etc.

My own preference leans toward protagonists who are human. Maybe my heroine's mouth is too wide for today's fashion, or too small; maybe she's a bit uncomfortable about her height, though the hero loves it about her (too short or too tall for most men, but not for him). Obviously, I'm not going to give my heroine acne and sweaty palms; not because there's anything *wrong* with either, but because readers who might live with either condition would prefer to think that they didn't. Whether you think it's unfortunate that our society places such great emphasis on physical attractiveness or not . . . we must keep in mind that we're writing to a specific market. Many women would agree that Danny DeVito and Michael Chiklis are attractive and magnetic, but neither would make a good hero in today's romances. Similarly, as compelling as Christine Baranski is, or as captivating as Fran Drescher, neither of them would make good heroines in the romance market. (Sorry, folks, we can't arbitrarily change the readers' preferences.)

If at all possible, try to avoid any flattering descriptives of your heroine through her own observation. You should certainly state what color her hair and eyes are, if she has an oval or heart-shaped face, but keep it just to the facts. That, or make a particular characteristic something the heroine dislikes about herself (impossibly curly hair, her eyes are too large); the reader will know that these are exactly the traits that make her attractive, but the heroine doesn't. Or if you wish, let *other* characters refer to her to reveal how very attractive she is, such as how the hero is always attracted to women with tilted-up noses—in dialogue, not in their thoughts. For my own part, I think a man with a slight overbite is very appealing; and I've known men who think a slight condition of knock knees is extremely cute or attractive. If it turns you on, go with it.

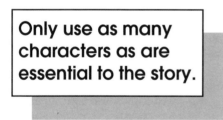

Only use as many characters as are essential to the story.

The heroine will, naturally, be embarrassed, or pleased—yet never take flattery casually or as her due. Though a secondary character may, if you want to make this person appear vain and superficial.

Perhaps the simplest guideline would be: <u>If you had to describe someone</u>

love to your best friend or parent, what qualities would you choose to stress and which ones would you minimize? It's what most of us do in real life, and to make your story believable, it's probably what your characters would do.

Your Characters

First of all, you must keep your cast to a minimum. We don't have to meet everyone's mother, aunt, brother-in-law, and high school chum; or know what peripheral characters are thinking. Only use as many characters as are essential to the story. Pretend you have to pay them Actors Equity minimum salaries out of your own pocket . . . watch the cast dwindle! I had to edit a manuscript once that had—count 'em—one hundred and three characters packed into a 60,000-word novel! It was utterly impossible to keep track of them all. Because the background was offbeat and interesting (the heroine was an airline stewardess), the manuscript had been purchased (or as we say in publishing, it was "acquired"). However it was a nightmare when it came time to edit it.

So I contacted the author, explained the editorial problem, and asked her permission to delete x-number of characters; which meant, of course, that she would have to provide me with additional material—centering on the main characters—to replace what was going to be omitted. She agreed, fortunately. So keep in mind that if you have too many characters, you're chipping away at your chances of making a sale.

With incidental characters such as gas station attendants, supermarket checkout clerks, and so on . . . we don't have to know their names. In fact, it's better if we don't. Or, if you wish to show that the heroine always shops at the same store and knows everyone's name—be sparing in how many you use. If you're writing about a small town, the heroine would probably know the greengrocer's or hardware store owner's name. It's to be expected. But the reader doesn't have to know why; just that it's so. If the character is only being used to move the story along, be brief; but of course, if the character is pivotal to the story line, devote more time.

Perhaps we can once again use the movies as an aid. As you watch a movie, any movie, observe the opening scenes—or what Hollywood calls "establishing shots." We learn right away where we are (city, country); are we in the present, the past, or the future; who the main characters will be; and very soon thereafter (if not at once) what the problem(s) is. These opening scenes "establish" what we're to expect next: thriller, horror, romance, adaptation of a novel, western, and so forth. We will see these primary characters throughout the film until its conclusion . . . unless, one of them disappears (is killed, has a heart attack, whatever), which then serves to *heighten* the interest in the plot. How does this affect the main characters? What do they do as a result?

The classic scene in "Five Easy Pieces," where Jack Nicholson tries to order a tuna sandwich on toast, is another good example. We don't know who the waitress is, and don't care. What's important is that it reveals a resourcefulness and ill-concealed impatience on the part of Nicholson's character. We never see her again, nor were we meant to. She was only there to give us insight into the main character. The screenwriter could just as easily have cut to the group entering or leaving the diner, with no scene involving the waitress.

The same is true in fiction. So as you write, decide if you really need this or that character. Do not assume that if a little bit is good, lots has to be better. It's not. The fewer characters you have, the more time you have to spend on delving into main characters' feelings and attitudes, or in strengthening your plot.

I've a couple of tricks that work quite well for me when shaping my characters. I pattern each of them after a well-known TV or movie star and make note of it in my log. Because I'm familiar with an actor's gestures, speech patterns, and so forth, I have no difficulty whatsoever in being consistent. How would Bill Cosby react to the situation in this particular scene. Or Corbin Berensen? Cicely Tyson or Suzanne Somers? Chad Everett or Valerie Harper? Do you see how much easier it is to imagine flesh-and-blood individuals as your characters on paper when you have real people to refer to? If I have a picture of the character in my mind, it's much easier to convey it to the reader.

Similarly, and also in the log, I assign each major character an astrological sign. I use *Linda Goodman's Sun Signs*, mostly because it's entertaining rather than ponderous. If I want a wishy-washy personality, that character is assigned Pisces. (Not all Pisces are nebulous, mind you . . . I'm one myself. But of all the signs, they are the most *likely* to be.) Pisces frequently have trouble with their feet . . . so that too can be part of the character's actions. If the heroine is a Pisces and has spent the afternoon at the mall, she'll be the first one to kick off her shoes and rub her feet. You don't have to go into elaborate detail; the mere fact that you mention her action will suffice. And unless I want a scene, perhaps a Beverly Hills party with lots of pompous and under- or over-developed egos present, I might have a casual character ask the heroine's astrological sign within the scene. But otherwise, it's only for my point of reference.

If I want someone to be headstrong, stubborn and taciturn one moment, and unable to refrain from lecturing the next . . . Scorpio. Heroes are ripe to be Scorpios. Moreover, it's the sexiest sign in the zodiac—so it's said. (*Hmm.*)

Here's an example. The scene is a New York City gallery hosting a one-woman show of our heroine's water colors. Midge is the heroine, and she's a Pisces.

Midge hung back slightly as she observed the guests slowly passing by her work. Keenly conscious of her own nervousness, she twisted the glass of champagne between her palms, hoping to hear something positive from the critics.

The background noises of the patrons and guests were a low rumble with an occasional hissing overtone. It was impossible for Midge to discern what they were thinking. No one smiled; no one frowned. They simply stared for a few moments and walked on to the next picture. *I begin to understand the psychological validity of rending one's garments*, she thought, chiding herself for permitting her work to be on display.

Slowly, Benjamin Taylor, of *The New York Times*, straightened before her framed "Water Lillies at Dawn." His expression gave her no hint of what was to come.

"Brilliant," he said softly. Then turning to the others, he proclaimed, "Absolutely brilliant! Who is this Midge person? Where has she been hiding?"

Her hands felt suddenly cold and she wished she had someplace to hide.

Why does this indicate that she's wishy-washy? Well, if you don't want to receive acclaim or derision, why would you put your work on display for top critics to see? It's a push-pull situation in this instance; she wants approval, but fears criticism.

Okay, same scenario but this time Midge is a Scorpio.

Midge moved along with the crowd in hopes of overhearing their reactions to her work. Even if no one had a kind word to say, Midge knew she was darned good. Perhaps even too good for these snobbish reviewers and critics. While she wanted to be accepted on her own merits, still if they didn't like her work...there was always Europe or Latin America.

She heard mumblings of "Interesting," "Provoking," but that was the talk of people who didn't know enough about art to even be able to spell the word.

Slowly, Benjamin Taylor, of *The New York Times*, straightened before her framed "Water Lillies at Dawn." His expression gave her no hint of what was to come.

"Brilliant," he said softly. Then turning to the others, he proclaimed, "Absolutely brilliant! Who is this Midge person? Where has she been hiding?"

Smiling radiantly, Midge took a step forward, her shoulders squared, her chin high. "I've always heard that you were perceptive, Mr. Taylor. Now I know it first-hand."

See how the reactions change? If you don't know your characters, inside and out, how can you possibly hope to make them believable to the reader? If you can picture your characters vividly, and you know what characteristics each possesses (with or without assigning an astrological sign), you can convey a sense of them far more easily.

And of course you can have a character doing or reacting in an uncharacteristic way. But you have to make that clear to the reader as well. What if our Pisces-Midge didn't wish there were someplace to hide? What if, instead of that last paragraph we said:

Her hands felt suddenly cold but she knew this was her moment. Perhaps the only moment she would ever get for recognition as an artist. Summoning all of her courage, Midge took a hesitating step forward.

Mr. Taylor noticed her at once. "*Ah-hah!* You must be the mysterious Midge." His smile was paternal. "Come, my dear, let's get better acquainted. Now...."

Midge could scarcely believe that *the* Benjamin Taylor was drawing her aside and barely heard him suggest an interview for a forthcoming Sunday section of the paper.

> # For the sake of clarity, keep the action of the speaker with the dialogue.

It's perfectly clear that Midge is still uncomfortable. And it's obvious to the reader that she wouldn't normally behave in that fashion. So it works. Just because someone's a Pisces doesn't mean that person has no gumption or spunk . . . s/he only has to work at it a bit harder than others.

Aquarians, I've found, are often a bit on the bossy side; and if they've ever been school teachers, you can rely on it. But to quote the syndicated astrologer, Carroll Righter, "The stars impel, they do not compel." In other words, just because you're born under a certain sign (or, for that matter, to a segment of society) doesn't mean you're stuck with it. You have the intelligence and the opportunity to change yourself or your circumstances.

But here again, there's a benefit you can reap. What if your hero or heroine has a habit s/he really dislikes and want to change? Part of your introspection, the development of your character, will be the recognition of a fault and the efforts to overcome it. Insofar as no one's perfect, how refreshing it would be if a heroine had traits she wanted to surmount!

Dialogue

It was once stated that, having read a book beforehand, good dialogue should be able to be read aloud, without mentioning who's speaking, and still the listener can recognize which character is talking. Good luck.

However, spend some time listening to your friends as they speak. None of us talks in precisely the same way. Some people use a lot of big words needlessly; some talk in short, declarative sentences; some speak falteringly; others tend to use a lot of overemphasis on key words (shown on the typewriter by underscoring the word . . . which translates to italics in the book—or if your computer is capable, go ahead and write it in italics); an example might be: "I told you so! Didn't I tell you so?" Some people use a lot of slang expressions, or (alas) ask, "Know what I mean?" repeatedly.

All of us have speech patterns and (often without realizing it) words or phrases that we use too frequently. *Wow, gosh, I'll be damned, what in tarnation, you don't say*, and so on. I knew a woman once who, anticipating what the rest of my sentence was going to be, silently mouthed my words as

I was speaking. Very disconcerting. Yet, a habit nonetheless.

It is best to keep such patterns predominantly for secondary characters lest it become tedious reading; and, of course, not overdone. If every single time you have Aunt Martha in a scene and she says "Really?" it can wear very, very thin. Give the reader some credit. Once you've established a speech pattern, the reader will remember and subconsciously build it into Aunt Martha's dialogue.

For what it's worth, I tend to have my heroes talk in brief, clipped sentences unless it's a tender scene. My heroines, though, are usually more verbose without being chatterboxes. If I have a possible second romance entanglement (the other man), he is generally more conversational and open than the hero.

But I'll give you a clue in case you've never lived in the South. Southerners are the most talkative people, as a general geographical group, I've ever encountered. Period. There's no such thing as "the strong, silent type" hereabouts. Fortunately, I've never had a Southern male as a hero in my novels; if I had (using the above-cited "brief, clipped sentences") my hero would have been totally false. Southerners are also the most touchy/feely population I've ever met. I mean, total strangers, men and women, will pat your arm or hug you. I witnessed with my own eyes, at a trade show exhibit in the South, a man who was a stranger who literally lifted up my female coworker and moved her bodily to another spot on the floor. She'd never seen him in her life. Up North, that man would have been flattened; and out West, in Southern California, he'd probably have been locked up!

I'm a relative newcomer to the South and it's been an educational eye-opener. If you haven't lived in this neck of the woods yourself, best stick to your own neighborhood for a background. You could be in a peck of trouble otherwise. Y'hear?

Good dialogue in a novel should be as readable as dialogue in a script. This was touched upon earlier, under **The Manuscript: Your Calling Card**, yet it deserves repeating. If I want the heroine to have an unexpected insight into the hero's character, I set it up so that it's an unusual situation. Perhaps they're both trapped in a log cabin during a snowstorm; maybe there's another character present, and maybe not. Or being roused from a sound sleep to attend to a sick animal; or maybe the heroine is stranded in the middle of nowhere with a flat tire . . . and along comes this pickup truck driven by a cowboy-type. Should she accept his invitation to give her a lift? What if he's some kind of deranged kook?

Still most of us, under different or unusual circumstances, will often let down our guard and reveal things about ourselves we might not otherwise discuss. This also helps the reader to see what our heroine finds so attractive about the hero—beyond just the physical. (In private, I often yearn for a homely hero and a plain heroine. Would it ever sell? No. But I'm entitled to my yearnings.) The hero might recall some revealing childhood incident, or confessing that he'd had a devastating love affair years before, or a host of other "insightful" revelations that build our sympathy for him. All bark and no kisses can be very dull reading indeed. (In many romances, I can't figure out what the heroine sees in the hero in the first place—I'd have told him to buzz off!) Some romance publishers are beginning to get away from the terse, taciturn, brooding type hero—and for my two cents' worth, it's about time.

Too often (and I blame the editors more than the authors—after all, it's the editors who let it get past them to publication), writers will affect written dialect or accented speech. Try to avoid this whenever possible. It's jarring and considered poor writing by just about everyone. If you really need it, though, give an example and give it only once. For instance, Spanish-speaking people have difficulty with words beginning with a "w"; those words are nearly always pronounced as if they began with "gw." They also tend to pronounce words ending in "d" as "th"—because that's how it's pronounced in Spanish. So if you absolutely must convey the phonetics of an Hispanic speaking in English, you could write:

> Maria was clearly searching for the right words. Only someone who knew her well could have interpreted what she finally said. "Gwell, *señora* Gwalters, 'e say dat de deener gwas pooty gooth."
> Midge had to smile to herself. She supposed that "pooty gooth," or pretty good, was better than no comment at all.

But having established what a foreign accent will sound like in English (if you must!) —drop it! The necessity of phonetically imitating an accent has been almost eradicated by TV and the VCR. Who hasn't heard what a French, German, or Russian accent sounds like? A good writer doesn't have to resort to phonetics unless out of sheer laziness.

And once you've made it clear what kind of accent is involved, you can have a character say, "But this is, how you say it in English, terrible!" Don't use "how you say it in English" again. Instead, your character may falter, grasping for the right word; or *tsk* in exasperation, or a host of other ways to indicate that English isn't that character's first language. For foreign characters, keep in mind just how frustrating it is...trying to recall the word, knowing that you do know it, but can't dredge it up; or searching to find an alternate word that will suffice. In both situations the other person is waiting for your reply. If you've ever been in a foreign country where you didn't speak the language fluently, instill in your character how foolish or irritable it can make you feel.

Or use sentence structure to indicate it. In Spanish (and indeed most Romance languages), adjectives follow the noun. So your character might say: "It's a lovely house white." You can also refer to this character's accent occasionally if another character asks for clarification. As an example:

> Midge could see that the woman was very upset. "Calm down, Maria. What are you trying to say?" She glanced from Maria to Richard, who seemed confused.
> "What's the problem?" Richard asked.
> Midge smiled uncertainly as she met his questioning gaze.
> "I don't know yet." Then she turned back to her housekeeper.
> "*Ay, válgame Dios*," Maria blurted, twisting her apron in

```
her hands, glancing furtively toward the gazebo beyond the
pool.  "El señor...!"
    "Maria!  Who?  Which señor?  What's happened?"
    The woman broke into uncontrollable sobs and Midge, not
knowing what or whom to expect, began to run toward the
gazebo, with Richard a few paces behind.
```

Now, granted, I know a bit of Spanish—enough to fake my way through a scene like that. The only word the non-Spanish-speaking reader might not get is *válgame*; but even so, since it's used with the Spanish word for God, it shouldn't be all that difficult to figure out (*válgame* means "save me," in case you're interested). And I didn't have to resort to written dialect to get the effect I wanted. You can sense that something terrible has happened. And if I used that short sequence at the end of a chapter, it would constitute a good cliff-hanger.

So, after you've established in the reader's mind that someone has this or that accent, or drawls, or whatever, you don't have to keep repeating it. The reader will remember it, fear not; and you need only occasionally make reference to it thereafter.

One more thing about foreign accents. Bear in mind that most countries in this world acknowledge a social or economic class structure. Although any number of people might be from, say, England, there are strong regional differences in how they speak. Once your ear is attuned, you can tell the difference between a Liverpool accent and a Londoner's; or someone who went to private schools (in England, a private school is the equivalent of U.S. public schools) or someone who attended Oxford.

In Germany, for example, there is what's called High German and Low German. High German is almost as melodic as a romance language; Low German, though, is gutteral. In Italy, it wasn't until Mussolini that the Italian language was standardized. Even today, people from certain regions speak their own dialects—they will not necessarily understand standardized Italian.

Clearly, before you decide to write a novel with a foreign setting, or have characters from other countries present, you had better be darned sure of your material. I once knew a woman who taught Italian at the university level; but when she went on sidetrips through the Italian countryside (i.e., outside of major cities), she couldn't make herself understood nor did she understand the locals.

Slang usage will also differ between the classes. Someone who grew up in a coal-mining community will not use the same argot as someone who's a member of parliament. So to wrap this up, if you're not sure of your ground (e.g., with foreign languages), then don't put your foot on it.

And as mentioned earlier, it's important—for the sake of clarity—to keep the action of the speaker with the dialogue. Wrong way:

```
Midge listened to Edith with disbelief.
She moved toward her, dark eyes flashing.
"I'm warning you...he's mine!"
```

```
"Don't you think that's up to him?"
She smiled sardonically.
"He isn't aware of it, but he does what I say."
```

Who's saying or doing what? You don't know because the action of the speaker wasn't kept with the dialogue of the character. Right way:

```
Midge listened to Edith with disbelief.
"I'm warning you...he's mine!" Edith moved toward her,
dark eyes flashing.
"Don't you think that's up to him?"
She smiled sardonically. "He isn't aware of it, but he
does what I say."
```

See how much simpler it is to keep track of speaker and action? Yes, I could have used names for each, but that becomes repetitive and slows the action and impact. Or, I could have said "the brunette" if only Edith is a brunette.

Another problem area beginners often have is interrupting dialogue or thoughts with a totally different subject, and then resuming the dialogue as if nothing had broken the train of thought. For instance:

```
"I see you've changed for dinner." He was wearing a formal
dinner jacket with a cummerbund that snugly revealed his
muscular physique. "You look very handsome."
```

It's jarring. How much simpler it would be if:

```
She glanced at him and saw he was wearing a formal dinner
jacket with a cummerbund that snugly revealed his muscular
physique. "I see you've changed for dinner. You look very
handsome."
```

Now we know that the dialogue belongs to the female glancing at him. There's no interruption in thought processes, but a smooth flow of observation coupled with comment. Yet all I did was add "she glanced at him and saw"; this establishes who the observer is, and who is observed. It goes without further definition who's speaking to the man.

Again, and it bears repetition here, read your dialogue aloud. Listen to yourself. Ideally, if you have a tape recorder, record the dialogue so you can play it back. Does it sound natural? Does it flow? Are you repeating certain words too often? While the use of contractions is important within the text itself, they're vital to dialogue. We all tend to run our words together in ordinary conversation. And that's what dialogue is all about: conversation. Unless, of course, you have some arrogant professor pontificating to the faceless crowd; or it's a lawyer's argument before a jury; or other less informal situations.

But in everyday usage, a character might say: "Long as you're up, switch to Channel 5, will you?" The character would not say: "As long as you are up, switch to Channel 5. Will you?"

Dialogue is conversation so it must sound like conversation: words omitted, contractions, and all. And when I use the word "sound," it's because so many readers actually "hear" the words they're reading. I don't mean they're moving their lips, but they are "listening" as they read. This is especially true if you've taken the trouble to make your characters human. Think about voices as you write. Do female characters have a deep, throaty laugh? Are their voices well-modulated with full lower registers or are they squeaky sopranos? What about your male characters? Are they tenors, baritones or bassos? Our speaking voices, vocabulary, and diction say a great deal about us; our schooling, what part of the country we're from; our ability to organize our thoughts and express ourselves clearly; and so on.

And in case you're wondering what I mean by "lower register," perhaps the best example I can give you is Henry Kissinger. Although he has a deep voice, his lower register isn't developed. When he gets into lower tones (not in volume, but in tonal quality), he speaks in a rasping monotone. Robert Wagner is another example of an underdeveloped lower register.

Women, in particular, often ignore developing their voices so that they're clear and well-modulated. Compare Kathleen Turner's speaking voice to, say, Roseanne's. Turner's is rich and vibrant; Roseanne's is twangy and lacking in tonal depth. These observations are not meant, by the way, as negative criticism . . . only to serve to illustrate how one's speaking voice can instill a variety of responses from the listener—or the reader.

The following is a sampling of frequent problems in writing. Most are some of the most commonplace errors made by beginning novelists. The list is far longer than what is included here, but these are some of the ones to watch for.

> **Readers don't want to be *told* what is happening; they want to be involved *in* it.**

Chapter Titles

Almost never used in contemporary fiction. Don't bother. And only nonfiction still has a table of contents.

The use of "for"

"Jerry stopped in his tracks for he had seen the problem immediately." Nowadays, it's less dated and smoother reading to use a semicolon instead of the word "for": "Jerry stopped in his tracks; he had seen the problem immediately."

Or in place of "for," use "since," "because," or even a verb: "Jerry stopped in his tracks, having seen the problem immediately." Or: "Having seen the problem immediately, Jerry stopped in his tracks."

Female Clichés

Try to avoid standard clichés about women. We don't all put our hands to our throats or mouths when surprised or frightened; I've never met a woman who stamped her foot in anger; and we don't all burst into tears if things aren't going our way. Not all female bosses (supervisors, department heads, etc.) are on mega-ego-trips pitting one employee (department) against another. Most women are safer drivers than men (verify this, if you wish, with a comparison of auto insurance rates between men and women under the age of twenty-five).

There are countless women who can't even boil water much less prepare an elegant meal; there are many women who don't feel like a failure because they're not married; and a surprising number of women who have no maternal instinct whatsoever.

Try to avoid reinforcing old clichés in your romance novel. Just because your heroine may be looking for marriage doesn't mean she can't have a best friend who thinks it's all a crock. And it certainly doesn't mean that your heroine should accept the first proposal she receives. Marriage is a job; it's work.

By dating, the heroine is—to all intents and purposes—soliciting bids on the "job" from eligible men. But being eligible doesn't mean he's the right man for her to marry. For too many years (would you believe centuries?) women have been subject to stereotypical thinking—both by male and female authors. Women haven't been portrayed as individuals, capable of breaking cliché molds successfully. In fact, quite the reverse. In most novels, even as late as the 1950s and 1960s, a female character who attempts to break out of the conventional mold had to pay for it in one way or another. So here's your chance to change that. Grab it.

Narrative

Whether in first- or third-person narrative, don't cop out with phrases such as "but more about that later." That's to impose yourself upon the reader; worse, how can your heroine possibly know what might happen in the future? She can't.

Try to avoid verbosity whenever possible. You're not being paid by the word, so don't milk your narrative. I read a novel some years ago where the author wrote: "It was not quite night, and not yet still day." Where I come from, we call that "dusk."

When writing about your heroine's thoughts, do not put them in quotation marks. Quotation marks are for dialogue, or to set a word apart from the rest of the text. A general guide is that thoughts are left in roman type (i.e., the same kind of typeface you're reading right now). However, if it is the heroine's exact thinking process, then this is set off in italics.

```
    Midge moved toward the railing of the ship,wondering
where Jerry might be at that moment.
    Or
    Midge moved toward the railing of the ship. I wonder
where Jerry is right now, she thought.
```

In the first, Midge is just sort of letting her mind wander and "wondering" in general. In this latter example, the reader actually sees what she's wondering. The difference is that in the second example we are silently articulating her thoughts; there's nothing vague about them. And as mentioned earlier, if Midge is thinking out loud, then and only then will her thoughts be in quotation marks. She is, after all, having a dialogue with herself, the mirror, or her cat.

Descriptives in Narrative

There are times when dwelling on descriptions of locale, weather, house, etc., can be very useful to establish the tone of a scene, or to be sure the reader is fully apprised so that some development later on doesn't come as an unfair surprise. The latter is generally referred to as "planting clues." And no, this isn't only used in mysteries; it's perfectly valid in general fiction and romances too.

However, too frequently novices will dwell endlessly and it totally stops the flow of the story. We don't really have to know that her blue dress was made of cotton, had a sweet yoke, with little buttons at the sleeves, and a Peter Pan collar, with a pleated skirt, and a matching belt, or whether her handbag and shoes were dyed to match. Unless you're writing a novel with a heroine who is a fashion model, give the reader a little credit for a good imagination. If a full description is vital, okay; otherwise a hint will suffice. And this is really another area where you, as "god," can give the reader a minimum amount of information that also reveals a great deal in a limited number of words . . . and without stopping the flow of the story.

Let's say, just for the fun of it, that your hero is a cattle baron who makes frequent trips to Chicago for livestock auctions. He would probably smoke cigarettes or even cheroots. If he lights up with a book of matches, we get one picture; if he uses an eighteen-karat Cartier lighter, we get quite another. When the heroine jumps into her car, is it a beat-up old Toyota, or a nearly new Chrysler LeBaron? We don't have to know what color the car is unless it's custom-painted to match her eyes—which no romance heroine would dream of doing, but wealthy secondary characters might.

For some reason, monograms seem to carry some significance for many authors of romances. This may be due to the fact that monograms aren't as commonplace as they once were, or that it costs extra to have them. But if Jerry can afford a Cartier lighter, he can certainly afford monograms—which means, unless it's a clue, don't bother to mention it.

Here's a typical beginner's way of describing something:

```
Jerry reached in his pocket for a cigarette.  Then he
pulled out a lighter.  It was a lovely, rich-looking one.
Midge was sure it was real gold.  She looked at him.  Jerry
was so wonderfully handsome in his dark blue, serge,
double-breasted suit.  It set off his dark blue eyes, and
the flame from his lighter made the color all the more
intense.
```

> The restaurant they were at was charming. Checkered
> tablecloths were on every table along with a fresh-cut
> flower. A candle flickered between Midge and Jerry, and it
> seemed very romantic. The restaurant was crowded, but Midge
> didn't care. She was with Jerry and that was all that
> mattered. Soon the waiter came to take their order.

Now, my parents, relatives, and friends might think that's a terrific description. They love me, they want me to succeed, and they're reading into it something that isn't there: scene and mood. But is it good writing? Another problem with that example? It's written totally in the past tense, so it conveys no action whatsoever. Let's try it again.

> Seated at the round, corner table of the charming French
> restaurant, Midge was delighted with the checkered
> tablecloths, flickering candles and fresh-cut flowers on
> every table.
> "I hadn't expected it to be so crowded tonight," Jerry
> apologized, lighting a cigarette with his gold Cartier.
> Glancing at him momentarily, Midge couldn't help noticing
> how handsome he looked in his dark serge suit. Her mind
> briefly wandered with romantic fantasies until the waiter
> came to take their order and her little game was interrupted.

See the difference? In the first version, it is the author who is telling us what everything is like. In the second, it's part of what the heroine is seeing and thinking—a much smoother way to present the same information, without interruption of the flow.

Beginning novelists often fail to realize that readers don't want to be told what is happening; they want to be involved in it. This means that you, as author, should stay out of the narrative as much as possible. See what your heroine sees, react the way your heroine would react—the flow must be from your heroine's perspective, not yours.

As stated before, take stock of what your heroine (through you as author) elects to notice. This can be highly revealing about her as a person. If all she ever notes is that cuffs are frayed, furniture needs to be reupholstered, buttons are missing, someone's teeth should have been capped . . . well, clearly, she is a rather negative person. Again, that's not to say that Midge won't notice negative things, only that there should be a balance—heavily weighted in favor of positive observations. Save negative observations for sad scenes, or disappointments, for contrast to her usual cheerful self. Remember that readers want to escape to a happier, more romantic "place"; they don't want to read a novel that might mirror their own lives. Yes, insofar as Midge is only human, she'll have her ups and downs; but being up, positive, determined, and so on, must take precedence over any temporary setbacks.

If you place your heroine in a depressing setting, be sure she observes her environs with sympathy, compassion, or even empathy. If she's a social worker who must spend considerable time on the wrong side of the tracks, then use this opportunity to lend your writer's talent to make the reader more compassionate. And I don't mean being a knee-jerk liberal (which I personally consider an arrogant, insensitive term).

Have you ever been so ill that you no longer cared if the furniture is dusted, or the windows are clean? If you have, then consider this: the mind can also be so "ill" (downtrodden, despairing, hopeless, etc.) that it too no longer cares. Just because a handful of minority people have risen above their origins doesn't mean anyone can do it; it only means that these select few had something unknown (an early influence, an inner drive most of us can't imagine) to overcome the quicksand of despair. Just because some people are able to stop drinking or smoking or taking drugs without help . . . does that mean anyone can do it? Of course not!

So let your heroine see peeling paint in tenements, or smell the mixed cooking odors in the hallway from many ethnic cuisines, or notice roaches, or even rats...but let her also see the courage, or even the sheer survivability, it takes to live in a ghetto! Let her see it, try to deal with it, and show us her grit. The bureaucracy must be dealt with: apathy, disdain, disgust, etc., etc. Is Midge a scrapper, a champion? Or simply a "just doing my job, ma'am" type? Or for that matter, turn in her resignation due to burnout. You decide; you're the one who's "god."

Just remember that, sure, there are people who take advantage of "the system," but those people aren't restricted to minorities. Crooks come in all sizes and varieties; from all walks of life. What? You never heard of insider trading? White collar crime? Politicians on the take? C'mon. You know it happens. If you've ever "taken" a box of paperclips from the office, who's paying for it? Hey, fair is fair. There are people on the dole who shouldn't be; yet the majority of recipients desperately need it and wish they didn't and are willing—eager, in fact—to find work and hold their heads high again.

So once more, what your characters observe, mention, and so forth reveals a great deal about them. Here's another example of the wrong way to write descriptives.

```
Midge crossed the room. She sat down on the red chair and
unfolded the newspaper she was carrying.  Her eye fell on
the note that was on the rectangular table next to the chair.
It was addressed to her. She picked it up and opened it.
```

With this example, all we know about the scene is that there's a red chair and a rectangular table. We get no picture, no visual sense, of where Midge is. She could be at the doctor's office, an airport waiting lounge, or her own living room. And once again, the above example is written totally in the past tense, also from the author's perspective instead of the heroine's. The author is "telling" us that or this happened but is not involving us so we can participate, to contemplate or discover along with the heroine. And if you're not going to involve the reader, you may as well be working on a book report or a treatise—but not a novel. So here's another way:

Crossing the large room, her footsteps muffled by the thick Oriental rug, Midge sank onto the red wingback chair, then unfolded her copy of *Romantic Times*. For a moment she let her mind wander, thinking of the beautiful job of restoration done to the Victorian house by its former owner. The stained glass window, placed strategically to catch the last rays of daylight, sent colorful patterns to the opposite wall, as if to echo the sunset. The graceful swoop of the damask draperies lent the illusion that the dweller was living in a different time, an era of grace and elegance.

Midge felt warmly welcome with the eclectic selection of antiques or replicas of the decor of the times. She could easily imagine the sounding of the door chimes, of the butler opening the front door to gracious and proper ladies and gentlemen, leaving their calling cards on the console within the foyer. Her flight of fancy caused Midge to smile for no special reason. Then, as Midge glanced about appreciatively, her dark blue eyes noticed a small white envelope propped up between the Chinese lamp and Tiffany ashtray on the end table. Her name was neatly written on its front, and Midge picked up the envelope, wondering what it contained as she opened it.

(A quick aside here. Note: in the book world, names of newspapers or periodicals are italicized. And in correct English, the word for a window covering is "drapery"—not "drape." Drapery is a noun; drape is a verb. To illustrate: She draped the draperies over the chair. So moving right along . . . .)

Again, it is not the author telling us what the room looks like, but the character. We see it as she sees it, through her eyes, through her own perceptions—not the author's. With this example, we get a very good insight into Midge's personality and her tastes. We know she's at least a little bit old-fashioned, with an appreciation for the craftsmanship of another epoch. And in dwelling even for those few paragraphs, we've also set a tone or a mood. She's comfortable; she feels secure. And she can laugh at herself. That's important if you want readers to like her.

Another reason for spending a bit of time with decor (or a sunset or a vista, etc.) is to establish a mood. Midge is cozy and secure at this moment. What you decide is written on that note can further the mood or shatter it. For example, if the note says, "Darling, can't wait to get back. I hate being away from you. Love, Jerry." Naturally, she's going to feel even more loved and content.

But if that note says, "My darling, I'm too much of a coward to say this to your face. I'm not really away on a business trip. I've gone back to my wife and three children. Please forgive me. I know I should have told you long ago, but I couldn't. I shall always love you, but must never see you again. Jerry."

Wow! Now that's a slap in the face! Midge's world has blown up on her.

Neither Midge nor the reader could have anticipated Jerry's confession. (Unless, of course, you want the reader to suspect Jerry even before Midge does; that would involve some clues along the way that the reader can spot, but Midge doesn't.) In all likelihood, with the original situation, Midge will never trust being so content again.

Just for fun, rewrite the above scene, except Midge hates the decor. What are her reactions and observations? How does this change the story line—if at all? And if she dislikes it so intensely, why does she live there? If the furnishings aren't

> **A novel should contain a moral, something the reader can learn from.**

a reflection of her personal taste and preference, then why is the furniture there? By keeping the same basic elements of that scene, but changing the decor, what happens to your heroine? How can you justify her living with something she hates and yet not make Midge seem like a negative person? Good luck . . . .

However, establishing decor—but not mood—could easily be done in segments hither and yon as opposed to one section. By that I mean that each time someone is in that room, a little bit can be described with the action of the story or dialogue. Midge might be standing beside the English antique secretary (it's then unimportant if it's mahogany or not—don't milk your scene—if it's English and antique, it's probably a dark wood); maybe Jerry goes to the window and moves the champagne-colored sheers aside; and so on.

If you're not using descriptives to set a mood, then keep them brief. Dole out such tidbits of decor as if unimportant . . . readers will still get a picture of the ambience without stopping the flow of the story itself. It can also be accomplished with brief mentions with dialogue. How? Funny you should ask!

```
Twisting the brown leather strap of her handbag, Midge
said, "Now see here!"
He turned from her, brushing at his gray flannel slacks.
"What can I say?"
She exhaled heavily and perched on the edge of his ornate
desk. "Why do we always have to argue?"
Jerry stood silently for a moment, as if studying the
composition of the Turner waterscape that hung on the wall.
```

That would be one of the ways to "subliminally" present the decor and attire. Strictly speaking, leather is the clue here; it's not plastic so it is more expensive. Maybe she spent too much money, but she does care for the real thing and not imitation. Also notice that both characters are "doing something" besides just talking. That keeps the action alive. Midge is twisting; then she perches. Jerry is brushing at his gray flannel slacks; the clue here is flannel. They are not polyester or poly-blend; so they would be more expensive than jeans or synthetic materials. Too, with flannel, his slacks would have to be dry-cleaned instead of machine washable. That costs money too. Another action is the fact that Jerry stands then seems to study. Both characters are doing something, they're not "frozen in space" with only dialogue to carry the scene. And anyone who can afford a genuine 19th-century Turner painting has megabucks! Jerry would have to be very well off indeed—a CEO, perhaps. But of course, if it's just a reproduction, that changes everything. It's this type of detail that separates the pro from the amateur.

Just to be absolutely certain we're still singing with the same sheet music, let me do it the wrong way for comparison.

```
Midge stood in front of Jerry's desk.  It was a huge
ornate, mahogany desk.  She wore a pale green dress, with
brown leather heels and a matching shoulder handbag.  She
twisted the leather strap of her handbag. Midge said, "Now
see here!"
    He turned from her. Jerry was wearing gray flannel slacks
and a dark blue blazer.  He brushed at his gray trousers
as he asked, "What can I say?"
    She exhaled heavily and perched on the edge of his huge
desk.  "Why do we always have to argue?"
    Jerry stood silently for a moment. He was gazing at the
Turner waterscape that hung on the wall as if studying the
composition.
```

Preterite! Static! Telling the reader instead of involving the reader! This version interrupts the flow of the story! Do not underestimate the intelligence of your readers. In fact, good, tight writing uses a minimum of adjectives or descriptives yet, like shadow lettering, still leaves an image with the readers. (What's shadow lettering? As you might guess, the letter itself isn't drawn or printed. Instead, the letter is invisible, but you get its formation from the "shadow" it might throw if it were a raised, three-dimensional letter.) Less is better, if written tightly. If you're being paid by the word, forget it.

However, by choosing what people surround themselves with, you can tell the reader a great deal about the characters' personalities. If the desk is cluttered, we know that Jerry is unorganized (but if everything else in the room is neat and tidy, then Jerry's just messy—he can find what he wants even if no one else can); it he's wearing jeans, he's far more casual than if he's wearing a three-piece suit. This saves you from having to tell the reader about such things; they're implied by the "props" you provide.

How people walk, how they talk, what fidgeting they do, what mindless habits they have, what they like to read, what movies they prefer, etc., etc. All of these things are insights into your characters. And in keeping, how much they know and/or remember is also an insight. If Jerry has memorized all the Superbowl scores for the past decade, we can be confident he's a football nut. If Midge can identify who George Raft was and what movies he was in, the reader knows she's a fan of old movies.

Think about when you meet someone for the first time . . . what questions do you ask? What questions are asked of you? As you get to know someone better, what else do you learn about that person? When you're writing a novel, it's no different. You're introducing strangers, your characters, to your readers. You don't have to stop everything as so many beginners do. For example: "Suddenly the sound of the telephone's ringing interrupted Midge's reading and she lay the novel, open-faced, down on the arm of her chair. " Okay. Now we know that Midge likes to read and probably prefers fiction. That's all the reader really has to know about that aspect of her personality— unless she's a librarian or researcher.

And again, never describe the same thing twice unless it's essential to the story. If you mention Victorian furniture once, you need not say it again. Instead, however, since the reader already knows that the room is in the style of that period, you might want to have a character move toward an inlaid, round table, playing with the brass pull of the drawer (or ceramic, or crystal, whatever). Decor can almost be treated as a "by the way" reference; i.e., "I've been meaning to tell you . . . ." It can be nothing more than an idle hint dropped into the story.

If you incorporate snippets of descriptive with dialogue or action, readers will be assimilating the information, getting a vivid picture, without having to stop the action or conversation. This is equally true of descriptions of your characters. Once you've said that Jerry is exceptionally tall, drop it. The next time, though, you may want Midge to be standing next to him, keenly aware that the top of her head barely reaches his shoulders.

But if Jerry is six-foot-two, and Midge is five-foot-ten . . . the images will change, as will the attitudes of your characters. While it's not as common-place today as it used to be, still men tend to prefer to date women who are shorter than they. And women who are taller than average may be extremely sensitive about their height, or even, maybe, have had difficulty in the past being asked out. Their height is intimating, perhaps. This will, naturally, affect her outlook on life and people. Some of you might even remember when it was an embarrassment for a woman to be too tall, or to have too ample a bosom. If you don't, ask your mother or grandmother about what it was like. Many a tall young woman in my youthful era walked with a stooped over posture to avoid the revelation of her actual height. (Today she'd probably be selected as a model for high fashion designers. Times change.)

Yes, I'm hammering at these things because they are so important to understand. So now, you rewrite the scene of Midge in her parlor reading the issue of *Romantic Times*. Make the decor Early American, or ultra-modern. What happens? A completely different opinion of Midge, of who she is, and what she prefers. If she prefers modern decor, we can pretty well establish that she likes sleek lines (furniture, cars, clothing, etc.); and that she wants the ease of simplicity and no-nonsense upkeep. Chrome, glass, straight lines. Wooden furniture must be "maintained" or cared for. You have to constantly wax it, or oil it so the wood doesn't dry out. Placing a glass of iced anything could totally destroy fine wood finishes—but only leaves a ring, easily wiped, on glass.

What colors are dominant in Midge's modern living room? Blues, greens, and perhaps mauve? Cold, remote, maybe a bit secretive. Change the colors to earth tones: ocher, sienna, rust, orange, etc. What happens? Warm, receptive, outgoing . . . . A heroine who prefers modern (regardless of color scheme) would doubtlessly have a sinking spell at the mere thought of how much more work is involved with antique pieces.

Even such relatively small details such as pets reflect the character's personality. Small, yapping lap dogs? Or huge, threatening dogs from the mastiff breeds? Pedigree dogs or saved from the pound? What about cats? Does she prefer them to dogs? Does she have one of each? How does the character behave around his or her pets? Are we witnessing someone who's "itski-witski" (my term for babytalk) with animals, or someone who treats them like equals or peers. Someone who gives the pet the run of the house, or someone who's a disciplinarian? The interaction between pet and pet owners is yet another strong insight into the character's personality.

And of course, there are many people who simply have no communion with animals of any sort. That doesn't make them necessarily bad—perhaps there's a very good reason for it. My grandmother, as a child, was attacked by a rabid cat and badly mauled. She conveyed her fear of cats to her own children. As a result, my aunt—who is probably one of the finest people in the world—is afraid of animals of any kind.

Just keep in mind that whatever external traits you assign to your characters are the indicators of who they are beneath the surface. That established, you really needn't embellish further. Put yourself to the test. The next time you meet someone new, pay attention to (1) what you observe about that person, (2) what your initial impressions are (on a scale of 1-10, representing dislike to like), (3) how you react, and (4) were you later surprised about that person's personality?

I'll give you a clue. My car is never as clean as it should be—inside or out. There's a roll of paper towels, glass cleaning fluid in a plastic container, an extra pair of windshield wipers, dry muddy seats, etc., etc. If you just met me and saw my car, your impression of me is likely to be that I'm neither tidy nor especially clean. However, the interior of my home is usually tidy, well dusted, vacuumed, and clean. Why the contradiction? Because 99% of the time there are at least two dogs in my car wherever I go. Trying to keep it clean is a waste of time. But do you see the opportunity here? How an initial impression may not be truly accurate? Then put yourself in the shoes of your readers. As you describe a character, remember that your readers will be "responding" to your character in the same way you do in real life.

And insofar as no one is totally right or perfect, it may add a little charm to your characters to reveal areas of "blind spots" or even weaknesses. As I recall, it was Oscar Wilde who stated: "I can resist anything but temptation." Okay. So what if Midge has a hollow leg when it comes to ice cream; or maybe Jerry collects something frivolous yet rather expensive—snuffboxes, perhaps. Your characters are not only allowed to have a bit of clay around their feet, it can make them more believable and winsome to the reader.

Failing to be aware of character development can lead to any number of false impressions about your characters. If you never saw Hitchcock's movie,

"Suspicion," (with Cary Grant and Joan Fontaine, 1941), I urge you to rent it on video and study how the characters are introduced, how they develop, and how you respond to them. For that matter, read Daphne du Maurier's novel *Rebecca*—which was also subsequently filmed by Hitchcock (this time with Laurence Olivier and Joan Fontaine, 1940). Both of these offer splendid examples of strongly delineated character development. Watch/read each first for the story elements. Then with paper and pencil, watch them again and note how the characters are introduced, interact, and evolve. Although both of these are mysteries, it doesn't matter. Good, solid character development is good, solid character development—whether it's for a western, sci-fi, general fiction, or . . . romances.

Let me backtrack for a moment. I'm blithely talking about character development on the assumption that you know what I mean. In case you don't, let me explain. Take, for example, Theodore Dreiser's classic novel, *Sister Carrie* (decades later made into a movie with Laurence Olivier and Jennifer Jones, 1952). It starts out with Carrie being exceedingly naive, just a simple country girl. Her character development is caused by what happens to her. She gradually loses her illusions; and although she triumphs ultimately, the price is high. By the end, Carrie is a well-known actress, sophisticated and perhaps even a bit jaded, though still vulnerable. Carrie is a success, yes; but she has lost her dreams of love and happiness.

> A novel must capture the imagination with vivid actions that reveal attitudes.

And if you're too lazy to either read (shame on you!) or see these old films, then let me give you a fail-proof simpler example. Think of Dickens' *A Christmas Carol*. What happens to Scrooge, via the three ghosts, is a splendid way to grasp what character development is all about. How he's transformed from a calloused, indifferent grouch to a warm, caring human being. What happens to him, and how he reacts—his conscious and subconscious responses—to these events is the nucleus of his revelation and metamorphosis. And that is character development at its simplistic best.

Your good guys should certainly learn something valuable from their experiences; bad guys may or may not, depending on what you're trying to accomplish. Earlier, I mentioned that a novel should contain a moral, something the reader can learn from as well as your heroine. Maybe the heroine has a kid sister who's always getting into trouble with the authorities—be they school authorities or the police. Perhaps only minor infractions, but a symptom of something needing attention and needing it at once (i.e., within the time-frame of the novel itself). How your heroine deals with the problem, what she and her sister learn, and how they "grow" is the character development in this situation.

As is true in real life, the chances of solving or overcoming a problem rarely happens right off the bat. Attempts are made that possibly fail or only partially succeed; one has to reevaluate the situation to see if there's another or better way of tackling the problem, and more attempts are made. And since problems involve the emotions as well as the intellect, there's the very real possibility that a character may realize what "ought" to be done (intellectual), but doesn't have the gumption or wisdom to accomplish (emotional). This emotional "failure" needn't be negative; far from it. By way of example, what if the heroine grew up in a poor family, always "in charge" of her younger siblings. Say she's frequently absent from school to tend a sick brother or sister; or has to help her mother with the paid ironing she does for others. As an adult, how capable would she be in a corporate setting? What about her social skills?

Create such a character in your own mind. Assign a situation (at the office, interviewing for a job, whatever), and then write it from the heroine's perspective. Does she feel intimidated? Threatened? Insecure? Because she's tended to the needs of others, she might well be a take-charge type of person. But there are ways to take charge and then there are ways . . . . How does she avoid being bossy or dictatorial? Does she even realize there's a difference? How does she avert hurting the feelings of others? If her business and social skills are underdeveloped, how does she handle the situation you assign to her?

Once you've written this scenario, take the same basic elements but have your heroine from a wealthy family, best schools, and so forth. What happens to her in that situation now? How will she react?

When you know your characters and their inner selves well, it will take less and less time to develop a muscle that aids you to write from each character's perspective without agonizing toil.

It is to be hoped, in real life, that we all have experiences—good and bad—that help us to grow into more mature, compassionate humans. Yet, most of us will know at least one person whose intellectual or emotional growth is stunted. To borrow a phrase from an Applied Psychology course: The average American dies at thirty but is buried at eighty. Translation: The average American ceases to learn anything new after the age of thirty—either intentionally or unintentionally. Given a choice, these people will cling to the familiar and never question how or why they are doing it.

> **Every chapter should end with a "cliff-hanger"; that is, a device that makes the reader want to quickly get to the next chapter.**

So, of course, in fiction, growth is a happy ending; succumbing to failure, giving up, is a sad ending. Inasmuch as any novel should have a message or moral to it, think first about what you want your characters to learn, or not learn. This is what's called character development. Again, they start out one way, and end in another. Not necessarily the reverse of what they were, but changed.

Pace and Rhythm

Rhythm? But this is prose, not poetry! Right. However, prose too must have pace and rhythm. Probably the most consistent error made by beginning writers is not to recognize this. Flip back and take a look at all the examples I've provided thus far. You will notice one thing in particular: Each of the "wrong" versions is slow reading, dull and lifeless. Each of the "right" ones has pace and rhythm, and is easily read, more visual or alive. Why are the former examples dull? Because they are written totally in the preterite. (Yes, we're back to that subject again and it will be repeated until you are fully aware of the difference between the "right" and the "wrong" way of fiction writing. Or, for that matter, nonfiction as well—unless it's a formal paper for school or a professional journal.)

Don't forget your novel is a moving mural on paper! Those black letters against plain white paper have the potential to kindle your readers' imagination; to make words transform what is being read into mental pictures. Or they can leave a blank screen . . . .

Break up the tenses. Instead of saying that Midge "had decided to go to the movies, then changed her mind" (all past tense), say: "Midge thought about going to a movie, then decided against it." In "thinking about going" you are projecting a possible future action; not just what didn't happen, all in the past. Or, "She wondered if she should telephone Jerry." Future action implied by what she might do, not what she's done. Interjecting the future is a solid way of keeping your readers directly involved; it aids readers to feel like an active partner in any such decisions—not a listless bystander.

When you write that your heroine is thinking about doing something, or saying something, you're hooking readers to think, "Yeah, that sounds like a pretty good idea." When you have her decide against it, though, changing her mind, this asks the readers to ponder why your heroine changed her mind. Then, depending upon what you want that decision to accomplish, you can either explain it further or just drop it as pretty self-evident.

Or, if your heroine is making the wrong decision, you have to decide whether or not you want the readers to anticipate a negative conclusion, or discover it only when the heroine does. All of us have known someone who, at one point or another, is about to make a stupid mistake. As often as not, it's impossible to intercede. You just have to let the person make the mistake and hope that he or she learns from it. You can present that kind of information for your readers too.

Remember when Midge was seated in the Victorian parlor and two versions of what that note contained were supplied? The first one was a happy missing-you note. You might want your heroine to continue with the following thought:

```
Glancing at her watch, Midge wondered just how far Jerry
had driven by then.  If he was almost to Nashville, Jerry
would be in Central Daylight Time.
     With a mischievous little smile, Midge moved toward the
replica of a French telephone. She lifted the receiver while
```

keeping the connection depressed as she thought about it.
Would Jerry be amused if she had a bottle of champagne
delivered to his hotel suite, waiting for him? Or would he
think it too frivolous...far from businesslike or even maybe
an invasion of his privacy?

Midge stared down at the telephone as if it might hold
the answer to her questions. Then, with a small sigh and
feeling just a bit foolish, she replaced the receiver but
left her hand resting on it indecisively. What if his client
should return to Jerry's rooms and see chilled champagne
awaiting? No. It would certainly not provide the impression
that Jerry was a serious businessman.

On the other hand, she silently argued with herself, it
might cheer him up, feeling less lonely in a Nashville hotel.

Okay. Do you see what's happening in this scene? Among other things, we
learn (if we haven't before) that Midge has a devilish side to her nature. And
we have projected a possible action implied by what she's thinking she might
do, and not what she's done. The reader is "thinking" about it with the
character. If you don't want it to be so important (which is to say, an insight
into Midge's character), then you could easily just condense it down to: "Midge
thought it would be fun to have a bottle of champagne delivered to his suite,
then decided against it." Period. Your decision. Will she or won't she send
the champagne to his room? Do you see how the reader is being kept part of
the scene? Do you have a picture of what Midge is doing, what her actions and
feelings are? Can you analyze how the preterite is mixed with the present
tense, and even with the future tense?

Take the second paragraph, for instance. Midge moved toward the
telephone (past tense); the fact that it's a replica of a French telephone is a
subliminal decor touch. She's keeping the buttons depressed, and that's
present tense. We can see her doing that right now. Then, again with a
projection into the future, Midge speculates how Jerry might react (future).
Note too how a one-word sentence can be used for effect. It keeps the pace
going. The reader's eye will glance right over the word, yet the message is
there. "No." It has a finality to it. But then she contradicts herself. This forces
the reader to wonder what she'll decide to do next . . . and that's what keeps
readers turning the page.

Also take note that the character is doing something, that there's action
within the scene. So let's take the second version of what's written on the note,
where Jerry admits he's married (the rat!).

Crumpling the note into her palm, it felt like a hot coal
against her flesh. A wave of nausea and lightheadedness made
Midge feel faint. She had trusted him implicitly, giving
her heart to the man she loved. But Jerry had betrayed that
trust...that love.

She felt the blood draining from her face, and her hands

became clammy as the realization sank in. Like someone who was drowning, images of their moments together flashed before her eyes. Jerry laughing, reaching out to touch her or hold her hand; Jerry basking in the sunlight on the lake's shore, his bare chest softly rising and falling...so many, many images came to her. Then they shattered. In her mind, they were now broken, just sharp shards stabbing at her soul.

Crumpling the note is present tense; that it felt like a hot coal is past tense. That Midge had trusted him is past tense, but giving her heart is present. That Jerry had betrayed her is again past tense. She felt the blood draining from her face is past but "sounds" immediate; and note how deftly (she said modestly) the present tense is mixed with the preterite with "flashed before her" and then immediately becomes present tense again with what she sees in her mind. Her images are shattered, past tense again.

Do you see how mixing the tenses provides rhythm and pace? If you want to prove to yourself how effective this is, rewrite the scene totally in the past tense. Then ask someone to read it back to you aloud, and follow up with the mixed tense version. If it's totally written in the preterite, it will sound as "vital" and "alive" as the predictable ticking of a metronome.

In fact, that may be a very useful analogy here. Metronomes may be set for any tempo you choose, be it 4/4 time or 3/4 time, etc. But think about it. Listen to one in your imagination. *Tick tock...tick tock...tick tock*—back and forth, back and forth, with nothing to break up the monotony. Then add some syncopation to it. Maybe: *tick tick-a-tick, tock...tick tick-a-tick, tock*. Do you hear the difference? Break it up some more, vary the syncopation: *tick-a-tick, tick-a-tick, tick-a-tick tock tock...tick-a-tick, tick-a-tick, tick-a-tick tock tock*. (Anyone for "The William Tell Overture" from whence came "The Lone Ranger" theme music?)

And that's what your sentences must provide: Pace and rhythm. Long sentences, short sentences, incomplete sentences, one-word sentences . . . past tense (preterite), present tense, future tense . . . and! That most precious resource for any good writer—introducing the gerund. *Ta-dah!* Had I the power I would hang a sign directly in front of your typewriter or display that says (in bold capitals, italicized, and with a florescent glow):

GERUNDS CAN BE YOUR FRIEND!

A what? A gerund. In school you may have been taught that the gerund is the same as the present participle. It's also called a "verbal noun." In brief, it's the form of any verb that ends with "ing." The difference between a gerund and a participle is in its use.

Gerund: Running for governor had been a secret dream. (Running, in this instance, is the subject of the sentence.)

Participle: While running for office, he met many obstacles. (Running, in this case, modifies he.)

I'm throwing this explanation in for those of you who are purists and really care about such things. The object here, however, is to get you thinking in visual, action ways of phrasing things. Instead of "she sat down," think "sitting down, she—" or instead of "she gazed out the window," try "gazing out the window, she— " It gives the writing a feeling of intimacy, as if we're right there with the heroine.

By mixing up your tenses, and prudent use of the gerund or participle, you take your novel out of the static past tense and breathe life into it.

Again: Do not overuse either. Too much is as bad as not enough.

Think about picture and action verbs, too. If Midge sits down, that tells us next to nothing. Anyone can simply sit down. It's how a character sits down that holds the reader. If she sinks onto the cushioned chair, we have a picture of what's happening. More than that, though, we can be pretty sure that she's very tired, or frustrated, or that the cushion is soft and deep. Verbs too can reveal the characters' moods, sometimes even more effectively than long explanations. Does Midge walk across the room? Or does she stride, amble, or saunter? If she's feeling tense or excited, why not have her "sitting tentatively on the arm of the chair"? *Hmm?* Teenage character who's just had a fight with Midge? He or she would slump, hands stuffed into pockets—yes, you can definitely slump onto a chair . . . ask any parent of a teenager.

Slamming a door makes quite a different impression from merely closing it. For that matter, so does "carefully closing the door so not to awaken him." You've got to provide images for your readers; not just basic information. Let your characters stretch to reach something, twist on their chairs, lifting a shoulder and rotating it as if to get a kink out of the back muscle, take slow and deliberate steps lest the full cups of coffee slosh over the rims onto the saucers, and so forth. Provide an image for your readers so they can be picturing the scene in their own minds.

Remind yourself constantly that a novel is not a term paper. It must capture the reader's imagination with vivid actions that reveal attitudes.

Another way is to introduce sentences with prepositional phrases: "In that case, Midge thought, she might as well have stayed home." Or: "Up till then, she'd had no choice."

Yes, the predominant part of your novel will be in the past tense—but break it up! You'll also want to be mindful of punctuation. We discussed this earlier, and it too can create an illusion.

Another area where the novice tends to lose the reader is with dialogue. It's as if writers think that nothing else could be happening just because someone is speaking. How often have you been on the telephone and made notes to yourself, or just spotted that dustbunny in the corner? Have you ever interrupted yourself to tell someone who's in the room something. Have you never been in the process of leaving a room, then called out a reply to the person you've left behind? Doesn't your mind ever wander while someone else is talking?

Just because a person is talking doesn't mean that person has ceased to exist other than as a disembodied voice. Some of us doodle while on the telephone; or glancing about, realize we're low on Kleenex; or have our memories jogged about something that happened long ago. Short of using a chain saw, most of us—at least momentarily—have thoughts that go beyond the immediacy of the moment. Have you ever cradled the receiver between chin and shoulder while removing leftovers from the refrigerator, gently kicking the door shut? To keep that pace and rhythm going, keep your characters busy with other mental or physical things—unless total concentration is required. Brain surgery, for instance.

Here's an example of what I mean:

> "How about a steak and a baked potato?" Jerry asked her, spreading the menu out before him.
> "The steak sounds fine, but I'll have sliced tomatoes instead," she replied, recalling all too well how long it had taken her to drop those extra five pounds.

Jerry's doing something as he speaks and Midge is remembering something. Then, if it's just the two of them in the scene, you can occasionally drop to almost only dialogue.

> "Worried about your weight?"
> She nodded.
> "You shouldn't be. You look great."

No problem keeping track of who's saying what . . . and it breaks up the pace of the book.

So do contractions. Many writers think it's permissible to use contractions in dialogue, but forget to use them in narrative—or erroneously believe they're not acceptable. To provide enough rhythm to hold your reader's interest, there's nothing wrong with using contractions in the narrative. (My sainted English teacher would kill me, but this is fiction, not a book report.)

> She'd have to move quickly.
> Wouldn't he ever learn?
> She hadn't thought of that before.
> Why couldn't he see reason?

Then too, there's the matter of "eye-stopping" words. Most of us read and assimilate information almost at a glance, not even particularly aware of the individual words. However, some words stick in our minds and we remember them if they are repeated too quickly. This can lead to lending a sense of repetitiousness, which can, of course, be boring.

Action and visual words, for instance. If you have a character trying to catch up with someone "at a trot," don't use the word "trot" for at least another fifteen to twenty pages. If someone "minces" his words, don't use "mince" again for a very long time. If you've used, say, "fascinat-

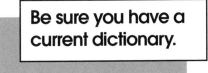

Be sure you have a current dictionary.

ing" in paragraph one at the top of the page, then don't use "fascinating" again in paragraph five. It's too soon. Wait at least another eight or nine pages before using it again (never mind Mr. Spock).

Any word that is not ordinary to our mental "ears" needs to be used sparingly. Unusal colors, for instance, will stick in the reader's mind. Mauve, vermillion, chartreuse, obsidian, etc., will leap from the pages and should be used very, very seldom. So will sounds. If somebody "hisses" a line of dialogue, don't use "hiss" again for at least another chapter—preferably several chapters later.

Whenever possible, don't repeat image or action words in the same paragraph or even on the same page if it can be avoided. Remember when Midge was in the Victorian parlor taking in her environs? I could have used "sunset" twice, but I didn't. Instead, I first phrased it "to catch the last rays of daylight" and later, in the same paragraph, used "sunset." Same soup; different noodles.

There's almost always a way to paraphrase something, or to find synonyms for any given word. However, there are two words that have driven me crazy for years. "Nightmare," for instance, has no synonym, per se; you have to substitute "a horrible dream" or some other phrase—but there's no one-word synonym. And the synonyms listed for "smile" aren't synonyms at all. A smile is not a grimace, nor a smirk, nor a laugh. So if you don't want your character to sound as if she's had a frontal lobotomy, be very careful with how often you use "smile."

Think in terms of responses other than physical. "She was amused" is another way to say "smile" simply because most of us smile when we're amused; or "she was pleased." For that matter, just having your heroine or character begin to hum to herself softly is an indication of a happy mood. Short of a funeral march, most of us are smiling when humming to ourselves . . . .

Cliff-hangers

This is just what it sounds like and generally applies to the end of each chapter. To varying degrees, every chapter should end with a "cliff-hanger"; that is, a device that makes the reader want to quickly get to the next chapter. When people refer to a book as "a page turner," you can be pretty much assured that the term cliff-hanger will apply equally. It can be in the form of a question, a statement, an unexpected development in the story, and any number of other things.

You've written, for instance, that Jerry and Midge have had an argument, and you're at the end of a chapter halfway through the novel. You might end that chapter with: "Midge sobbed her heart out." Well, yeah, that tells it like it is. Yet it doesn't pique the reader's curiosity. But if you wrote: "Midge sobbed her heart out. His words had been so angry! Would she ever see Jerry again . . . .?"

All right. Now you're asking the reader to ask the same question. Will Midge ever see Jerry again? Just how will those two get together after what's happened? Note too that an exclamation point was used only once. Exclamation points and the boy who cried wolf are interchangeable—don't overwork it. And while I could have simply put a question mark after the last sentence, I used the ellipsis first. Do you see how that lends a sense of dangling uncertainty? The ellipsis serves to heighten the reader's awareness and desire to read on.

Okay. How about a really dreadful stormy night and you've reached the end of that chapter. Instead of saying "Midge curled up with a good book," why not say "Midge curled up with a good book, soon caught up with the story. Suddenly, she heard a knock at her door. *That's funny*, she thought. *Who'd be out on a night like this?*" Well, now the reader is equally curious. Who is at her door on such a night?

Now mind you, you won't be able to pull off cliff-hangers for every single chapter. And not every cliff-hanger needs to be in the form of a phrased question . . . it can also be a sense of anticipation that keeps the reader going. Let's say that Midge has decided to go to Jerry's office following that argument, to attempt to sort things out and rekindle their love. You don't need a question at all. Instead, you need only write: "Midge paused in front of the door, her eyes fixed on the nameplate with raised brass letters: Jerry Hayden, Executive Vice-President. Squaring her shoulders, she took a deep breath, then turned the knob of the door with silent determination." See? No question needed. But the situation she's in subconsciously asks: Will Midge succeed? You, as author, don't have to put the words in the readers' minds; just make sure the scene you end the chapter with leaves the reader wanting to know more.

And I may as well again cover how thoughts are handled in a novel. Take a Post-it labeled "Thoughts" and stick it to the right-hand margin. Thoughts are not conversation or dialogue, so no quotation marks are used. If the thought represents precisely what the character is thinking, then the entire thought is underscored or italicized. See the paragraph above for an example. If the thought is simply a general one, such as "would she ever see Jerry again," then no special punctuation is required. Here are a few more examples for your quick reference.

```
#1: Midge idly played with the edge of her napkin, glancing
around. She felt terribly ill at ease. I should have dressed
up, she silently chided herself, feeling very out of place.
```

Her exact thought is presented here, so it's italicized. That she's feeling ill at ease and out of place isn't a thought, per se, but a general bit of information.

```
#2 : Midge stood at the jeweler's display window, admiring
an antique gold necklace. It's got to be at least eighteen-
karat gold, she thought. She shrugged, wondering if the day
would ever come when she'd be able to afford such luxuries.
```

Her exact thought is italicized. Wondering, though, isn't a precise thought but a general bit of speculation. If you want it to be her exact thinking, then you would have to rewrite it as: *I wonder if I'll ever be able to afford such luxuries?*

Now, there are times in all of our lives when we are talking to ourselves, if only in a mutter, and in those situations there is audible sound. Therefore, we need quotation marks. It's not a thought anymore, it's a monologue. How you handle this is often a very good glimpse into a character's personality. For instance:

> #3: Midge held the brown suit up to her chin as she slowly turned in front of the mirror. "Too businesslike," she said, tossing the garment onto her bed. She went over to the closet and removed a pale blue dress, then spread out the full skirt as she glanced at the mirror again. "Hmm. Feminine, demure, but no frills."
>
> She lifted the dress in front of her to inspect that it didn't need ironing first. "Well, that pretty well sums me up," she said to no one. "Feminine yet no frills. As for demure . . . well that depends on my mood." Then Midge laughed at herself. *Maybe I should get a cat. At least I'd have someone to talk to!*

See how that was handled? Midge is talking aloud—quotation marks. She does so again, then laughs at herself. Her silent yet exact thought follows and is italicized. Okay, but what else have we learned in just those two paragraphs?

She's obviously going to meet someone and doesn't want to appear too businesslike—yet she owns businesslike suits, so probably holds down a job with responsibility. And in case the reader hasn't yet figured it out, we also learn that Midge prefers feminine dresses but nothing fussy or flouncy. We learn that she is aware of speaking aloud and laughing to herself about it. And we now know for sure that she doesn't have any pets or we wouldn't need the last line. So we haven't merely described clothing, but have been given insights into Midge's personality. Throughout those two paragraphs, Midge is doing something—not just staring into her closet. That she tosses the suit onto her bed? She's not a fuss-budget about such things; a fastidious person would have taken the suit back to the closet and put it back in place, probably with all the hangers facing in the same direction. Do you see how much can be learned about a character with very few words, and without impeding the flow of the story?

Now if the first two examples were at the end of a chapter, how could you end them with a cliff-hanger? Actually, #1 leaves ample opportunities for all kinds of cliff-hanging sentences.

> She cringed when the waiter approached and asked with slight disapproval, "Party of one?" He placed the oversized menu before her, an obsequious smile on his face.
>
> For a moment, Midge was tempted to get up and flee the restaurant. Fortunately, Jerry had just entered the dining room, looking for her.
>
> "No," she told the waiter, unable to totally hide her

discomfort, "my escort has just arrived." *Someday*, she thought, *no one will ever dare speak to me that way*. Even as she thought the words, Midge had to inwardly smile. Someday? Who was the unknown benefactor who would leave her a million dollars?

Now, that could be a "plant" or clue to what's to come, or just an observation. But it does pose a question on two levels: Would her circumstances ever change (i.e., through power or authority), or will she inherit a vast sum of money? You'll have to flip that page to find out.

With #2, it might be all right as it stands—depending upon what's going on in the story or has led up to this moment. But #3 needs some help to be a cliff-hanger. Maybe the phone rings and Midge hopes that it's not Jerry calling to beg off their date; or there's a knock at the door when she's not expecting anyone. If you want to get melodramatic, perhaps a rock is hurled through her bedroom window, with a note tied around it. What's written on the note? Why would anyone want to break her window? Again, think soap operas. You have to leave your reader wanting more . . . .

I can't tell you how many romances have remained on my coffee table, opened to the second or third chapter, and I never finished reading them. I lost interest. I didn't care what happened next simply because the author failed to make me want to know. Remember that editors read with a highly trained eye; they won't be so forgiving as someone who knows you well. It's the book that counts, and only the book. If you lose your editor's interest, you've just lost a sale . . . .

Pull out some of the romances you've enjoyed the most and reread the endings of the chapters. What held your attention? What made you want to read more?

Details

One of the reasons I'm so very fond of editorial work is that it permits me to be an armchair detective. You're halfway through a manuscript and the writer mentions the red-haired niece. Wait a minute! Didn't the author state

> **If you don't need a drink to write a letter, you don't need one to write a novel.**

that the niece was bald a few chapters back? *Flip-flip-flip*. Right. Gotcha.

Some years ago, I was reading a romance wherein the heroine was a guest in someone's home. Shown to her bedroom, she was pleased with how sunny it was, but the adjoining bathroom had no shower; only an old-fashioned claw-legged tub. Guess what? The heroine took six showers in that same bathroom before the book was finished. (Now that should have been caught by the editor, but wasn't. You can't trust anybody these days!)

My own way of solving this little problem is quite inexpensive, simple and I don't have to clutter my mind trying to remember every single thing I've said on paper. Though I mentioned it earlier, it's worth repeating here. I have a looseleaf notebook. For every single character (unless it's one who's a one-shot and will never appear in the book again—like a train conductor or an usher), I keep a log of everything I've ascribed to that person: physical appearance, gestures, pet expressions, favorite colors, preferred mode of dress, where that character lives (I even make a crude drawing of the floorplan so I don't have her turning left into the kitchen in one scene, and turning right in another) along with the decor, background (family and personal), education—everything! Consider it an FBI dossier for each of your characters.

This saves me hours and hours of having to double-check myself. It also means that if the editor who is assigned to my novel happens to have a hangover, I don't have to worry about him or her not catching my mistakes.

But don't throw a wrench into your creativity. Don't make these notes as you're writing your scene or chapter. Do it later, and allow some time to get some perspective on what you've written. My own way is to wait till when I'm rereading yesterday's material for content and mistakes (proofreading). I write down what I've said about every important detail of decor, locale, and the characters themselves. Some authors will wait weeks before doing this, so you'll have to establish what works best for you.

And just because your manuscript has been sold, don't discard the note-book, or other reference materials, until after the novel has been published. It's generally about a year between signed contracts and actual publication. And that's not counting the months and months of waiting while the manuscript was being submitted to the editor(s). Who could possibly remember a question about some small detail all that while later? Much less where the information might appear in the manuscript.

For example, I had a novel published a few years ago. Just a little more than twelve months had passed since it was contracted for and finally scheduled for publication (and the actual publication date was still several months away from the current date). When it came time for the editor to go to the art meeting with regard to the cover, she telephoned me with a hasty request for a refresher on what two of the characters looked like. No problem. Out came the notebook, and I was able to tell her anything she wanted to know.

Unlike bearing a child, you should never wait till one book has been published to begin another—your career would be thwarted and you'll starve to death. Writers write. So when that editor telephoned me, I already had another four books in varying degrees of completion. Without my notebook, I could easily have given her a bum steer. There isn't enough time in a harried editor's life to reread a manuscript prior to a cover art meeting, or a sales meeting, etc. You'll be far more appreciated if your editor knows s/he can count on you for last-minute refreshers about the story and its cast or locale. It will also greatly reduce the chances of the cover art showing the hero as a blond when he really has sandy/brownish hair.

If I had never been an editor, it probably wouldn't have occurred to me to also do up a "style sheet." Every conscientious editor draws one up before beginning to read any manuscript for copyediting. (Note that I qualified with "conscien-tious." That doesn't guarantee your editor will fit that description.) While authors don't have to do this, still it would make an editor's life happier thus ensuring you receive a figurative star on your forehead for being thoughtful.

All that's involved is taking a standard sheet of typing paper and drawing lines to create quarters. At the top of each quarter, you list how many letters of the alphabet will be covered in that quadrant. Since there are 26 letters to our language, you can't divide it precisely by four. But that's okay. For words that are less likely to begin with a particular letter, unload the extra two with the others. For instance, upper left quadrant is for words beginning with the letters from "a" through (and inclusive of) "f"; upper right quadrant is for letters "g" through "q"; lower left quadrant is for letters "p" through "u," and the last quadrant, lower right, is for letters "r" through "z." You can divvy up opening letters in any way that suits you, as long as it's easy to find what you're looking for.

Why is this beneficial? Well, for openers, there are an awful lot of words in our language that can be spelled more than one way; sometimes that's due to the British usage vs. American usage, and sometimes it's simply because our language has changed and continues to undergo additional changes. An example is the ever-increasing usage of spelling "can not" as one word (cannot). As long as the Merriam-Webster dictionary sticks to the original usage, so shall I. If you spell "can not" as one word, it means the reverse of your intent. As one word, it's almost always followed by the word "but." Example: If I find out that you're guilty, I cannot but go to the police. Spelling it as one word means you must, not that you can not. That's changing, of course, but hasn't been officially permitted yet by some dictionaries.

If you want to, instead of spelling it as one word, simply use "can't." And if you're as adamant about this as I, then alert your editor to it on the style sheet. It may turn out that the publisher's house style is to keep it as one word, but at least you strove valiantly to save the language.

To give you yet another example, I wrote a novel for Doubleday eons ago. In hardcover, authors are given the courtesy of seeing the copyedited manuscript before it goes to press—a courtesy often not extended by paperback houses. Okay. So I'm reading along, nodding my head with some of the editorial changes, and then came to a particular line. I had the heroine being upset by the hero's "affrontery." The editor had changed it to "affrontedness." Affrontedness? I don't think so. But grudgingly admitting, albeit silently, that I don't know everything (!), I went to my unabridged dictionary. Nope. No such word as "affrontedness."

However, to give credit where credit is due, I also looked up "affrontery." Nope. That too doesn't exist. So to avoid editorial hassles, I simply rewrote the line to eliminate the word altogether. It wasn't till months and months later that I learned where the problem lay. The infinitive of the verb is spelled "affront." Or even as a noun, it's spelled with an "a": It was an affront to his years in office. But! When using it as a term to indicate a state of boldness or insolence, it's spelled with an "e": *effrontery*. So I misspelled it, the copyeditor invented a new word, and we were both wrong. You've gotta watch copyeditors!

When I was growing up, "judgement" always had an *e* in the middle. Today, the British have kept the "e" but Americans have left it out. Technically, both spellings are "correct" but if you're writing for Americans, then use the

American spelling. As mentioned earlier, the British still hyphenate "co-operate," while Americans dropped that hyphen decades ago. Just to give you a short list (far from a complete one!) . . . .

British	American
agonise	agonize
centre	center
cheque	check
favour	favor
humour	humor
Mr or Mrs	Mr. or Mrs.
Mr	Dr.
scheme	plan
realise	realize
theatre	theater
towards	toward
travelled	traveled
wants	needs

In the '60s and '70s, Americans still hyphenated teen-ager; not anymore. Take it another step, if you wish. In the 1920s and '30s, the word wasn't "airplane," but "aeroplane"; "today" was "to-day." Be sure you have a current dictionary or you could come across as an antique hermit who hasn't kept up with the changes in usage.

There will be times (at least, when I'm working on a book) that the American spelling "looks wrong." It's an arbitrary decision, usually involving single or double consonants. If there's more than one way to spell it, then I keep my style sheet within reach and jot down which spelling I've used.

Here again is a splendid reason not to rely on your spell-check. The above-cited spellings are equally correct, depending on your readership. Many spell-checks will contain both versions and not differentiate between American and English usage. Beware! And when the manuscript is accepted for publication, make a duplicate of your style sheet and send it along to the editor who'll be working on it. This is exceedingly helpful. However, editors are only human and yours isn't the only manuscript in the hopper. Things do get lost, no matter how careful someone is. So be sure you hold on to a copy of everything even remotely connected to your novel. It could save the day.

Another thing to list on your style sheet are foreign words and usages. You can't expect your editor to know these things, so be agreeably willing to provide this information. In English, for instance, we capitalize Mr. or Ms. when used with a character's name. In Spanish, though, they're not capitalized. So if you're following Spanish usage within the text, you would write: "*dona* Alvarado" or "*el señor* Martinez."

In fact, there's a very popular reference book that I read about six or seven years ago (it's still in print and going strong). Neither the author nor the editor caught a very important error. (Okay, so maybe it's not so important and I'm just a stickler.) In the book, the author referred to Don Quijote (or sometimes spelled in English as Quixote), the legendary hero of tilter-at-windmills that was subsequently converted to the musical, "Man of La Mancha." Later on, the author referred to Don or Donna Quijote. I was conscience-bound, even compelled, to write the author a letter. If he had known that *don* isn't capitalized except at the beginning of a sentence, he would also have known that it wasn't Quijote's first name, but indicated the hero's title or rank. In turn, it would also have been clear that there couldn't possibly be a "Donna"—a woman's first name, and an English one at that. Fortunately, the author took it as I intended and said he would fix it for subsequent editions of his book. That's comforting. So often, authors are extremely touchy about their work—rightly or wrongly.

Speaking of author's egos, and to digress once again, there's an old joke told in publishing circles that illustrates the "typical" author's ego. It goes like this:

```
An overbearing, egotistical, yet highly successful male
novelist was at a New York City, chic cocktail party. He had
managed to find a young female guest who clearly wasn't very
sophisticated, and had been telling her yarn after yarn
about his adventures in life, and how they were incorporated
into his fiction.
    Finally, removing his arm that had held her trapped in
a corner, he smiled in a self-deprecating way. "Well, let's
not talk about me anymore. Okay? Let's talk about you! Tell
me, what did you think of my latest book?"
```

Yup. An author's ego can be an awesome thing. Try not to let success go to your head. But moving right along . . . .

In addition to a style sheet and your looseleaf notebook, if you decide to set even just a part of your story in a locale that's not familiar to you—or, for example, if you haven't lived there in a long time—contact the Visitors and Convention Center for the area; almost any city in America has one. Smaller communities could probably help you via the Town Clerk. I'll give you a good example. I haven't lived in Greater Los Angeles since 1977. Beginning a novel recently, I set it in Laguna Beach and had the heroine on the balcony, overlooking the Pacific and the Victor Hugo Inn. The Victor Hugo Inn had been there since before I was born. However, a chum telephoned who happens to live in Laguna. To my chagrin, he told me that the Victor Hugo Inn had been Las Brisas for at least a decade! Oh, boy! I'd already sent the partial to my agent . . . too late to change at that stage (although it will be easy to fix before the novel reaches the copyediting process).

The "problem" with having to alert your editor to necessary changes is that it tends to indicate—no, it does indicate—that you didn't do your homework first. Not a sin, but also not a feather in your cap either. It means the editor must fix your mistakes that you didn't catch in the first place. Not nice.

Who knew that shanty-town Tijuana, just south of the border at San Diego, now has a modern shopping mall? Who knew that the "nowhere" downtown area of Burbank had been razed for about ten years but that a mall would soon be constructed on the site? For that matter, I lived in Spain for roughly six months, in a small, dusty suburb of Barcelona. At the time, the most exciting thing that could happen was the arrival of the Coca Cola truck making its deliveries. The town had two paved streets. Imagine my shock when I learned that the Summer Olympics were to be held in the stadium in Badalona—that same dusty town where I had lived. Stadium? What stadium? So check your geographical information before you start your novel. Twenty years ago, there wasn't a McDonald's to be found outside of this hemisphere. Now they're in Paris, Moscow, and so forth. Things change. Check your facts.

If you're going to set it, or even just a scene or two, in a foreign city, see what kinds of brochures your local travel agency has. (And if you're going to take up a travel agent's time, but you're not going anywhere, be sure to explain why you're asking for help . . . and be sure to use that travel agent for any future trips.) Or, write to the country's consulate and request help.

Almost any city worth its name has a public library large enough to house telephone directories from other major cities throughout the country. Use this resource to locate embassies, consulates, Visitor and Convention Centers, Town Clerks, and so forth. Bigger libraries today even offer video travelogues that can be enormously helpful. The library is probably the best friend your writing endeavors will ever have . . . and you don't have to send a thank-you card! Though common courtesy would suggest you at least write a positive note to your

> All bark and no kisses can be very dull reading indeed.

local newspaper's Letters to the Editor, commending the librarians' assistance. They need all the good press they can get.

Writer's Block

I believe it exists because I am so frequently told that it has happened to writers. However, it has never happened to me, nor to the majority of professional writers I've known over the years. Writer's block should not be lumped in with emotional trauma or illness. If you've just lost your wedding ring, or your husband is sick in bed, or you're coming down with a cold . . . that's not writer's block. That's a very good reason for not being able to think clearly enough to work on your novel; other pressures prevail.

Now I don't want to seem like a hard-nosed taskmaster, but I genuinely believe that—more often than not—anyone suffering from writer's block is simply self-serving and too precious for words. If you've outlined your romance, know what it must contain, there's not a reason in the world why you can't write it. A raging case of spring fever does not equate with writer's block. Writers write; amateurs or self-pampering pros find excuses.

Still, putting aside my own prejudicial thinking about this, let's assume you have a bona fide case of writer's block. My only advice to you is to keep on writing—no matter what. Even if you have to throw that day's or week's output down the drain, keep on writing. If you give in to yourself, it could become a permanent case of mental paralysis. You'll come out of the block ultimately, and probably with even better ideas than before it happened.

And should it happen that you fail to take my advice about plotting out your romance before you write a line...even that's not a good excuse for writer's block. Let me give you a true-life example. Because I'm not a "morning person," I spend the first few hours of coming to grips with the day by doing menial tasks: run the vacuum cleaner, wash up those crystal goblets that look as if they'd spent the winter in the barbecue pit, or whatever. Since I'm lazy about outlines and don't have one to refer to when I'm ready to work, I let my mind wander over yesterday's scenes or chapter, review what went on before then, and idly wonder what might be fun to have happen next.

Unfortunately, I too often box myself into a corner with this lack of discipline. Writing *With Fate Conspire*, I was typing along productively and found myself at the end of a chapter (more or less) and had to figure out what to do next for a cliff-hanging scene. I don't know why (temporary insanity, probably), but I decided that the mistress of the house should be stabbed.

So I stabbed her. There she was, poor old thing, standing in the doorway with a knife handle protruding from her abdomen, telling the heroine to flee.

Now what? I hadn't planned for this to happen at all!

Sighing with self-disgust, I telephoned a friend and we chatted aimlessly. She asked how the novel was coming along. "I just stabbed *señora* de Lorca," I said.

"You what? But why?"

"I don't know. Seemed reasonable at the time."

"But what are you going to do next?"

I mumbled something about not having the foggiest idea. We hung up. I made a cup of coffee, then stared at the pages I'd just written. Okay, smartie . . . is the *señora* going to die? I had no reply for that. Shrugging, I decided that the *señora's* fate could be determined later. I'd set it up that the heroine had to flee—and flee she did. Okay. Once back into the story, it again began to write itself.

Yes, I could've knocked off for the day with the excuse of "writer's block," but it wouldn't have been true. The truth, clearly, was that I hadn't written an outline first and had thus made my life more difficult. (And no, I didn't kill the *señora* off—I liked her too much for that.)

Another myth you'll hear from any number of writers (surely none of you, however!) is that they can't write a line without a drink beside them. A real drink—booze. To this I say: Cowpuckie! (A little feminist humor.)

If you don't need a drink to write a letter, you don't need one to write a novel. Mind you, I enjoy my evening cocktail as much as anyone else; but alcohol does not make me a better writer. In fact, quite the reverse. Absolutely stupid ideas take on the veneer of Tolstoyian brilliance; yet when rereading in the cold light of sobriety, I have to admit I simply wasted my time. Worse, with a couple of drinks in me, my manuscript reads as if it had been typed on a Russian keyboard; my fingers get caught between the keys or are on the wrong line of keys, and what I should have done was take either a cold shower or a nap. So if I know I have a luncheon engagement with someone, and that there's likely to be more than one Bloody Mary consumed, I already know that it will be futile to attempt to work that afternoon. Better that I should spend the time reading or telephoning all the friends I've neglected because I've been on deadline.

If you don't want to write that day, don't blame it on writer's block or because you might need a drink to rev up your creative juices. Just admit you don't feel like writing. Period.

This next list consists of words that are often confused or misused, and how and when to use the apostrophe. Many are common mistakes and you should be aware of them. Why, you ask, should these teeny-tiny words be so important? Well, they're *very* important and this anecdote will explain why:

Several years ago, Sharon Jarvis—book editor, agent, writer and publisher—was a guest at a writers' conference. She was on a panel which analyzed the impact just the opening three pages of a novel had on an editor—how publishing professionals can make judgments about a book based on merely those pages.

One of the samples proffered by an attendee was the first three pages of an historical romance. Panelists had to read the pages out loud and comment on them. It took considerable effort for Sharon not to laugh aloud at the following, which was the first line of the very first page:

```
In those days, there was a wild beauty in the hills of Rome.
```

To which another panelist quipped, "Did they catch her?"

Of course you know that the line should have read, "In those days, there was a wild beauty *to* the hills of Rome." Right. Now you also know why publishing professionals can make editorial judgments not only based on the first three pages but on the first page and even the first line!

Affect/effect

"Affect" is a verb; "effect" is a noun or a verb, depending on how it's used. You are affected (verb) by the loss of a lover, a cut in salary, or the weather. However, the effect (noun) of any of these events can be profound. When is "effect" a verb? When it's used to indicate bringing about a change of some sort: He strove to effect a change in bylaws.

Apostrophes

Apostrophes are used to indicate the possessive (Dick's cat), or that something is missing ("wouldn't" instead of "would not" indicates the "o" is missing from "not"). And of course, they're used as single quotation marks within double quotation marks ("And then she said to me, 'I am not.'").

When you're referring to decades, using numerals instead of spelling them out and dropping the century, you'll need an apostrophe; for instance, The

Roaring '20s. To place the apostrophe between the numeral and the "s" is incorrect. Think about it. What's missing? The century. So the apostrophe is there to make it clear we've dropped the 19 from 1920. You don't want an apostrophe before the "s" since there's nothing possessive about it.

You *would* want a possessive apostrophe if you were to write: She was dressed in a '20's style bathing suit." Now that requires the apostrophe to indicate the missing 19, and an apostrophe to indicate the possessive. But it looks cumbersome and awkward, so in your shoes I'd rewrite it. "She was wearing a bathing suit reminiscent of the '20s."

You'll see the apostrophe misused frequently. That doesn't make it right, and you should know better.

Blond/blonde
Technically, since the word comes from the French, "blond" is masculine, and "blonde" is feminine. Many publishers are just dropping the "e" altogether; however, you should know the difference.

Continual/continuous
"Continual" is like blowing your nose when you have a cold; you do it lots, but not constantly, without interruption. "Continuous," however, is without interruption—like a continuous line. Or let's say it's raining. If it has rained, without cessation (perhaps a monsoon), then it has rained continuously. If it's been raining off and on, then it has rained continually (often clarified for a specific period of time—for a week, a month, etc.).

Eager/anxious
If you're eager, you're looking forward to something or wanting to get to something as soon as possible. You might eagerly await the arrival of a loved one; or your children might be eager to open their holiday presents. However, when you're anxious, you are apprehensive, concerned, perhaps worried. You could anxiously await a loved one—especially if there's been a five-car pile-up on the freeway that's the route your loved one usually takes. You could even anxiously open a gift—hearing a rattle and fearing it may be broken. You might be anxious about attending a school reunion for the first time;either because you've aged or you fear your classmates will no longer be recognizable. But if you're really looking forward to it, you're eager . . . not anxious.

Everyone/they
As commonly used as a toothbrush, still, few people use it correctly. You can't say: "If everyone knew the facts, they would believe her innocent." Why? Think about it for a second. "Everyone" is singular; therefore, to use "they" with it is incorrect. Similarly, you can't say: "Each person knew where their seats were." Each is singular; their is plural.

Ferment/foment
The dictionary is currently allowing either to mean inciting to riot. But if you want to be correct, you should know that ferment comes from *ferentum* (Latin

for yeast). So if you want to be accurate, foment means to motivate the mobs.

Flout/flaunt
This one really gets four stars for misuse. To "flout" is to be scornful or to mock; to "flaunt" is to indulge in conspicuous display. You can flout someone's political platform, or flout the rules. However, when you drive home in that new Rolls-Royce and deliberately leave it in the driveway so the neighbors can see . . . you're flaunting.

Founder/flounder
Contemporary dictionaries are permitting the use of either to indicate—either figuratively or literally—being stuck or sinking, yet there is a significant difference you should be aware of. A "flounder" is a type of fish. To go aground, or to sink, requires "founder." So if you want a character to be stuck for an answer, you might write: "Jerry's lips moved as if searching for the right words, but he soon foundered and gave up."

From/than
Though you'll hear it all the time, it is not correct to say "different than." An object or person is "different from," not "than." In conversation, you can probably get away with "different than" (even though it's incorrect, most of us are more lax when talking than when writing), but with the written word try to be correct. Most of us (myself included) will make grammatical errors when speaking, but we should be more careful when writing. We are, after all, role models for those who are less secure about correct usage.

Further/farther
Further is used today more in the abstract than in Olden Times. One discusses a problem further. Farther is now used almost exclusively to indicate distance. So further is abstract: "How much further can we endure this?" And farther is measurable: "Don't take another step farther."

Hung/hang
The laundry has been hung to dry (and we all know what it means in slang usage, don't we?). However, a person is hanged (to death), not hung (unless you mean it in the slang sense—better suited to males than females).

In/on
Another common mistake is characters who "sit in chairs" or dogs "jumping in laps." You sit on a chair, not in it. To be in it, the upholstery would have to come undone and you would be "inside" the chair instead of on it. The same is true for animals jumping on furniture or people.

Lie/lay
Ah, yes . . . everyone's nemesis (even some editors have yet to get the hang of it). And for sure, the problem is shiftier than most espionage novels. However, if you keep it clear in your head just what each word means, you'll

86

find it simpler to deal with . . . and which tense to use.

To lie is to recline; to lay is to put down, or set something. Contrary to the convenient guideline that it has anything to do with animate or inanimate objects, it is the meaning of each that determines which is correct. If you picked up a small statue and decided to put it on its side, you are going to lay it on its side. If you are referring to the statue's position, it is lying on its side.

If, though, you are moving a magazine from the coffee table, it can't possibly stand on its own—you will lay it elsewhere. A chicken lays an egg because it is "placing" the egg somewhere. But when a kitty curls up for a nap, it is lying. To "lay" is to place or set, as in setting the table: You lay the flatware and other necessities. But when indicating the position or act of reclining, you or some other object/person is "lying." "She was lying on the chaise longue." (Note: It's not a chaise lounge, but a chaise longue. "Lounge," as we all know, is to sort of hang around, not doing much of anything but relaxing, or a room for that purpose. The French word, *longue*, means "long" and that's what a chaise longue is; a long chair.)

Anyway, I've pulled the following together and you may wish to put a Post-it on this page for ready-reference:

Verb	Present	Perfect Past	Perfect Participle	Present Participle
lay	lay	laid	laid	laying
lie	lie	lay	lain	lying

Where I still have a problem, though (and maybe one of you will be kind enough to set me straight), is with which to use when your job is terminated. Are you "laid" off, or are you "layed" off . . . and is there such a word as "layed"? Since "layed" isn't in the dictionary, I'm guessing that one is "laid" off . . . .

Loan/lend

A "loan" is a noun; "lend" is a verb. You can't loan anything to anyone; you can only lend it. So, when you've applied to your bank, and they lend it to you, you then have a loan to pay off.

None

Another very frequently misused word. "None" is a combination of "no" and "one." Therefore, it's singular. Yes, you'll read it and hear it all the time, but if you want to be correct, remember that "none" is singular. Therefore, you can't write: "Although it was a three-car accident, none were hurt." "Were" is plural. It should be "none was hurt." If you don't like the way that looks, then rewrite your sentence. Or to put it another way: "Of all the attendees at the opera, none were more impressed than Midge." Nope. "None was more impressed," etc. Again, we're getting mixed signals from the media, who so frequently misuse the correct singular; but as a writer, and a role model, it's up to us to maintain the correct usage.

Organizations or groups
If you're not referring to a human being or several humans, the pronoun is "it." This applies to clubs, groups, or audiences as well. Although they are comprised of people, once clumped together the ensemble becomes an it.

Example: The audience rose to its feet for a standing ovation. Not: The audience rose to their feet . . . . Or: She works for Provident in its Claims Department. Not: She works for Provident in their claims department. If this reads awkwardly to you, then rephrase it: The members of the audience rose to their feet (and so forth).

Plurals of certain words
Many words are either singular or plural without adding an "s" or anything else. Employment, deer, personnel, apparel, for instance, are both singular and plural. If you're uncertain, check the dictionary.

Preventive/preventative
Due to common usage, preventative is now in the dictionary. However, to be correct, drop the extra syllable. It's preventive.

Proved/proven
I'm probably so outnumbered with people using these interchangeably that, for all I know, maybe it's okay as a result of common usage. English is, after all, a living and ever-changing language. Occasionally, no matter how it grates, we simply have to give in to common usage. However! you ought to know what's correct and what isn't. Proved is the past tense or preterite; proven is the past participle and requires the use of "has" or "have." Example: It was proved to be correct. But: It has been proven to be correct.

The moment you use either "has" or "have," you need the past participle—not the preterite. This applies to any verb. "Jerry hanged the draperies," but "Jerry has hung the draperies."

Again, if it looks weird to you, simply rewrite the sentence to avoid it. You're allowed.

Rather/prefer
We've become so accustomed to it that many folks have lost sight of the difference. Rather is usually a modifier; it's a rather nice day, a rather nice crowd turned up, and so on. Or it may be used to indicate a correction (such as "May I introduce my brother . . . or rather, my step-brother?"); or to indicate something is the opposite of what might be expected (such as "His fortune, rather than multiply, soon dwindled."))

It was never intended to be a synonym for one's preferences.

So bumperstickers that proclaim "I'd rather be fishing" are grammatically incorrect.

She/he

Okay, we're all keenly aware of sexist language these days. Even though it is grammatically correct to use "he" or "man" in terms of general reference when the gender is unknown. For instance: When one is shopping for a suitable gift, he should keep the recipient's hobbies in mind. Another example might be a reference such as: "As someone in a cafeteria line, mindless of a selection, he would choose the chocolate pie every time." It might not be a "he" in the line, but that's correct (traditional) usage. Today, it's not politically correct. So to avoid this, try writing in the plural. For instance: People in a cafeteria line, mindless of their selection, will almost always choose chocolate pie. It won't work every single time, but the plural will help reduce the s/he syndrome most of the time.

In fiction, you're not too likely to have the problem, but it can arise. Substitute "humanity" for "mankind," for example. If, for instance, your heroine is attending a PTA meeting, you may find it more convenient to use all plurals to avoid the pitfall/repetitiveness of s/he, him/her. It's become quite acceptable to refer to a "chairperson" instead of a "chairman"; and instead of mailman or mailwoman, just say "mail carrier" and you'll upset no one.

There is always a way to rephrase something to avoid offending; but it's very difficult to retract what you've written once it's published.

That/which

This has to do with restrictive and nonrestrictive, and all that complicated stuff. To borrow from editor-friend, Shirley Peterson, think of it this way: "The cow, which has four legs, ran across the meadow"; however, "the cow that has three legs tried to run across the meadow." The first example is "nonrestrictive"; cows usually have four legs.

Notice too that when "which" is used, it is like an aside, and could be set off with commas. "That," however, is "restrictive" insofar as it sets a three-legged cow apart from the others.

That/who

Another pet peeve of mine . . . the word who is practically disappearing from our language unless used in a question. Nonhuman things or corporations, etc., are that; people are who. A corporation is an "it," not a "their." For example: In its 1994 fourth quarterly report, Glaxco showed its profits and investments favorably. Glaxco showed "its" and not "their." On the other hand, if Glaxco's annual report included all of its subsidiaries, then "their" would be appropriate.

Common sense wins out here. Just beware the difference between humans and non-human entities.

Till/until

Maybe this ought to have been included with apostrophes, but it happens so often that I felt it necessary to give it its own space. "Until" is a whole word; so is "till." Both mean more or less the same thing; i.e., they're synonyms. Where the "problem" arises is with "'til." Again, the apostrophe is to indicate that something is missing. If you spell the word "till" with two "l"s, nothing is missing. But if you spell it with one "l" then the "un" is missing and requires an apostrophe.

Titles/captions

When to capitalize and when not to: First you should understand that different media have different rules; often referred to as "house style" This has led to considerable confusion over the years. Newspapers, for instance, will almost always use single quotation marks instead of double. Magazines, however, vary in what each would prefer.

Since we're concentrating solely on the book publishing industry, I've invented an acronym for you: CAP. When capitalizing titles, remember that Conjunctions, Articles, and Prepositions are never capitalized unless they appear as the first word in the title or caption. The word "and" is a conjunction; "the" or "a" are articles; and "with," "by," or "for" are prepositions. If you're not all that sure of your grammar, simply check the dictionary before typing up your title page. Some sample titles might be:

By Love's Command (preposition is first word)
The Love Potion (article is first word)
Love for Hire (preposition between two words)
And the Waltz Played On (conjunction is first word, article is not capital-ized between two words, and "on" in this instance is an adverb so is capitalized).

If you're unsure, then simply capitalize everything and claim it's house style.

Troops

If it weren't for the consistent misuse of this word in the media, I probably would have let this go. But it is so often misused by TV and newspaper reporters, I simply can't. A "troop" is automatically more than two people; even as a squadron is. To say that we're sending thousands of troops somewhere is categorically incorrect. We're sending thousands of military personnel—yes. But not troops.

Were/was

Another one of those confusions that probably arose from an oversimplistic guideline. Many of us were taught that when the word "if" is used, we need the subjunctive, or "were." It has zilch to do with the word "if." Ixnay. Instead, it depends on the meaning of your sentence. If it's contrary to fact, then "were" is correct. If it isn't contrary to fact, then "was" is used. Example: If I was invited to the party, I never received the invitation." Okay. There's the word "if."

Since the speaker isn't sure one way or the other, we need "was" and not "were." Another example might be: If I were in your shoes, I'd . . . . Well, clearly there's no room for your feet and mine in the same pair of shoes—it's contrary to fact.

Double consonants

If you're anything like me and can never remember which verbs take two "r"s or two "t"s when converted from the present tense to the past tense, here's a rule of thumb to save you time from double-checking yourself with the dictionary. Alas, I didn't learn it till only a few years ago. But . . . if the first syllable (or next to last) of a verb has the accent, use only a single "r" or "t". If the last syllable has the accent, the use a double "r" or double "t".

For instance, al-ter (altered); pre-fer (preferred); ac-quit (acquitted); mas-ter (mastered); and so on. But of course there are exceptions—we are dealing with the peculiarities of the English language. "Elect," for instance, comes to mind as an exception; the past tense doesn't require a double "t". There are bound to be others, so bear in mind that this is only a rule of thumb. It's similar to "*i* before *e* except after *c*"—yeah, right, but not always. A case in point where it doesn't apply? Try omniscient.

As you might gather, I'm a bit worried about how lax we've become with our language. In the late '40s and early '50s, it was the advertising agencies that were mutilating the language by adding *ize* to nouns and converting them to verbs. Over the past couple of decades, it's technology's rapid advances that have not only introduced new words, but have also converted nouns into verbs.

Today, access and impact are used as verbs instead of nouns. Before computerese, one (or something) didn't "impact" a situation or "access" anything. One has an impact, or one gains access. While I lament these changes, still one has to be flexible.

But when glaring errors are made, I have no compunctions about writing to network anchor people, or *Advertising Age*, or anyone else about the responsibility of media personnel to uphold good usage in our language.

We are rapidly losing the hyphen for compound adjectives. Graphs for TV weather reports will often omit the hyphen from "five-day forecast"; Oldsmobile has dropped the hyphen from its "eighty-eight" model; and so on. A good example of the importance of a hyphen can be found in a seafood restaurant's marquee I recently spotted: "Come see man eating shark." Without the hyphen, we would expect to watch a man eating a shark. With the hyphen, however, we would expect to see the species of shark known to eat people: a man-eating shark. Hyphens are needed to make our message clear, until such time as they are deleted to convert the two words into one, which also eliminates confusion. In England, for example, they still hyphenate the word co-operation. In the U.S.A., we quit using the hyphen and combined the words with no devastating aftereffects.

The illiteracy rate in our country is appalling, and if the average citizen can't turn to journalists (TV or print) as reliable sources for usage . . . then what hope is there? If you agree with me, then write your own protest letters. It's not true that "more hospitals use" this or that painkiller. Hospitals aren't using them. Patients are. Doctors are perhaps recommending them. But hospitals are nonanimates and can't "recommend" or "use" anything—unless it's electricity, or other utilities. If all of us write in our protests about misuse, maybe we'll have some voice to remedy the situation . . . and make our alleged role models more responsible. And if you're into nostalgia, I can still remember when *New Yorker* magazine offered a reward to any reader who found a typographical or grammatical error in its publication. The editors don't offer a reward these days; they're not crazy.

And if you need considerable more help than just these few examples, I urge you to go to the library and borrow *Thirty Days to Better English*, and *Better English*, both by Norman Lewis. (Both are currently out of print, but with any luck at all, perhaps some smart publisher will republish these two books.) Also vitally important is Strunk and White's *Elements of Style*—a gem of a book that, in a nutshell, emphasizes that simple is best; do not use a big word if a smaller one will do just as well—unless, of course, it suits the character to use big words. This book is currently available in paperback.

We shall now have a brief musical interlude . . . .

CHAPTER FIVE

The Worst Is Over . . . Or Is It?

To people who have never written a novel, it would appear that the hardest part of all is the writing. That's not necessarily true. Granted, that's the part that involves all the hard work, but not the whole ball of wax. As I'm wont to say, you can raise the best hogs in the country, but if you can't get 'em to market . . . what good are they? (Not exactly a refined, ladylike observation, but there you are . . . .) So this section deals with getting your manuscript to market. If it isn't sold, isn't published, then the time and effort to write it can swiftly bog you down unless you know what to expect and how to go about selling it . . . and yourself.

Writing a book is a gamble, no different from putting your money on Red 16 in roulette. Except that placing a gambling bet takes but moments—writing a novel can take months and years, even if you needn't do any research. You have to have a strong stomach, a healthy heart, nerves of steel, and an Olympian sense of humor. Your attitude and professionalism—which this book is intended to bolster—can make this next stage bearable. Otherwise it can be sheer agony.

Your romance novel is completed, typed neatly and ready to send off. Send off where? Directly to the publisher? Or maybe you should find a literary agent? You don't know a thing about the book publishing business, and what if the publisher tries to cheat you? Let me give you some historical background first . . . .

In the alleged good old days (before WW II) literary representatives generally had an excellent education, a sincere love of words and literature, an understanding of how the publishing industry (yes, it's called an "industry") functions, and a genteel, congenial manner. Even as was true of most book editors, literary agents were quite Dickensian: soft-spoken, erudite ladies and gentlemen. You may put that quaint picture out of your mind.

That was before the paperback revolution followed by widespread conglomerate takeovers. Prior to these two events, almost anyone connected with the book world possessed the above-cited qualities, and the publication of good literature was more important than profits. (In England, for example, book editors had to be independently wealthy. Salaries were really nothing more than stipends, covering the cost of transportation to the office and little more. You were expected to be a book editor because you loved books, not to earn a lot of money. In the mid-1960s, it was still the same.) The aim, originally, was to encourage writing talent; even if the first book or two lost money, agents and editors and publishers had faith in the writer's abilities. Enough faith to put up with slow sales or even a dud.

I was a kid during World War II. The only paperbacks I'd ever seen were the Armed Forces editions of popular hardcover books. And then Pocket Books (the very first successful paperback company . . . though there had been paperbacks in this country since the Civil War) burst upon the scene. I read James Hilton's *Lost Horizon* and Pearl S. Buck's *The Good Earth* in paperback. Paperbacks then cost 25 cents at retail, so I was thrilled to be able to afford my own books. Still, only reprints of hardcovers were in paperback; no original material.

The reason paperbacks hadn't become successful previously was that they were being marketed the same as hardcover books. It just didn't work. Retailers would buy the quantity of a hardcover title they were confident would sell. There were no returns for credit. If the buyer overestimated, the leftover titles were put in a bin and discounted to get rid of them. Historically, paperback publishers tried to retail their own titles in the same manner and it failed miserably.

> **Writing a book is a gamble, no different from putting your money on Red 16 in roulette.**

Pocket Books, though, came up with a "new" way of marketing their books. They distributed them in the same way magazines were distributed. The retailer says how many copies s/he wants of any given title (or in some instances, are floorplanned) and it was on sale for one month. Four weeks, one moon . . . just the same as if they were time-dated and obsolete after four weeks of being on sale. What didn't sell was returned to the publisher for a refund or credit. It was a win/win situation for retailers. And Pocket Books implemented this approach with books and they took off like an oversexed rabbit.

It's also the explanation of why you might see a paperback on the rack, but if you don't buy it right away, it's no longer on display when you return. Its time has come and gone. Some publishers may redistribute the books to secondary outlets, but more often than not, the books are shredded. The cost of warehousing is staggering and the sheer numbers of returns can be monstrous.

To round out your journey into paperback history, back then, they didn't varnish the covers; instead, a type of cellophane was affixed to the cover, giving it a glossy look, and had a most irritating way of curling at the edges like the peeling of a sunburn. I had been a good reader as a kid, but when paperbacks became available, I was hooked and upgraded my status to an avid reader.

The paperback business has come a very long way since then! And to a large extent it's become a situation of the tail wagging the dog. Only the most esoteric of hardcover houses (or specialty publishers) will accept a manuscript that will have little chance to sell to a paperback house or a book club. That's

94

when the real profits to the hardcover house start to kick in (unless a book becomes a bestseller in its own right before sale to paperback).

Another thing you should know is that there were—and still are—no colleges or universities that gave a diploma on how to be an agent, or an editor, or a publisher. It was a seat-of-the-pants business. It was expected that your Ivy League liberal arts education would have heightened your awareness of what was fit to publish and what wasn't. Sounds lofty, snobbish, and clique-ish? Well, it was. It was, after all, a circle of the literati, the intelligentsia. And yes, there was a thinly disguised tolerance of literary agents—they were, after all, in the business to make money and not for the unsullied love of literature. How crass! Still agents were useful to editors. It was like having manuscripts pre-screened and only those works that were likely to be of interest to the editor were submitted. But before you feel a cold sweat of fear trickling down your spine, let me remind you that Jack London and William Faulkner never finished high school, and they were both fine writers.

Today there are some few colleges that are offering seminars or special courses (one even offers a certificate in publishing) about specific aspects of the business. A case in point was a class I taught at UCLA entitled "The Editor's Side of the Desk." It was an accredited course, but no certificate or diploma was available. You still (as far as I know) can't get a degree in publishing, but at least you're not coming to the job cold-turkey. In my day, you got a job in publishing and you learned. You had to have at least two years of college to even be hired as a receptionist in a hardcover house. So I opted for a job in paperback publishing; I didn't have any college behind me and knew I'd never find work in a hardcover house. (So how did I manage to teach at UCLA? They have a special program called Extension. You don't have to be a certified teacher or professor, only an expert in your field.)

Okay. So how does all this affect you, as author? Simple. You are going to be dealing with individuals, not clearly defined company policy. You will be subject to each individual's personal whim, opinion, and extent of learning. There is no right or wrong—only subjective reaction that one hopes is based on expertise and open-mindedness. This applies to agents as well as editors. If an agent has a rotten cold, or an editor was just told to shape up or ship out . . . these influences can and do frequently determine how either will look at your work. We're not selling oranges here, but words, and words are subject to interpretation. Therefore, what determines the acceptance of your writing (either by an agent or an editor) is based on how your work is subjectively perceived. Which is another good reason not to give up just because your book has been rejected ten or even fifteen times. You certainly ought to reread it to see if there is a valid reason for rejection; or you might want to regear it toward a romantic-suspense market. But don't give up.

Because I've been a published writer, a book editor on salary, and an agent, believe me when I say that this is a business that depends largely on the frames of mind of the people who read your material. Unlike the auto parts business (if you need a muffler, you need a muffler), you are going to try to sell your "creation." Its reception will vary depending on whether the agent has gout, or the editor just got a raise in pay, or any of the other daily events that mold a person's emotions and attitudes at any given moment. If you are not prepared to accept this, you are in for a lot of shattering disappointment.

Well may you ask: <u>"You mean, after I spend months and months of working, honing, rewriting, polishing . . . that my book may or may not be accepted on the basis of digestion?"</u>

<u>Answer: "Yes."</u> That's the bad news.

The good, though, is that almost everyone in this business has had years and years of experience and knows if it's a good day to read manuscripts for evaluation, or to put it off till another day. More importantly, when you "read for a living" (as agents and editors do), you acquire the expertise to swiftly spot a good or a bad manuscript in very short order.

There's an anecdote told about the late Bennett Cerf (a legend in publishing circles). Apparently, one of his readers at Random House returned a submission with a standard rejection form (just a printed slip, with no explanation). The author, irate, wrote directly to Mr. Cerf in protest.

```
Dear Mr. Cerf:
    I was aghast at the return of my manuscript when it wasn't
even given a complete reading.  I know no one there read the
entire book because I stapled some of the pages together
before sending it to you.  It came back with the pages still
stapled!
```

As gossip has it, the letter went on and on in furious indignation. And as the story goes, Mr. Cerf allegedly wrote back:

```
My dear sir...one does not have to eat the whole egg to
know that it is rotten.
```

While that wasn't very nice of Mr. Cerf, if you knew how many weird submissions publishers receive, crank calls, even threats, you'd understand his side of the story. But let's talk about the different routes available (agent or editor) so you can decide which one would be best for you.

Agents

Dealing with agents isn't too terribly different. They too receive dozens and dozens of non-requested manuscripts every week. And whether or not you like the idea, a lot of writers are just downright crazy—which makes it harder for the rest of us (Sharon Jarvis once received a death threat because she didn't read a submission fast enough). They'll phone agents in the middle of the night, try to trap them as they leave a restaurant, and are more persistent than a rabid terrier. Writers can have egos that top the Empire State Building (as noted previously), and this definitely puts them in the TBA class—To Be Avoided.

An agent is a psychologist, a bill collector, a moderator, a confidante, a negotiator, and a salesperson. If agents are connected with large agencies, they may be on salary or draw against commission. If they are self-employed, their livelihood depends solely on their judgment about a book, and the ability to sell it. Books that do not sell do not earn an agent's commission; and agents have hefty overhead expenses, especially in New York City. Anyone can become a literary agent; not anyone can make a decent living at it.

This should tell you something. In plain language, that no agent is going to represent your work unless s/he believes it can be sold to a publisher. Yet again, do not forget that this decision can be subjective. If an agent declines to represent your work, it could well be an agent who is unable to see its merits...not that your work isn't any good. Too, it may also be that the agent is representing another manuscript that's too similar to yours. A super story idea doesn't always surface from just one source; there may be surprisingly more writers with the same basic concept.

Traditionally, an agent never charged a reading fee; wasn't so concerned if you'd been published before or not; submitted manuscripts to editors with a polite note expressing hope that the editor would find it suitable for his or her list; and if the book sold, the agent took ten percent off the top of any monies the book generated (inclusive of magazine serialization, movie rights, book club rights, and so on). Agents spend a reasonable amount of time (and money) lunching with authors and editors, or going to cocktail parties—all of it pure business, not for fun. It costs money to be an agent, just as it costs money to be in any other business. Although you may find it interesting that honorable editors don't permit agents to pay for lunch or drinks; it may leave them vulnerable to feeling beholden to accept what an agent submits, regardless of merit.

Things have been changing. Not radically, but changing. More agents are beginning to charge reading fees—particularly if you've never before been published. While it's not as yet standard practice, I have to agree that agents spend an awful lot of time reading pure unsalable junk—they're entitled to a fee. Many of them will apply this fee against the earnings of the book, so in the long run the author pays nothing.

Find an agent with the facade of Cecily Tyson or Hector Elizondo, but with the heart of King Kong.

Some agents simply refuse to represent an unpublished writer; they won't even read your work "just in case" it might be good. Some will consider representing partial manuscripts; others will not. Their rules and regulations differ and are usually rooted in personal experiences with writers and editors.

There is also a swing toward charging a fifteen percent commission for domestic sales; it's standard for agents to charge twenty to twenty-five percent for foreign sales because they usually have to split the commission with a foreign representative. In brief, most have formed a liaison with an existing literary agency in many major European countries—a split commission is cheaper than having to go abroad all the time just to try to sell foreign rights. However, with ever-expanding technology, I can foresee a time when manuscripts, on floppy disks, will be submitted directly to foreign publishers via modem or some other electronic means. But for today, that's not the case.

And nowadays, some agents are telling authors what to write, making demands upon writers to revise to their specifications. With rare exception, I am very much against this practice. An agent (usually) is not a writer . . . nor, in all likelihood, an editor. If an editor wants me to change my novel, I am very glad to do so; however, the editor is the one who will be contracting for my book—not the agent. Since agents do not purchase manuscripts for publication, but sell them, I am leery of agents who tell writers how to write. On the other hand, if my agent makes suggestions that I can readily see would improve my book, then I'd have to be insane to refuse.

If you're going to take the agent-first route, and if you can possibly afford to do so (since most of them are in New York City), I would recommend going to the expense of meeting with them before making a commitment. Why? Because there are simply too many agents who accept your work for representation, append a note and send it off to an editor. That's little more than a postal rerouting. You need to know how they work, how well connected they are, and if they'll fight for a better contractual agreement than you could possibly get on your own. It would be rude, of course, to bluntly ask . . . but in person, getting to know one another, the information can be obtained without offending.

Finding "good" agents is far more important (and difficult) than simply having representation. During your initial contact, ask if they have a list of their clients, which publishers they deal with the most often, if they have TV/movie co-agents in L.A. (another instance of split commissions), what some of their biggest successes have been (bestsellers), if they attend book fairs or have a rep who does. In a very real sense, "interview your babysitter." Your agent is your book's babysitter until it's sold. How conscientious is the agent you're hiring? My quest over the years has been to find an agent with the façade of Cecily Tyson or Hector Elizondo, but with the heart of King Kong. No luck so far on that front. . . .

A reasonable question to ask yourself is: "So what do I get for the ten or fifteen percent commission?"

Technically, you should get someone who knows the business well; who is on a friendly basis with as many editors as possible; and who stays on top of which editor is looking for what, new trends in the making, and so forth. Some agents keep apprised of what's happening in the motion picture and television industries or have co-agents in Los Angeles. A good agent should be able to read your manuscript and know that it is, for instance, too unsophisticated for one romance line, but if expanded to meet the word-count requirements of another romance line, it might sell there.

At that point, the agent will be in touch with you to give you your options. Or possibly, the agent might telephone one of the editors at a particular romance publisher to say that, though the manuscripts needs to be fleshed out, perhaps the editor would like to see it anyway. The advantage in this approach is it gives the agent the opportunity to present your novel in such a way that it conveys a sense of urgency ("Don't let this one get away from you!"); it can also lead to a contractual commitment before you've actually done the work. From the editor's perspective, it gives him or her the chance to give you editorial guidance before you do the work, possibly going off on the wrong tangent. However, both the agent and the editor would have to have considerable faith in your ability to provide what's needed . . . and that seldom happens with first-time novelists.

Or, especially if you've never been published before, the agent may insist on receiving the additional material first—just to be sure you really can do it. Or worse, that you're a flake. While it doesn't happen often, it occurs often enough to make agents and editors wary: Author signs contract, accepts first half of the advance as a binder, and never completes the book. Hard as that may be to believe, it does happen. Of course it's unscrupulous! And yes, word travels fast in publishing and the offending party will have a bad reputation and swiftly be blacklisted. But it happens nonetheless.

So let's take a simpler scenario. The novel needs no further revisions or additions, the agent likes it and accepts it, and a sale is made to a romance publisher. Some publishers insist on a percentage of all monies earned through subsidiary rights (see Glossary) sales; some even insist on controlling those sales — i.e., they have their own subsidiary rights people, in-house, and will pursue those sales internally. Smaller publishers will still want a percentage of the sale, but would prefer the agent to handle it.

Depending upon the terms of the contract, a good agent will pursue subsidiary rights and in every other way nurse your novel along until nothing more can be done for it. In reality, most romances never see any additional monies other than what they earn in paperback book form. Don't expect the book to have a big TV-movie sale or to become a book-club selection. There are simply too many romances to choose from, and in truth, few are well-written enough to warrant any additional sales. To my knowledge, other than Barbara Cartland or Danielle Steel, I've never seen any other TV-movie adaptation of a romance novel. And at that, from what I hear, Danielle Steel doesn't consider her novels to be category romances . . . .

Now, what I've enumerated are the things you should hope for when you have a good agent. But remember that I said anybody can become an agent? That's where you've got to be on your guard. There are a disconcerting number of people who have set themselves up as literary agents . . . and they don't know the first thing about the business. I've even met agents who can't comprehend a contract, who can't tell a good book from a bad one, and—to all intents and purposes—are little more than a mailroom clearing house for unsuspecting authors. Granted, the inept ones are in the minority—but they do exist.

I met an agent once—thank the fates, only once—who had a genuine scam going. It was legal, but immoral and unethical as all blazes. To avoid a lawsuit, I'll call this agent "It" instead of "he" or "she." It would receive submissions of manuscripts from hopeful authors. It had proper stationery, offices, a secretary, and so forth—there was no way for anyone to assume anything other than a legitimate business operation. However, whenever It could get away with it, It would tell an author that his or her work really wasn't salable . . . but, that It would be willing to buy the manuscript and take a chance, absorbing the loss should It fail to sell the work elsewhere. Well, naturally, a lot of first-time amateur writers fell for this; they were thrilled to make a sale of any kind. And of course, not knowing better, they simply assumed that if It sold the work, that they would at least see their names on the cover.

The scam? It would then put a new title page on the manuscript, with Its own name as author, and sell it to an established publisher (having first acquired a bill of sale, all very legal, from the original author). So for an outlay of anywhere from $50.00 to $500.00, It kept all the excess profits for Itself plus getting the credit for authorship!

So before you sign anything with an agent, make certain you know exactly what you're putting your name to. (Actually, that really applies to signing any kind of agreement—even a lease.) Many agents today do ask authors to sign a letter of agreement, or a mini-contract. But that's to protect them. Novices simply aren't aware of publishing protocol. It's not uncommon for a beginning novelist to be in discussion (by letter or phone) about representation with one agent, and in the interim, sign up with a different one. The first agent has then wasted an awful lot of precious time!

If you're asked to sign a letter of agreement with an agent, ask if there's a cap on how long the agreement's for. That is, will the agent let you out of the agreement if the work hasn't sold, for instance, in two years? And that's not a farfetched period of time. It takes at least six weeks for the agent to get to your submission; often longer. Then it's submitted to an editor, who may or may not get to your novel for another eight or nine months! Even if accepting it, there are negotiations, the legal department has to process the contract, and so forth.

If it's not accepted, the manuscript is returned to the agent who then has to take it from Square One, repeating the entire process with the exception of reading it in the first place. Two years isn't unreasonable; even three years would be acceptable. These things just plain take time. Add t-i-m-e to your list of four-letter words.

You might also want to inquire about adding a clause with regard to the agent's ability to perform suitable representation. Let's say it's a one- or two-person agency. What happens to your novel if that agent becomes seriously ill, or even dies? Book contracts automatically have a clause for termination for failure to publish within a specified time. I don't think it's untoward to ask for the same clause with an agent's letter of agreement. And I doubt that a reasonable agent would deny including such a clause. Fair is fair.

However most established agents accept that the agent-author relationship is more of an affaire than a legal marriage. It would be ridiculous to make an author stick to an agreement if the author isn't happy. Unhappy writers rarely produce salable books, so good agents let the author out of the agreement. ("Unhappy" in the sense of with one's agent, not emotionally despondent.)

And you should read the agreement carefully to see if any of the agent's expenses will be charged back to you. They shouldn't be. Those expenses are part of the cost of an agent's business and are tax-deductible. Even as you took a risk when deciding to write a book, the agent takes a risk when accepting it for representation.

Yet again, and I can't stress this too much, if you're in discussions with one agent, don't switch mid-field. Agents encourage their writers nobly; they spend hours on the telephone, write many letters, and really work at making a sale. Don't waste their time, proving to one and all that you're an ignorant nerd, by courting one agent then marrying another before anything has been concluded.

Then there are agents who will submit a work maybe two or three times, and if it hasn't sold, they'll bounce it right back at you. Because romances are category books, and each line has its own specifications, you and your agent will be more likely to make a quick sale if you, the author—having determined what kind of romance you want to write—stick to the publisher's guidelines. But keep in mind, that if you gear your novel to a particular set of publisher's guidelines, and it isn't accepted, the chances of selling it elsewhere dwindle measurably. That's one of the biggest risks in writing to a specific set of guidelines; what one publisher wants rarely, if ever, overlaps into what another publisher is seeking. My advice, at that point, is to revamp your novel to a more generic market, such as romantic-suspense or even a straightforward mystery. (Which is why I've provided you with considerably more information than simply what is required for romances. You may well need it.)

However, agents spend a great deal of time with their authors bolstering egos, cheering you on, guidance, etc. This too is an expense—if not in actual money, then most certainly with time. For every minute spent with their authors, it's time not spent courting editors, getting to other submissions, performing follow-up tasks, and so on. Professional and considerate writers recognize this and leave their agents alone unless it's unavoidable to be in touch. And the same applies to editors. Too many writers behave as if they are the sole client, which means, of course, that they become more of a nuisance than an asset. They also tend to behave as if agents and editors have no personal life.

Another thing that happens, much to an agent's chagrin, is that writers are nursed along and when they become a big success, they dump their original agent to go with someone "bigger." Not fair; not fair at all. Remember your origins and who stuck with you during the hard times . . . that agent deserves your loyalty.

All right, next question. How can you tell a good agent from a bad one? You can't. Not really. While it would be easy to say that you should stick to those agents who have been around for a long time, that would be grossly unfair to new agents who might be every bit as competent, if not more so. (For that matter, old-time agents might be slowing up or just getting bored. That's not an ageist observation, but a strong possibility.)

It would also be a disservice to state that agents in New York City are superior to those in smaller cities. I've known several agents across the country—some of whom have never even been to The Big Apple—who make very comfortable livings and do quite well by their authors. However, I must admit to a certain amount of prejudice. Agents who are based in New York

City have greater routine access to editors, and it is therefore (presumably) more likely that they will know what editors are looking for. There's no guarantee of that, naturally.

Well then, how do you select an agent! If you can't have one recommended to you, it's no different from finding a good physician. Open up the Yellow Pages, close your eyes and see where your finger lands. That's one way. A better way, however, is to spend some time at your local public library and each week read Paul S. Nathan's column, "Rights & Permissions," in *Publishers Weekly*. This is the publishing industry's official source of weekly information, and most libraries subscribe. If you're very nice, the librarian may let you read it as long as it's on the premises. While this column is devoted to who sold what to whom (inclusive of the agent involved), it can't possibly cover every sale that's made. But you'll begin to notice that certain agents' names appear more frequently than others—a sale here, a deal there.

Another way is to join your local Romance Writers of America chapter (assuming there's one in your community). Or subscribe to *Romantic Times* Magazine; it has a column entitled "Agent News." If you can afford to do so, attend Romance Writers conferences and mingle. At least via these routes, you're meeting people who have similar interests to yours in the types of fiction they enjoy reading and are writing. In most Romance Writers of America chapters, at least some of the members have been published and are happy to share information with beginners.

Getting back to agents.... Be prepared to learn that some agents simply don't handle romances. Not enough money in it. So don't take a "No" personally.

Another thing, a good agent should be able to negotiate a contract in your favor. However, in the romance market, there's very little latitude for negotiating clauses. Some few concessions may be made if the book is head and shoulders above other submissions, but the concessions may not be enough to really brag about.

For the most part, category fiction isn't subject to a lot of wheeling and dealing. Editors have been given ceilings on what they can pay authors, so the advance against royalties is negotiable to a point. And if an agent begins to insist on a change in this clause, and striking out that clause, an editor is just as likely to say, "No thanks." They receive hundreds of romances from hopeful writers who don't care what the contract says at all, as long as their books are accepted for publication.

Too, a "good" agent to one author may not be for another. If the agent is regularly selling your work, you'll probably think he or she is a good agent. And to some extent that's true. But if you become successful, another Danielle Steel, you'll need an agent who can hammer out contractual details that benefit you and your career direction. If the publisher's standard contract stipulates that the company will get fifty percent of, for instance, a book club sale . . . your agent might be able to whittle that down substantially (but only if you are a famous writer with clout . . .).

However, let's say you've found that good agent and your romance has been sold. The contracts are all signed and you have a copy for your files. Your agent will—if you're short of money—do a bit of nagging at the publisher's accounting department (or directly to the editor who will do the nagging) to hurry that check for the first half of your advance along. And when it's time for your royalty accounting, your agent will see to it that there's no unreasonable delay; and if monies are due to you, nag again. But be realistic about this. All the agent can do is ask, cajole, beg, etc. No agent can physically go to accounting and write a check. (Accounting departments in the publishing business suffer from a notorious reputation for dragging their heels. I've never found out if it's truly warranted across the board, but I've worked at some publishing companies where I swore accounting was jealous of writers, arbitrarily withholding checks when they were already overdue.)

Do not think that because you have an agent you're going to be best friends, even if you live next door to each other. Your agent is a business associate, not your chum. And again, you are not your agent's only client! Be as businesslike as is humanly possible, taking your lead from the agent for deportment. Don't start getting cute, sending birthday cards or trinkets of appreciation—unless you'd do the same thing for your dentist or auto mechanic.

Upon opting to contact an agent, send a straightforward business letter (ideally not to exceed one page). It should outline your reason for writing; and if you can say so honestly, that you have quite a few other ideas for books (this alerts the agent that you're not a one-shot author). If you've been published before (anywhere!), on a separate sheet list the titles and dates of the publications, who published it/them, and the names of the publishers. If you've never been published, don't say so—wait till you're asked. Or if you've only been published once or twice, that can go on the query letter. On a separate sheet of paper, provide a synopsis of your novel. And enclose a copy of your resume. Then you wait for a reply.

One final word regarding the agent-first route. It is extremely difficult for the first-time author to be accepted for representation. Not impossible, but difficult.

Editors

All right, so what happens if you decide not to have an agent at all—at least, not for now. Surprise! There are many editors who actually prefer to deal directly with authors, eliminating the middleman. This is particularly true with category fiction such as romances.

Let's face it. This is your very first novel. Are you going to nitpick over the contract (even if you knew how)? In all likelihood, you won't even know what you're signing! Fortunately, crooked editors are the exception, not the rule. One of the easiest ways to spot a crooked editor is if s/he tells you that your romance is a borderline situation for acceptance . . . but for ten percent (or any kind of sum) the editor will tip the balance in your favor. Ye olde kickback, plain and simple. Get your manuscript back as quickly as you can—though taking pains not to anger the editor. Angry, crooked editors have been known to do very nasty things—like besmirch your reputation, "lose" your manuscript in the wastebasket, and so forth.

I can't overly emphasize how unlikely it is that you'll run into this type of person. With over thirty years of being in, over, under, through, and around this business, I've only heard of two editors like that, and both of them have been run out of the business. Publishing is a rather small clique and word gets around very quickly.

Some beginning writers worry unduly that an editor will steal their ideas. First, as I've said before, the current copyright law protects your novel the moment it's finished (more accurately, at the moment of its creation). Second, very few editors are also writers. As stated earlier, it's much more likely that another writer will steal your novel after it's been published. In a field as crowded as romances, you'd probably never know it even if someone stole your story.

Keep in mind that romances are written to a specific formula. If you decide to write a romance with bullfighting as the backdrop . . . don't you think there are at least a dozen other authors who've also had the same idea? Nobody "stole" your concept. It's a matter of the odds that with so many people writing for the romance market, ideas will and do overlap. So relax. Paranoia is unbecoming to a writer.

> **A query letter should be free from error. If just a letter has a lot of spelling and grammatical errors, God knows what your manuscript will look like!**

So let's get back to taking the editor-first route. You have already decided that your romance was going to be for, say, Silhouette Books. Obviously, that's where you start. You can go one of two ways: (1) Send a query letter first to inquire if the editor is interested in seeing it (same information applies to what you would send an agent); or (2) just send the manuscript in cold turkey—what we call "over the transom" submissions. Sometimes a publisher's guidelines will tell you the preferred way of handling this; sometimes not.

In my experience, most editors prefer the query letter, generally accompanied by a brief outline of the novel (not more than six pages; less is better). This saves me time, shelf space, and alerts me to the fact that the author may well have something better than I might have expected (an unusual plot, a background that isn't overworked, or the heroine has an interesting career and the author seems to know a great deal about that business).

Query letters are also in your best interest:

(1) There's no rule about how many editors to whom you can send query letters. If you think your romance might fit just as well in some other publisher's line, it's perfectly all right to send a letter to that firm as well. However, there is a rigid rule against submitting your manuscript to more than one editor at a time! Never do that. If your agent wants to, okay; but not you!

(2) If the editor says yes, and you send your manuscript along, return postage is on the publisher—unless otherwise noted. If you send in your manuscript "over the transom," you must enclose a self-addressed stamped envelope suitable for returning your work. Again, if you want to know that

your manuscript arrived safely and when, either mail it certified mail, return receipt requested; or enclose a self-addressed postcard.

(3) Time. An editor can answer your letter in a matter of days; but if your manuscript has to be read first, it can be months and months.

The query letter

Why it should be so, I don't know—other than the fact that the act of writing a letter is becoming a dying art. However, most writers are scared silly of the query letter. It's fundamentally simple; and the simpler you keep it, the better.

If the publisher's guideline doesn't provide the name of its romance editor(s), then go to the public library and ask to see *Literary Market Place*; it lists all the primary editors, and if the romance line is a separate imprint, the editors, names will be provided. Often, imprints aren't listed in the main directory of publishers; but there's a section especially for imprints that will refer you back to the parent company.

Your letter should always be typed single-space; a handwritten letter will probably be thrown away since it shows that the writer is an amateur who hasn't taken the trouble to find out some of the basic etiquette of publishing practices. The letter should be free from error. Why? Well, look at it from the editor's point of view. If just a letter has a lot of spelling and grammatical errors, God knows what your manuscript will look like! Consequently, the neater and more professional your letter, the more receptive an editor will be.

As stated previously, the query letter should be brief. All it has to do is introduce who you are, and why you're writing to the editor. Editors don't give a darn how many children you have, what your husband does, or how talented your mother thinks you are. Just the facts that pertain to the reason for writing and nothing more. (Remember that the synopsis will be on a separate page.)

A query letter, then, is nothing more than a request for permission to submit your manuscript. It should be calm, reasonable, un-cute, and if you have any special qualifications, include them in addition to the accompanying résumé. By the way, if you've never held a job, then just provide some background information about yourself such as hobbies or interests. You don't have to be a "fascinating" person, with degrees out of the Yin Yang, world-traveled, etc.; it's your novel that counts. There's no stigma in being a housewife and mother; it's a career of its own.

If you happen to have any special qualifications, include them. In the following example, it's computer technology; but if you've worked in a veterinarian's office, the mortgage department of a bank, or any other area that you're using for a background, it's important to tell the editor. (Many writers of romances invent interesting careers for their heroines and then fail to tell the reader anything about this side of the heroine's life . . . probably because the authors know nothing about that profession.)

Whatever you can bring to the query letter that helps to sell your romance—without giving yourself hickies for excellence—should be part of the query letter.

As stated in the letter, enclose a copy (not the original) of a two- or three-page synopsis of your novel. If you need five pages, okay; but try to avoid

Sample query letter:

Jane Doe
000 Main Street
Centerville, U.S.A.

(Date)

Name of editor (don't use Ms. or Mr. if there's a title)
Title of Editor (Associate Editor, Senior Editor, etc.)
Super Romances, Inc.
Valentine Lane
New York, NY 10000

Dear Ms. (name):

   As an avid reader of your line of romances, I have written a romance of my own entitled, *Romance of My Own*. I have perused your guidelines and believe my novel fits your requirements.

   Set in Lower Slobovia, it is the story of a young American woman on an exchange program for computer technologists. Mary Smith, the heroine, is instantly attracted to the American manager of her division, Greg Swell; however, he seems to resent her presence and she can't figure out why. A detailed synopsis is enclosed for your convenience.

   The completed manuscript is estimated at 58,500 words. May I point out, Ms. ___ that I have worked in computer technology and know my subject well. Consequently the background information is completely authentic and with so many women going into this field, I believe readers will find added interest as a result of the background.

   With your permission, I would like to submit *Romance of My Own* to you and look forward to your reply. In the interim, thank you for your consideration.

Sincerely,

Jane Doe

Encl: Synopsis, Resume

anything more than that. Shorter is faster—therefore better.

   Anything that facilitates an editor's workaday is appreciated and will probably result in a more favorable impression.

   By the way, it's considered poor form in business letter writing to begin paragraphs with the word "I," especially the opening paragraph. See the sample for a typical query letter.

If, however, you are asking the editor's permission to submit a partial manuscript (partial is exactly what it sounds like—incomplete), then the letter will have to be altered slightly. Obviously, you will not say "complete" nor give the estimated word count. Instead, you will talk about "my manuscript in progress, of which I now have the opening four chapters completed" and address yourself to the book's "projected length of between 55-60,000 words." And if you want to send in only a partial, then add to your query letter that you're doing so in order to get his/her editorial guidance prior to completing the novel. You will, of course, still enclose the synopsis.

A word or so about submitting partial manuscripts, though I touched on it earlier. Many writers do not understand how to go about this. I have received "submissions" of a single, random page from each chapter of a book; or the fifth and seventh chapters, but nothing else; and so on. An editor can tell nothing from this type of submission other than that you're not a pro.

If you want to send a partial, send the opening chapters, complete and in sequence. Otherwise, it's like walking into the theater during the middle of the movie; the viewer can't tell who's who, what went before, why this scene should matter, and so forth. If at all possible, send at least five or six chapters; but never fewer than three.

Over-the-transom submissions

Whether a partial or a complete manuscript, it will still require a cover letter (which, as far as I'm concerned, means you might just as well have sent the query letter and saved time). The cover letter should say everything the query letter does, except that you're not asking if it's all right to submit . . . you've submitted.

Again, do not send suggested artwork for the cover. Do not write jacket copy. Those two things are taken care of by the publisher. It is a good idea, however, to enclose a synopsis even with a completed manuscript. It saves the editor time. It's not imperative, but it's helpful.

And to repeat, your manuscript should be sent in a sturdy box or in a padded mailing bag. It shouldn't be bound in any way other than a couple of rubber bands around it, and possibly a cardboard stiffener to protect the manuscript pages' edges.

The primary problem with over-the-transom submissions is how long it takes for an editor (or a reader) to get to them. Usually, there are bookcases filled to the brim, or a huge library table where they are stacked until threatening to tumble. The quantity of manuscripts awaiting a reading is usually referred to as a "slushpile." That should indicate in what "high regard" uninvited manuscripts are held.

Editors will usually read agented manuscripts first, or those they have asked to see directly from the authors. And yes, over-the-transom submissions are read in order of their receipt . . . but not till it's a slow period (Ha!). Manuscripts asked to be seen get priority; slushpile waits.

A word of warning. If you decide to submit directly, and engage in negotiations for the book, then do not bring in an agent later to conclude the deal. Nothing turns an editor off faster (other than learning it's a multiple submission), and you may find yourself with no sale at all. Bringing an agent in on a deal after discussions have begun is no different from being five feet tall and picking a fight, then just before it begins, you bring in a seven-foot-tall muscleman to do your fighting for you. Don't do it! You began the whole process; you finish it. Should you happen to acquire an agent in the interim, then that person should handle your next book . . . not this one.

However, you can bring an agent into this at the moment an editor expresses interest in buying your book. You can explain apologetically that— in the time between submitting the manuscript and hearing from the editor— you have acquired an agent. Also, while you'd be more than willing to discuss any editorial suggestions, you'd prefer the agent to handle any negotiations. You can say this even if you don't have an agent! Tell the editor you will have your agent phone her—because then you can turn around, call any agency, and ask them to handle the deal. No agent will turn down a deal where the legwork has already been done! But to pull this off you need nerves of steel. If playing Meryl Streep is not for you, then stay away from this.

What you must be prepared for, agented or otherwise, is waiting. You will do an unbearable amount of that. The sheer volume of manuscripts is amazing. And reading submissions can only take place around the actual editorial process and meeting deadlines. Too, writers manage to come up with some highly creative excuses for not meeting their deadlines: broken wrist, breakup with a lover, it's tax time—you name it. Editors have heard them all. If a deadline is missed, a substitute title must be found immediately, and that's unnerving, vexing, and will count against you if you want to sell that editor anything else. <u>A deadline is sacrosanct. Miss it and you're figuratively chopped liver.</u>

What is permissible, though, is if you can anticipate a problem with meeting the deadline before your manuscript has been scheduled for production. Editors are, after all, human beings and know that everyone encounters personal problems occasionally. So if you give your editor ample forewarning that you may be late, then the editor will not schedule your novel until it's been received.

Although editors know perfectly well that it's best not to schedule a manuscript until it's been completed . . . some editors are under such tight deadlines that this becomes a luxury. Ideally, the completed manuscript should be read (it may need revisions) before contemplating scheduling it...but that's just not always possible. If the editor you're working with is on that kind of tight schedule, be prepared to literally "drop everything" to do the revisions instantly. Instantly!

Were I in charge of the world, no one should be hired as an editor until that individual has spent two years—without outside income or help—as a writer. It'll never happen, of course; but at least editors would come to understand just how awful it is to wait and wait and wait.

And then there's their side of the story . . . .

CHAPTER SIX

The Editor's Side of the Desk

Whatever most of you think is typical of a paperback editor's day at the office, forget it. They are the most grossly underpaid and resourceful people in America; they are also frequently overworked and pressured to the point of ulcers. Their bosses think they spend too much money, waste a lot of time, and buy too many duds from authors. Authors think they don't spend enough money, waste a lot of time, and buy lousy books from other writers instead of buying everything from only a handful of authors. Agents, because they can see both sides of the issue, straddle the fence.

Sure, some editors are more fun to work with, or more candid about internal problems (such as delayed royalty checks), but editors don't run the company; they are only responsible for editorial output. They buy the best quality of writing they can find, but quality has to play second fiddle to a production schedule. If an editor is responsible for seeing ten books a month to press, s/he is going to buy ten books—not nine, not eight, but ten. If the editor can find more than ten good romance manuscripts, and it doesn't exceed budget, then the editor might buy more than ten to be ahead of the game for a future schedule.

Let me remind you once again. Since conglomerate takeovers have occurred, there are almost no independent paperback publishers left. For example, Fawcett is owned by Ballantine which is owned by Random House; Pocket is owned by Simon & Schuster which is owned by Paramount which is owned by Viacom—and that could change at any moment. If you peruse *Literary Market Place*'s directory carefully (also known simply as *LMP* in the industry), you'll swiftly see that virtually all publishing firms are owned by a non-publishing major company. So what does that mean to you? It means that "policy" is being dictated by people who don't understand traditional publishing; the edicts from on high are based on the profit-and-loss bottom line. Period. This means that editors must operate from a teeter-totter position: Is it a good book; will it sell; can enough manuscripts be found to meet the monthly quota; will deadlines be met; and the All Important question of will the novel earn out its advance and production costs plus make a profit?

This is in addition to knowing how to: edit; copyedit; proofread; write jacket copy and sales kits; interface with the art department, salespeople, advertising, publicity, and other departments—all departments think theirs is the most important; get authors to willingly revise their work (the key word here

109

is "willingly"); meet with agents, writers, and outside vendors (freelance artists or photographers); and so on. It's quite a balancing act.

They also need managerial skills to run their departments (if in charge), and how to interface with accounting, the legal department, support staff, and of course, the boss. Organizational skills are imperative! Meeting deadlines is no easy matter even when the authors have met theirs. Anything can happen; anything at all. Printers are on strike, the bindery machines are down, 25,000 copies of a book have been run with the covers upside down (so must be run off again, throwing off the schedule all the way down the line), editorial staff is out with the flu—Murphy's Law most assuredly applies here. Being an editor means you have to wear quite a few hats, and look good in all of them. Good luck!

Generally, their offices are woefully small, often windowless, with never enough bookshelves or tables; their desks are almost always a complete mess. Do not be deceived; they know precisely where everything is. They have to— there's nowhere else to put anything. Show me a paperback editor's office that's neat and tidy, and I'd be willing to put money on that person not being a very good editor. Not a hard and fast rule, but still . . . .

It's Monday morning. Edna Editor has just climbed two flights of stairs from the subway in New York City. She's embattled from shouldering through the hundreds of people also three minutes late to work. She still has to walk/run four blocks (regardless of weather) to her office building, keeping an eye out for muggers yet striving for a cheerful attitude before greeting her coworkers with a pleasant "good morning." Edna Editor is in charge of her division of the paperback company: Raging Romances.

She may have a secretary, but it's unlikely. She will probably type her own book contracts (if there's no legal department) and correspondence and do her own filing—after hours or on weekends. She also has to be sure all manuscripts received are entered into the log (book or file listing authors alphabetically, title of the manuscript, date of receipt, and when appropriate, final disposition of the manuscript—rejected or accepted). However, Edna works for a smallish company and is responsible for seeing four romances per month to press. So she will probably have an editorial assistant. For only four books per month? You better believe it!

Unlike hardcover houses that have "seasons" (the fall list, the spring list, etc.), and infinitely fewer books to publish per year, paperback houses operate on very tight monthly schedules, *simultaneously* working on as many as six months' worth of books at a time. For those of you who are genuinely interested in this, I'm including in this chapter a copy of how I set up my own editorial working schedule for ease of reference. Once a manuscript is put into schedule for publication, it gets preference over everything else—everything.

What does this mean? There are a number of things that must be done before the manuscript is copyedited:

(1) Edna, ideally, will have completely read all four manuscripts for that month.

(2) She will prepare a list of alternate titles, either for approval by committee or her immediate boss's. Paperback companies love to change

titles; usually they're quite right. Authors, even old hands, are rarely objective about their own work.

Then too, there's the matter of a romance already published with that same title you provided; or a romance on Edna's list of forthcoming titles that's either the same title, or too close. Don't be surprised if the title of your book is changed.

(3) Jacket copy—sometimes called "blurbs," though that's technically erroneous—must be written for front and back covers. Then the frontispiece (also known as front sales) must be written; this is the first page of the paperback where either review excerpts or a condensed scene from the book appears.

(4) A synopsis of the story must be written at the same time, along with any salient information that would prove beneficial to the salesforce, to provide a sales kit—unless Edna is lucky enough to have a publicity department to do that for her. In a small company, that's highly unlikely. But let's say the romance has a cruise ship setting, from Miami to the Bahamas. So? So what? A good salesperson and/or the publicity department (Edna) will contact cruise lines with that route and push stocking copies of this romance in their gift shop. If Edna's sharp (which of course she is!), she'll recommend to the author to contact a real cruise ship line (or Edna might do it herself, adding to her tasks) and request permission to cite their line in the book instead of a make-believe cruise line. If they agree, they'll stock plenty of copies to tout their own line. Smart. Very smart. So if there's something special about the romance that lends itself to sales beyond bookstores only, she'll go for it.

> **Romance editors *want* to accept your work; they are desperate to feed the voracious schedule they must meet.**

(5) Edna must also come up with ideas for the art department on how to illustrate the book. This will include descriptions of the main characters, where the book is set, and several thumbnail "scenes" that may serve as the cover's illustration. You may have noticed, from time to time, that the illustration on the cover has no bearing to what happens in the book. Usually it's because the art director has ignored Edna's suggestions. Frustrating, but not worth getting an ulcer over it.

The reason all of this is done in advance of copyediting a manuscript is that the art department must have covers run off at least four months ahead of publication date (also known just as pub date). The cover goes into the sales kit and the salesforce is out there pitching the book long before it's printed. Having pre-sold copies gives the publisher a pretty good idea of just how many copies to print of any given title. In turn, one hopes, there will be fewer returns or warehousing due to printing too many.

Remember, please, that this is for four books simultaneously. While she's doing this, she will also be: (1) copyediting manuscripts due to the production department; (2) proofreading manuscripts set into type; and (3) checking the signatures before the book is printed and bound.

In the meantime, Edna is answering correspondence and telephone calls from agents, authors, her boss, questions from other departments, and making lunch dates with agents, hardcover editors or subsidiary rights people, magazine editors, going to editorial and production meetings, and if she can find four minutes to make an appointment with her dentist, she's lucky!

Then Edna has to meet with you while you're in town, along with other authors on her lists, and make each of you feel very welcome and special. Never mind that she can't see you over the clutter on her desk. While you're there, a writer telephones to complain that her contracts haven't been received. The writer is put on hold (and so are you) while Edna does a quick search to be sure she really did mail off the contracts. If she can't find her copy, then she'll have to do it all over again. Or a phone call complaining about not receiving a royalty check or questioning the accuracy of the royalty report . . . . It's time-consuming no matter how you look at it.

As if all this weren't enough, there's that table over there with dozens and dozens of solicited and unsolicited manuscripts to be evaluated. I have found that it takes reading about twenty submissions to find *one* I can accept. That's a lot of time spent to read nineteen submissions you can't use.

Mind you, romance editors *want* to accept your work; they are desperate to feed the voracious schedule they must meet. Nothing would make them happier than if they could accept every manuscript they read—but it doesn't happen that way. Everybody wants to be a writer; few people are disciplined enough to become one. (That's the whole purpose of this book . . . to help you!)

We've already discussed how to be sure your manuscript arrived safely and when. However, it's traditional to allow at least eight weeks before you send a polite inquiry about its status. Next in line to be read? Ten submissions from the top?

In today's rush, give Edna ten weeks before you make any inquiries. An agent can generally call after about six weeks, yet agents know how very busy editors are and try not to interrupt their hectic workdays. Let me repeat: For every interruption in an editor's day, that's time away from reading submissions.

If you remember nothing else, keep in mind that there are thousands of writers out there wanting their romances to be published. If you antagonize your editor, you will lose the sale no matter how good your romance might be. The last thing in the world an editor needs is an overanxious or whining writer! And just to reinforce just how strange some writers are, I once received an eight-by-ten-inch glossy photograph—typical "author's" photograph, heavily shadowed and posed. There was no letter with the photo, but on the back of it the man had handwritten:

```
This is my formal author's photograph.  You will never
be able to use it because I wouldn't dream of sending you
```

112

my novel. It's much too good for the company you work for. All editors are jerks in the first place and would not be able to appreciate what a superior writer I am.

It wasn't signed and there was no return address. What was I supposed to do with it? Naturally, it was thrown away with a shake of the head.

All right, Edna finally gets around to reading your romance. It's been on that table for anywhere from three to six or seven months. Most editors date the manuscripts when they come in and try to read them in order of their arrival (unless the editor has asked to see it, in which case it gets preference—maybe it'll be read in five months instead of seven).

She reads your romance and loves it. She must now write to you and tell you that she is interested in contracting for your work. Maybe it needs some revisions—are you willing to do them? For that matter, are you capable of doing them? Not all writers can revise their work; and some simply refuse to do so.

There are thousands of writers out there wanting their romances to be published.

At that point, Edna may have well wasted her time reading your manuscript. And if you ever submit to her again, no matter where she's working, she'll probably remember your name and reject the manuscript outright. There's no point to reading a writer's work if that writer is a known uncooperative person. This is equally true if you've submitted your manuscript to another editor at the same time. If Edna reads it, then finds out you've sold it to some other editor—well, I wouldn't want to be in your shoes!

But after you've read this book, you'll have a far better grasp of what's expected of you and what isn't. So you listen to (or read) what it is Edna wants changed, and you agree to do it. A modicum of *polite* disagreement is permissible, but don't forget this is your very first sale—don't alienate Edna, who already has plenty of problems. If you genuinely don't like the requested changes (and give the suggestions some time to filter down so you don't argue needlessly), then make two or three counter-suggestions. This will show Edna that you are not a "deathless prose writer" (nothing can be worse), and that you're fully willing to cooperate with her for the betterment of the book . . . only that you have a few ideas of your own. Most editors will compromise if they possibly can. They still have to meet those schedules and they must have manuscripts to do so. Some will remain adamant about what changes are required, and that's that.

So you've now agreed on the changes. This is *not* a guarantee of a sale to Edna. She first has to be sure you really can do it. It's not unusual for a first-time author to founder, getting sidetracked and off onto another direction. Naturally, you are confident that you can, and your husband sweetly offers to cook dinner for two weeks while you work on your revisions, and your oldest son says he'll do the laundry. Dusting and vacuuming can wait (unless you can assign the tasks to your other children). If you live alone, nothing matters as much as rewriting your romance to please Edna.

The revisions are done and you send them off to Edna. At this point, she will make a genuine effort to get to them as quickly as possible. Not only is Edna a considerate individual, but she has to buy manuscripts for publication or have gaps in her schedule . . . and probably lose her job. And Edna is very eager to find out if you've pulled off the changes satisfactorily so she can send you a contract. (I sincerely hope that every editor who reads this book will show this chapter to her or his boss and ask for a raise!)

You've done your work well and Edna sends you her company's standard contractual agreement. A few weeks later, you'll probably receive an Author's Questionnaire. Not all paperback houses do this, however. Fill it out and return it as quickly as you can, and be sure to avoid laboriously long answers.

You have now delivered your baby, and have turned it over to an adoption agency. From this moment on, you have *nothing* more to do with your romance! That's it. It's over. You've done your part, now the adoption agency will do its. To illustrate this point, what follows is a checklist . . . .

Hard facts checklist

You will have no say in a title change. You can, however, suggest alternative titles. You may also wish to know that a title can't be copyrighted. The only legal recourse is if someone uses a title that has been a bestseller previously. For instance, you can't legally use *Gone with the Wind*. That's to capitalize on the success of a different book and leaves you open to lawsuit.

You will not be consulted about the sell-copy on the covers nor the illustration. Unless invited for your opinion (not likely), what you get is what you get.

You will not appear on television talk shows nor have a national author's tour—unless your book will be Edna's lead title, or it really sells exceptionally well, or the publisher's faith in it warrants such an expensive push. Again, not likely. But Edna might take you out to lunch because she's very nice or because she wants to encourage you to submit more manuscripts by providing editorial guidance.

You will have nothing to do with the style of the typeface for the book, its layout, and/or minor editorial changes.

It will probably be at least a year before your book is published; often longer. Smaller companies may go to press in less time, but most of the romance publishers work far, far in advance.

You may or may not see the copyedited manuscript or the pageproofs (or the repros or the galleys) of your book to proofread before it's printed. Publishers vary, and you'll need to ask about their procedures. If that courtesy happens to be extended to you, you may make changes in the copyedited manuscript. But make no changes reading the galleys other than corrections of printer's errors or extremely minor changes. Any changes you make that aren't as a result of an error will be charged back to you. This is no time to start rewriting! Besides, it won't be possible to add much text because the signatures for the book have already been set.

It's unlikely that you'll see what the cover looks like in advance, despite the fact that they're ready months before the book's official publication date. Why? Too many authors, over the years, have complained so much that it doesn't pay to send advance covers. You'll see the cover when you receive your advance copies of the printed book—several weeks before pub date. Handling writers' complaints takes time and it's a bore. (But if you're lucky, the publisher will send you one cover.)

You can expect your romance novel to have a retail shelf life of approximately four weeks.

Outside of publications devoted to romances, it's unlikely your novel will be reviewed—unless it's in your own hometown. Ask permission from your editor before submitting a review copy on your own. It may be that the publisher has already sent a copy to the publication. (For every copy that's given away, for whatever purpose, that affects your royalties and the publisher's profits.)

Your romance novel is competing with dozens and dozens of other romances published in that same month. **Don't expect miracles.**

Editorial/production terminology

Although most of these terms will appear in the **Glossary** for ease of reference, let me explain some of the words I've been tossing around as if everyone already understands them. And I'm providing them here in sequence, just as your manuscript is handled once it's contracted for.

So let's back up for a moment. In large companies, with big payrolls, employees tend to become compartmentalized and perform the same specific job over and over. The books may be different, but the duties are not. An editor edits, a copyeditor copyedits, and so on. Some companies have specialists in writing jacket copy, some do not. However, we've set up Raging Romances with just Edna and her editorial associate or assistant. This means the two of them must do just about everything without any extra help. So here's their professional vernacular so you can sound knowledgeable when discussing your manuscript.

Editing

This is when you read the manuscript for content. Is it well written? Does the story hold one's interest? Are the characters and their actions believable? Has the author thrown away a scene that could be infinitely more powerful? In short, "editing" is reading the manuscript to find out if the overall premise works and is entertaining for the market it appeals to.

My own way of working at this stage is to make notes on ruled paper about things that bother me. Unless the manuscript has been contracted for, an editor should not mark it up in any way. What bothers me might well not bother someone else. Even misspellings or grammatical errors are left alone. If the editor hasn't received a signed contract from the author, the manuscript doesn't belong to the editor and s/he should not make changes.

Copyediting

You need good eyes, a superb memory, and a love for detail. This is where you try to catch all the author's mistakes and correct them on the manuscript itself. Sometimes the copyeditor will spot a detail or concept that seems doubtful or questionable, and will flag that line to double-check with the author or, in larger companies, with the contracting editor. If Edna has kept her initial notes about the manuscript during the editing phase (she has), that is extremely helpful to the copyeditor. The copyeditor will have drawn up a stylesheet for the proofreader's benefit later.

Many editors today do their copyediting on the display screen. (I'm entirely too old-fashioned for that. I'll do a preliminary copyediting on the display before printing, but I still have to read hard copy if I want to be sure I've caught all errors.) In some cases, the floppy disk is sent to the printer instead of the manuscript on paper. But other than facilitating the process, the production stages remain pretty much the same.

Once the manuscript has been edited and copyedited, it can go back to Edna for verification of the copyeditor's questions, or to the author, or both. Usually, questions will be done by letter or phone since it is too risky to send the manuscript itself back to the author; it can be lost, the author's too busy to get to it right away, or any other delay-causing situations. Generally, if questions arise, a phone call will answer them easily. (Don't forget you still have your notebook with all the pertinent details of your novel. You do, don't you?)

Another thing copyeditors must be concerned with (though not particularly with romances) is when they're working with renowned authors. In the mid-sixties, a respected and venerable poet's work was compiled into a slim volume. The copyeditor had deleted a comma from one of her poems. Not omitted, but deleted—it was intentional because the editor thought the line read better. The outcome? The poet sued on the basis that her work had been sullied, destroying the effect she'd intended. She won. If an editor is working with a famous author . . . s/he must be very careful to obtain permission before changing anything.

I don't mention this just as a publishing anecdote. <u>My point is that until an author has a bestseller to his or her credit, writers are pretty much powerless regarding the treatment of their work.</u> But once you become famous . . . you've got power, kiddo, real clout. Nobody's going to kick sand in your face ever again! That's the good news. The bad is that fewer than five percent of all books published annually ever reach bestseller status. Since approximately 40,000 books are published in this country per year, the odds are against bestsellerdom.

Production

Once all editorial work is completed, and everyone is happy, it goes to the production department. That may be in-house (the plant isn't on the premises [Heaven forfend! Printers mingling with editorial staff? How gauche!]) or it may be farmed out. Either way, there's a production manager who's Edna's contact with regard to seeing the book to print. The production department is in charge of seeing the copyedited manuscript through all phases of

116

physically converting your manuscript into a book, at varying stages.

Even with today's computerized production methods, as noted above, the process hasn't changed all that much. Whether with desktop publishing or traditional typesetting, the manuscript is set into type. Very few companies get galleys anymore, but you ought to know about them.

Galleys are very long, narrow sheets of paper (about 16-18 inches) with the book's typeset text on them. The galleys are not paginated. Previous to the computer, they were sent to the editor for an initial proofreading. Because new errors could be made while correcting the original typesetting errors, the editor would have to reread at least a few paragraphs prior to the correction, and following it, just to be sure no new errors were made or that anything had been left out. That step has pretty much been eliminated today, sparing editors having to proofread twice.

Today, Edna is more likely to receive "repros"—short for "reproductions." (Prior to the computer, they were called pageproofs. They were still long narrow strips, but at this point they were paginated.) Repros contain all the typeset information and have already been pasted down on oblong, horizontal light cardboard strips. Usually with several pages per strip, and paginated. What's sent to Edna is a copy pulled from the original—no chances are taken at this point. No coffee spills, no curling edges, no pages askew due to the proofreading process and sweaty palms.

Printers make mistakes. No matter how excellent they are, they will still make mistakes. Sometimes paragraphs can be left out, even a chapter. I once worked at a publishing firm that used a printing company more accustomed to girlie magazines than paperback books. I was proofreading a Western novel and there was (of course) the scene where the Indians had raided a community of settlers. The lieutenant had ridden his horse all night to tell the fort's commander. The line from the book should have been: `"Send for the messenger,"` the commander barked. However, when I received the repros to double-check, the line read: `"Send for the massagers,"` the commander barked. You've got to watch printers.

Proofreading

This is critical. Even more so than with copyediting, you really need very good eyes because typeset material is generally smaller than typewritten. You still need a superb memory and a fetish for detail. So Edna or her associate will proofread the repros. At one of my editorial jobs, I had a two-person situation such as that. To reduce the risk of not spotting mistakes, my associate and I would take turns. You can read something so often that you no longer see errors. So if I copyedited it, my associate would proofread it; and vice versa.

Another benefit to working that way is that it served to train my associate on my editorial preferences; and it provided an easy opportunity to double-check her work to be sure she was staying on top of things.

The proofreading phase is the very last chance there is to catch any errors—whether the printer's or one's own. And again, that original stylesheet is a blessing!

It's also when you check to make sure there aren't any "orphans" or "widows." A widow is the top line on the page that doesn't extend at least halfway across; an orphan is the same, but it's the last line. Either looks terrible on the printed page. And they're the cause, occasionally, of your sentences being extended or cut, without altering the meaning. You'll probably never even notice that it's been done, but the purpose is to eliminate widows or orphans.

Long, long ago, if a book was published with more than three errors in it (of any kind), heads would roll. You're outta here! In fact, a major hardcover house had an entire floor devoted to copyediting and proofreading. No speaking was allowed. Quiet as a tomb. Nothing could interrupt the level of concentration. With the crippling costs these days, that is a thing of the past. And of course there are more mistakes in books than ever before.

Once the proofreading has been done, the repros are sent back to production to correct any errors. The corrected repros are returned to Edna again. Nowadays, with the computer, it's very difficult to make a new error while correcting the first error. Editors will still make a cursory check, but it doesn't involve as much re-proofreading as before.

So when we talk about proofreading, we mean making sure that the typesetter has set the manuscript as it was supposed to be, without error (some will always slip by the author or the editor), and that the book is as perfect as it can be.

Signatures (brownline or blueline)

Repros have been corrected and this is the next-to-the-last stage for the text of your novel. A signature is thirty-two sequential pages of the book. They are printed on a flat piece of paper and then folded to show how they will appear once bound. And it's the signatures that are later bound together, not individual pages. As an aside, because of the 32-page format, a paperback book's length (number of pages) must be divisible by eight. They technically can be shorter (in four-page increments), but that means you've got to guillotine the leftover pages, or leave them blank, and paper is expensive. Sometimes, when a manuscript simply can't be fitted into a 32-page format, the publisher will announce upcoming books in the back just to utilize the paper.

Sometimes signatures will come to the editor with brown ink, and sometimes with blue. Hence the "brownline" and "blueline" reference above. Signatures must be checked in case, between repro and signature, pages have been transposed, chapters have fallen out, or large portions pasted upside-down. And it's the last chance to be sure the pages are numbered properly. Checking the signatures, Edna will make sure that the last line on the bottom is followed correctly by the first line on the next page. Yes, the text was already pasted down with the repros . . . but it's a cheap paste, the pages can easily fall off, and if not repasted carefully errors can occur. I once worked on a nonfiction book that continually referred to a specific chart. Throughout all the checks and counterchecks, not I, my boss, the author, or the printer caught the fact that the chart had been omitted at the typesetting stage.

The book was published, and then had to be recalled from retailers. Another company I worked at did an updated edition of a highly successful cookbook (fortunately, I wasn't involved with that fiasco). The authors were well-known in culinary circles, and the cookbook has been on sale for better than three decades! Never out of print. Well, when the updated version was published, it turned out that the ingredients for recipes had been transposed with instructions for other recipes. To clarify, let's say it was a recipe for lasagna. The list of ingredients were for meatloaf, but the instructions on how to cook lasagna had been transposed with meatloaf. This occurred throughout the book. The authors sued—and won. The publisher had to recall all editions it had sold, and completely start all over again. A very, very costly oversight!

So all that aside, the above are your basic editorial terms in the book publishing business.

Scheduling

It doesn't happen very often, but sometimes a book in schedule has to be pulled, leaving an empty slot on Edna's schedule. Panic time. Then she remembers your book is "ready to go" and slides it in.

Let's say it's now October. Edna is working on repros and signatures for the forthcoming December list of books; getting copyedited manuscripts to production for the January list; and completing all cover information for the April list. Let's also assume she has slotted your romance to be a May title to fill the void left by the pulled title. Cover information won't be due to the art department until next month—November of this year.

It's already been explained why the covers have been done first. Paper must be ordered, press time reserved, costs projected, and a host of other factors—most of which will affect how many copies of your book will be printed. Or, if there's retailer resistance (for any reason), fewer copies will be printed.

As explained before, paperbacks are sold on consignment to retailers. Formerly, unsold copies were returned for credit; however that's changed due to the ever-increasing cost of postage/shipping. Today, it's more likely that the covers will be torn off and only they are returned for credit. What happens to the coverless paperbacks is anybody's guess—probably sold at half price, but neither the publisher nor the author will see any profits from that.

Okay, let's get back to the production process and Edna's schedule. Keep in mind that it's now October and look at the schedule Edna must work with. Her department is all through with Raging Romances' list of books through November, and almost everything has been taken care of for the December list. (Not all publishers have such tight schedules, by the way, but this will at least give you a very good idea of what kind of pressure Edna is under.)

"No." refers to the book's number (dropping off the ISBN prefix—ISBN stands for International Standard Book Number, useful to librarians and retailers). "Title" is obvious. "Due" refers to when Edna must have that portion of the process completed in order to meet deadline; "actual" refers to when she really turned it in (no cheating, either!). Edna, at a glance, can pace her own work, predict areas of possible chaos and keep tabs on how her department is doing. (And you thought all we did was read manuscripts and have lavish luncheons!)

Clearly, when it comes to editorial deadlines, Edna is pretty on top of things. Something must have happened this October, though, because she was late with all her April cover information. Perhaps she was out with the flu; or nobody liked what she had presented so she had to do it all over again. However, once that manuscript is sent to the typesetter, Edna is now subject to pressures from that department, along with whatever else might go wrong in her own department.

December's titles, as you'll note, seemed to have been held up in production; that department was very slow in getting those proofs to her. And with one book, even though it was due to Edna with sufficient time for her to proofread and get the proofs back to production by September 27th . . . production still hadn't given her the proofs for one title. That means that when they finally do come in, Edna will have to skip a lot of lunches or stay after hours (or both)—for which she is *not* paid. (Another benefit to keeping a schedule is to serve as Edna's alibi—*she* wasn't late, production was.)

And as you can see, since your book is slotted for May publication, Edna has one month to come up with cover information while taking care of everything else in schedule . . . *and* reading manuscripts for possible acceptance.

Now you know why it takes so long to get decisions from editors, and why such emphasis is placed on meeting your deadline. If you don't, and Edna was counting on you, her entire month is thrown off—and so is the production department's (they tend to yell a great deal).

To repeat, some publishers will send you a copy of the repros to proofread your own book. However, if you are asked to proofread your own novel (Edna's doing it simultaneously), do not make any unnecessary changes. It's too late. You should have thought of those additions or deletions or rephrasing before you submitted your final manuscript. If you see a mistake that the copyeditor failed to catch, that's one thing. If Edna cut some of your manuscript (this frequently happens) and it reads poorly, point this out to Edna . . . but don't write on the repros themselves. Use a separate piece of paper. (The end of this chapter will provide standard proofreaders' marks for your benefit.) And make sure that any corrections you make on the repros (typos) are in the margins—*never* between lines, even if you can find the space.

Remember, it is very costly to make changes at this stage, and *you* will be billed for any alterations (called "author's alterations" or AAs) that didn't appear in the original manuscript. Moreover, your changes are likely to affect the pagination and that too is costly. So don't cut, add, or revise now, for Pete's (and Edna's) sake!

To give you a better idea of what's involved, let's backtrack for a moment. Let's talk about the basics of formatting a book's text. If there's an art department, the decisions will be made there. If there's no art department, then Edna will decide. As you've doubtlessly noticed, there are all kinds of different typefaces (also called "fonts"), and sizes they come in. Some publishers of romances want each book to be "styled" individually; some have a set format.

Styling a book refers to what typeface is used; how much air there should be between the lines; do chapters begin on right-hand page only or right and

Work Schedule: October

No.	Title	COVERS		MANUSCRIPT		PROOFS		REPROS		BROWNLINES	
		Due	Actual	Due	Actual	Due	Actual	Due	Actual	Due	Actual
3114	DECEMBER	6/10	4/28	9/6	8/11	9/27	9/2	10/6	9/14	10/18	10/18
3115		6/10	5/12	9/6	9/2	9/27		10/6	9/3	10/18	10/17
3116		6/10	4/27	9/6	8/3	9/27	8/30	10/6	10/12	10/18	
3117		6/10	5/12	9/6	8/24	9/27	10/5	10/6	10/6	10/18	
		6/10	6/14	9/6	8/16	9/27	9/29	10/6		10/18	
3118	JANUARY	7/9	6/4	10/5	9/29	10/26		11/5		11/16	
3119		7/9	6/4	10/5	9/23	10/26		11/5		11/16	
3120		7/9	6/15	10/5	9/24	10/26		11/5		11/16	
3121		7/9	6/7	10/5	10/11	10/26		11/5		11/16	
3122	FEBRUARY	8/10	7/30	11/5		11/24		12/3		12/16	
3123		8/10	7/30	11/5		11/24		12/3		12/16	
3124		8/10	7/29	11/5		11/24		12/3		12/16	
3125		8/10	7/29	11/5		11/24		12/3		12/16	
3126	MARCH	9/10	8/30	12/6		12/27		1/5		1/17	
3127		9/10	8/23	12/6		12/27		1/5		1/17	
3128		9/10	8/23	12/6		12/27		1/5		1/17	
3129		9/10	8/23	12/6		12/27		1/5		1/17	
3130	APRIL	10/4	10/8	1/5		1/26		2/4		2/18	
3131		10/4	10/8	1/5		1/26		2/4		2/18	
3132		10/4	10/7	1/5		1/26		2/4		2/18	
3133		10/4	10/4	1/5		1/26		2/4		2/18	
3134	MAY	11/10		2/5		2/25		3/4		3/14	
3135		11/10		2/5		2/25		3/4		3/14	
3136		11/10		2/5		2/25		3/4		3/14	
3137	YOUR BOOK HERE	11/10		2/5		2/25		3/4		3/14	

left, or even in the middle of a page. Is there a "running head" (see **Glossary**)? If the book's running a bit short to fill out the 32-page signature, running heads may be used. Or possibly a "half-title page" (see **Glossary**).

If Edna asked you for 60,000 words of manuscript, and that's what you gave her (give or take a couple of words), then Edna can pretty well rest assured that—using a particular typeface, margins, etc.—she will have a 176-page printed book. If she wants to run ads in the back of the book, she may have to use a smaller typeface to gain the blank pages, or run the chapters together, or both.

So once you get your repros, if you start cutting or changing, that could throw off the number of lines per printed page . . . which in turn could wreak havoc with the signature. Perhaps you never noticed, but except with the end of a chapter (where the text doesn't necessary come to the bottom of the page), all facing pages match across the last line. Theoretically, you could end up with a book that has blank pages between chapters—though Edna and production would never permit that to happen.

Instead, assuming that Edna had designated that she wanted each chapter to begin on a right-hand page, this might suddenly have to be amended. Everything has to be pasted down yet again to meet the changes, and quite possibly, even need to be typeset again. A most time-consuming and therefore costly process.

That's why AAs (Author's Alterations) are billed back to the author. Again,

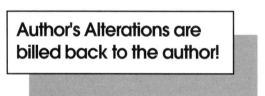

Author's Alterations are billed back to the author!

if it's not your error (you wrote "there" and they typeset "their"), then by all means indicate the error on the margin. This type of correction will not be billed back to you. Or, though it happens infrequently, sometimes the typesetter will set the same line twice, drop out a paragraph and so forth. This too is not billed back to you. Only your own changes that veer from the original manuscript will be held against you.

The main reason paperback companies rarely send a copy of the repros to the author is simply a matter of time; not that they're inconsiderate. Those monthly schedules are gruelling.

So if your image of an editor was of the tweedy sort, twirling a rose whilst gazing out the window, you now know just how wrong you were.

Oh! Edna will have bound copies of your romance sometime in April. She will send you your free author's copies at that time . . . and you can start bragging that your novel will be on sale in May. "Yes, I'm available for autograph parties. Aren't you a dear to ask!"

To review the sequence of events:
(Note: I'm bypassing the galleys stage since it so seldom occurs anymore. Were it still commonplace, it would squeeze in prior to repros/pageproofs being received in editorial.)

1) Manuscript received and logged in. This can mean a notebook, an index card file, the computer, or whatever. Your name, title of the manuscript, and the date it was received will be written down.

2) It's placed on the slushpile by date of receipt—unless it was requested by Edna (either directly from you or your agent).

3) It's ultimately read by either Edna or her associate. If not suitable, it is instantly returned to the author or the agent. If a "maybe," Edna might ask her associate to read it too. Final disposition: Yeah, with revisions; or nah, more work than they have time to give it.

4) Letters or phone calls outlining what terms they are prepared to offer; or explaining what changes will be expected first.

5) Copies of the contracts sent to author or agent for signature, and return. An executed copy (signed by Edna or someone else in authority at Raging Romances) will be sent to author or agent later.

6) The manuscript is either shelved for future scheduling, or pending receipt of author's revisions.

7) When in schedule, the manuscript is copyedited.

8) Copyedited manuscript sent to production department with all pertinent instructions regarding styling of text, front and back matter, etc.

9) Months later, pageproofs (repros) are returned to editors.

10) Ideally, whomever did not copyedit the manuscript then proofreads the repros.

11) Proofread repros returned to production department for corrections.

12) Corrected repros returned to editorial to be double-checked lest new errors were made while correcting mistakes.

13) If everything is okay, repros returned to production.

14) Signatures sent to the editors to be sure no pages fell out. Too late to change anything short of a disastrous oversight.

15) If signatures okay, they're sent back to production...usually initialled by Edna or her associate. This is production's safeguard. If there's a mistake, but it's initialled by someone in editorial, production will disavow all responsibility.

16) Editorial receives advance copies of the bound book, and sends

off author's free copies. Usually a month before on-sale date.

Samples of typical proofreading marks:

_e   delete: remove ~~remove~~ it

C   close up: shou⌣ld be a⌣ll one word

ing / et ∧   caret: insert miss∧word, letter, or pun∧ation here

requires space∧between words or letters

tr.   transpose the order of letters or words
as th∪is or upon a time once,

/   slash is used to separate two or more
proofreading corrections on the same
line, or to indicate upper-lower case (see below)

Proofreading example:

o/t   She was to∧close to it to no∧ice

¶   symbol to begin new paragraph

cap.   should be a capital letter, or the entire
word should be in capitals(CAPITALS);or
three lines under letter(w)

l.c.   lowercase: letter or /ord should not have
a capital; or slash through letter

ital.   italic: should be set in *italics*

=   hyphen required

$\frac{1}{m}$ em: a one-em dash; longer than hyphen

⌃   comma

⌄   apostrophe

⌄⌄ ⌄ ⌄   quotation marks (double and single)

⊙   period

⌃⌄   semicolon

⌄⋅   colon

124

CHAPTER SEVEN
Details, Details . . .

Understanding your contract—or even a portion of it—takes some explanation. Of course, if you have a good agent, you won't have to know any of this. But what if she or he isn't a good agent? Or you're between agents? Or you can't find an agent who'll accept you? Better you should know.

I'm not going to cover every single detail that most paperback contracts contain; that would be a book unto itself. Moreover, contracts vary from publisher to publisher; it all depends on whose lawyer is trying to confuse you more. So I'll list those clauses you really should understand before you sign a contract. The ones that genuinely affect you . . . .

And we can talk about negotiating clauses as long as you want, but the bottom line is: Sometimes you win, sometimes you don't. The way the mop flops is pretty much determined by how much authority or latitude the editor has to make such decisions, and just how badly he or she wants your romance novel. With a first-time novelist, the reality is that there's little room for negotiation—especially with category books.

By the way, if a contract is altered in any way, both your publisher (or Edna) and you must initial where the changes occur. Otherwise there's no proof that all parties agreed to this change.

Grant of rights or territory

This says where the publisher may distribute your novel in the English language. Generally, paperback companies want the right to distribute your romance in any English-speaking country in the world. This is usually listed as the "United States, Canada, the Philippines, and the open market outside the British Commonwealth." (The British Commonwealth is often considered part of the foreign market.)

Nowadays, most romance publishers also insist on being given control of foreign-language markets, for which they will take a chunk of money (usually anywhere from 25-50%). (If you've been published before, successfully, and you're agented, your agent may want to fight to restrict the publisher to distribution of your book throughout the USA only.) In the case of Harlequin/Silhouette, part of the deal in selling them your book is you *must* let them have foreign rights. That's because Harlequin already has a worldwide network in place for reprinting its romances in foreign languages.

Most of the major paperback houses have their own distribution network.

125

But smaller publishers, not affiliated as an imprint of a larger one, are likely to use an independent distributor that handles several lines of books from various publishers. If this is the case where you've submitted your novel, does the publisher retain direct sales? This is important to know.

Direct sales are those made to outlets other than major retailers: a small, neighborhood bookstore; stores that don't usually sell books (if the heroine is a hair stylist, why not try to place copies in beauty salons?); or sites that you might approach directly because you're a local resident; or any other outlet not serviced by the distributor.

Most independent distributors try to withhold direct sales in order to protect their own profit flanks. And once a publisher has signed an agreement with an independent distributor, it's written in stone for the term of the agreement. There's nothing the publisher can do about it until the contract is about to expire . . . and even then, the publisher doesn't have much negotiating latitude.

However, direct sales can accumulate and often represent a hefty extra profit for both the publisher and the author. If your prospective publisher doesn't control direct sales, you may want to reconsider selling to that firm. Let's say your local high school or college, from which you graduated, has a bookstore but it doesn't stock romances. The distributor's salesforce isn't going to drop by to pitch your book; but you could because you're an alumnus, and they just might stock your novel to promote the success of one of their own. Without direct sales being controlled by the publisher, your hands are tied and you can't approach the bookstore manager.

A word of caution here. Never attempt to have your book stocked anywhere without first getting the publisher's permission. There may be plans afoot whereby your "interference" could shoot the plan in the foot.

Delivery of manuscript

This is usually quite easy to understand; if the contract says "typescript," that's the same as manuscript—more frequently used in England than here. In the event that you're selling the manuscript as a partial, or revisions are still due, this clause outlines when the publisher expects you to provide what's required. Don't lock yourself in with unrealistic deadlines—be sure you can reasonably meet them. Allow for the kids getting sick, or other possibilities— in short, if restricted only to your spare time, how long will it take you to do what's requested?

If your editor asks why you can't get the material to her sooner, reply: "I probably can. But I don't want to make a promise I may not be able to keep. Or leave you in the lurch. So this is just my 'at the latest' even though I may get the material to you much sooner." Simple.

Revisions

If the contract you receive doesn't cover this subject, you might want to request that it be added. In essence, you are agreeing to any ordinary editorial changes in your manuscript, consistent with reasonable publishing standards and practices. This will usually include your consent to a change of title too.

If you're dealing with an established, reputable company, you really have nothing to fear. However, should you find yourself dealing with an "unknown quantity" (or just want to be absolutely certain), you may want to ask for a more specific Revisions Clause. Try to get a clause that limits and specifies the extent of any revisions of your work. Something like: Author agrees to grant Publisher the right to correct all typographical and grammatical errors within the Work; any other revision or changes in the original Work's text shall be subject to Author's written approval.

Now, you might not win that point. And again, reputable, established publishers _never_ substantially change a writer's book without discussing it with the author first. However, I'm concerned with some of the fly-by-nights whose integrity hasn't been proven. And sadly, in the romance field, there are some editors who take liberties . . . mostly just to save time, but still . . . .

I once had a novel accepted for publication (not a romance) and it was published while I was out of the country. When I saw the printed book, I nearly broke down and wept. Some editor had added five and a half pages of totally needless, prurient sex and completely changed the ending of my novel from upbeat to a downer. It was too late. There was nothing I could do. Why didn't I sue? I tried. I called the best publishing lawyer in the USA, and while he was sympathetic, he made it very clear that it would be impossible to _prove_ that my work had been altered. A carbon copy isn't "proof"; I could have typed a different one at another time.

This is another good reason to join your local Romance Writers of America. Talk to members who have sold their work to a particular publisher to learn if they're satisfied with how that publisher and its editorial staff operate.

So try to figure out a polite, discreet way to inquire just who you're dealing with if you're not already familiar with the line. It won't be easy, and you certainly don't want to risk besmirching a perfectly innocent company's reputation . . . but do your best. One way to go, maybe, is to smile sweetly at your editor and explain that while you have implicit faith in him or her . . . editors change jobs so frequently that you want the clause for protection in case you have to deal with someone else later on. Works for me.

Author's alterations

Pretty clear, and for the most part, already covered in this book. However, as already explained, anything you change (other than a typographical error) after the book's been typeset is an AA. You will be charged for each and every such change (usually beyond a certain percentage, which will calculate out to a certain number of total pages based on the number of pages in the final book). If the contract doesn't stipulate what the fee-per-change is, or list the percentage, ask that the sum and/or percentage be included in the contract. Usually, it's not a big deal. Maybe it's only $4.00 per change. But fees can and do go up, so stipulating the sum beforehand might save you a few bucks. If you're squeaking by on a shoestring, it can make the difference in your world of having ground round for dinner or a New York strip steak.

Guaranty and royalties

This is probably one of the most misunderstood clauses. "Guaranty" can also be termed "Advance Against Royalties," and is more commonly used than "Guaranty."

An Advance Against Royalties is tantamount to a loan from the publisher to you. In category fiction, there is generally a ceiling on what an editor can offer you (especially if you're a first-time novelist). The advance can range anywhere from a scant $500.00 (yes, five hundred, especially with very small publishers of romances) to $1,500.00 or as high as $5,000.00. If you have a proven track record, this might (and only "might") go up to $10K. (A usage aside here. The letter K is used with sums of money to indicate thousand; in any other usage, such as tons, the letter M is used. Just thought you'd like to know.)

> **The advance is based on how well the editor and publisher think your novel will sell. It is not repayable. Even if only one copy of your book sold—to your mother, for instance—you still do not have to repay that money. (Should a contract state that you do have to repay it, watch out!)**

The advance is based on how well the editor and publisher think your novel will sell. It is not repayable. Even if only one copy of your book sold—to your mother, for instance—you still do not have to repay that money. (Should a contract state that you do have to repay it, watch out!) And you should keep in mind that traditionally, publishers pay the first half of the advance upon signature of the contract (a misnomer because accounting doesn't work that quickly—it could take weeks, even months for that check to be cut). Depending upon the publisher, the second half of the advance could be paid either upon acceptance of the complete manuscript, or upon publication date. Since the publication date can be months and months away, strive for getting the second half upon acceptance of the manuscript.

The advance is a "loan," however, to the extent that it is later deducted from how much your romance earns in royalties or other sources of profit generated by its publication. Candidly, I'm opposed to contracts that include "other sources." It's not fair. Deducting from the royalties only is fair. Let's say (we can dream, after all) that the novel is sold for a TV-adaptation. That has nothing to do with what was advanced to you based on the predicted sales of the novel itself. But again, negotiating this is not only tricky but your chances of winning are slim and none. If that's policy and standard contractual terms for that publisher's romance imprint . . . there's very little you can do about it.

Anyway, whenever you read that a Big Name author is getting hundreds of thousands of dollars (or even millions) as an advance, there are two things you ought to keep in mind: (1) It means that author will not see another dime until the book has earned that much money; and (2) it means that author will have to pay taxes on a big chunk of money instead of spreading out the income over the years. Some famous writers do, by the way, have clauses added that indicate an annual payment schedule to lower the taxes. While the contract may say, for instance, that the advance is $500,000.00, the payment clause will indicate how that's to be paid out, in what increments, and when. Not too dissimilar from the way the lottery operates.

For my own part, I think this is foolhardy. Why should I let the publisher make money on my money? Instead of the advance earning interest in my bank account, it's earning interest in the publisher's bank account. And I'm confident that were I to become rich and famous, I could come up with a few tax shelters of my own . . . thank you very much. Of course, every situation is different and only one's accountant can advise the best way to go. A non-related example is an acquaintance of mine who has made so much money in theater that her accountant occasionally tells her to refuse work—the taxes are so high it isn't worthwhile for her to accept additional work for a while. We should all be so lucky!

All right, the term is Advance Against Royalties. (In show business, these are called residuals.) <u>What are royalties? They are a percentage of the retail price of your book—or of the net monies received by the publisher.</u> Most publishers have a break in the royalty rate after a certain number of copies of the book have been sold. Do not confuse how many books are printed, or distributed, with actual sales figures.

You'll hear agents and editors talk about "she got four and six, breaking at 150 thou." Translation: The author receives four percent of the retail price of the book, for the first 150,000 copies sold; she will receive six percent of the retail price for all copies sold beyond 150,000. Take heed: We are talking about the number of copies sold. It's a distinction too many writers fail to grasp. A publisher may print 30,000 copies of your novel, but that does *not* mean that all 30,000 will be sold.

Some paperback companies offer six and eight percent, breaking at either 100,000 or 150,000 copies sold. Some very lucky authors (and only if the editor is burning to buy that manuscript) might even get eight and ten percent. Other companies might offer a sliding scale of four, six, eight, and ten, breaking at every x-number of copies sold.

This is among the areas where contracts can usually be negotiated. The operative term here is "usually." Obviously, you have to have a good track record before any editor will discuss such matters; or a good agent. For the sake of conversation, let's pretend you've already had three romances published. Each of them sold well enough to go back to press for a second or even a third printing (that rarely happens in romances by unknown authors, but it can). Let's further imagine that you're dissatisfied with the treatment you've received from your former editor and publisher, and you want to go elsewhere with your newest romance.

Your agent has sent the new one to Publisher Z, who can only offer you

$10,000.00 as an advance. Okay, it's just a loan anyhow. But, as a concession for letting your new book go "so cheaply," your agent pushes for a higher royalty rate, breaking at smaller increments. That doesn't mean the publisher will concede to everything your agent asks for, but because you have an established and popular following, there is room for negotiation.

Let's say that your earlier contracts specified four and six percent, breaking at 150,000 copies sold. Publisher Z is willing to offer you (via your agent's hard work) six and eight percent, breaking at 100,000 copies sold. Until you know what the retail price will be, you know it's a better deal, but you can't estimate your potential earnings. Some contracts will specify what the retail price will be, some don't; if not, it's quite all right to ask. Most romances are generally within a fixed range. So just to keep the arithmetic simple, let's say you're told the retail price will be $4.00.

So you go to your files and pull out the last royalty report (check the column for cumulative sales) for each of your earlier novels. Your first one didn't do all that well primarily because you were an unknown author. Maybe it sold about 25,000 copies. Your next romance novel did better—closer to 40,000 copies. And your third one was the novel to tip you over into a "valuable author" status; it sold close to 75,000 copies. So to be conservative, you'll do your computations on the basis of at least 75,000 copies likely to be sold for your newest novel. What does this mean to you in dollars and cents?

6% of $4.00 = 24 cents per copy for the first 100,000 sold
8% of $4.00 = 32 cents per copy for all copies sold beyond 100,000

Okay, you're figuring you can safely expect to sell at least 75,000 copies of your newest romance. At six percent, that's $18,000.00 your book will have earned in royalties. Sounds pretty good, doesn't it? Ah, but did you remember that you received an advance of $10K? You'll have to subtract (actually, the royalty department will do it) the advance from the book's earnings.

If your book surpasses the 100M break, then you'll earn just that much more. But, much as I hate to rain on anyone's parade (she said with a heavy sigh), few first novels ever earn more than the advance paid. Romances frequently fare better because they're so very popular. All I'm suggesting is that you act with prudence. If you run out and open up a bunch of charge accounts, or overextend yourself on what "can" happen, you could be in a peck of trouble. Wait till you've got your royalty check and it's cleared your bank before you spend a dime of it—*please!*

You should also be aware that most paperback publishers always withhold a certain amount from your royalty check against "returns." As discussed before, paperback books are sold on consignment; retailers return for credit any unsold books (or their covers). This is a very touchy area with retailers, distributors, and publishers alike. The book is printed and bound, shipped to the distributor (along with the other books for that month), and the distributor sees to it that the number of copies ordered by each retailer is delivered. However, that retailer is also receiving that month's shipments from numerous other paperback houses, magazine publishers, and so on. It is not rare for a carton of books to be "temporarily" placed out of the way . . . and then forgotten, never even opened to be put on the retailer's shelves. A few months down the road, and somebody suddenly discovers this unopened carton. It's too late to put the book on sale. Other books have been delivered and there's simply no room to squeeze in even one more book. Ship's sailed, folks.

Even if this doesn't happen (and it is quite seldom), the publisher has no way of predicting just how well your book is selling. Until all retailers have sent back their "returns," the basis of computing what is due you in royalties is little more than an educated guess.

It's traditional in paperback publishing to withhold as much as twenty percent or more (though fifteen percent would be fairer) from your royalty check against unforeseeable returns. I would like to see the percentage specified as part of the contract, but few publishers will agree to do that.

If the publisher has more than one division, your contract may include what the royalty rate will be should your manuscript be published under a different imprint; this isn't very likely, but it looks impressive, as if you might earn royalties from a variety of sources for the same book.

And there's usually a different royalty rate for any copies of your book that are sold as premiums. This could be a bulk sale of the book as, say, a giveaway for a new perfume; or a bulk sale to your local bank as a public relations gesture; and so forth.

You will not receive any royalties for books that are given away for purposes of review, or for promotional purposes.

Royalty statements and payments

This often confuses beginning writers. So pay attention. Most paperback contracts state that the publisher will provide the author with a royalty statement on a semi-annual basis. Let's say the time-frame will provide royalty reports each April 1st and October 1st. Your novel must have been on sale for six months as of the previous royalty statement date. On sale. Not following its publication date.

Okay, it's not all that hard to grasp. If your novel was published in February, for example. It will not have been on sale for six months in April, but for two months. Consequently, you won't see a royalty report until the next statement date in October. And the October report will include sales made as of publication date; or put more simply, all copies sold between February through the end of September . . . less the sum of money held in reserve against returns and less the advance. And just because the report is due to be issued on October 1st, don't forget it might fall on a weekend or national holiday. The report will go out as close to the first as possible; not necessarily precisely on that date.

Some publishers cover their bases by stating precisely what period will be included in the report. For instance, while the royalty statement will be issued on October 1st, it will only cover sales made during March 1st and August 1st. Don't worry about it. They'll make it up to you with the following report. It's an accounting thing . . . .

If you have an agent, these statements and checks will go directly to the agent who will then deduct his or her commission and issue you a check from the agency.

Subsidiary rights

In show business this is called ancillary rights. Same color, different fabric. What it does is set forth the split between you and the publisher of all profits made from any source *other* then the retail sale of your romance novel: book club, movies, magazine serialization, merchandising, and so forth. As popular as romances are, I fail to understand why it is publishers (or some clever independent soul) aren't offering tee-shirts with pictures of the better-selling authors or covers of their books. That would also come under subsidiary rights as part of merchandising. This "oversight" is probably due to nothing more than the sheer volume of paperback romances published annually. Just glancing at the wall of a retailer's romance section is enough to intimidate anyone . . . .

Today, of course, there's a big push to get into electronic publishing—i.e., transferring books onto floppy disks and selling them to be read on the computer's display. My resistance to this practice is understandably huge. Outrage! It's the end of civilization! I, for one, am a book-lover. I want to hold it my hands, turn pages, smell the ink, turn it face down if I'm interrupted; in short, a book, in my book, should be tangible. (However, fair is fair. If books were to be kept solely in their tangible form, then we wouldn't have movie adaptations.)

Then too, there are all the computer-related illnesses to consider (cataracts, abnormal births, and so on). We live in an extremely litigious society . . . wouldn't this open the door for readers to sue publishers due to supplying books on disk?

Still, don't be surprised if electronic publishing is included on the list of subsidiary rights. This is a highly controversial issue between agents, the Authors Guild, writers vs. the publishing/electronic industry.

But back to subsidiary rights practicalities. Most paperback publishers like to get a fifty-fifty split on all such earnings. The Authors Guild (an organization devoted to protecting authors' legal rights) has been fighting it for decades, and agents snicker derisively at such lofty but futile hopes. The Guild's stance is that publishers should only receive profits from the publication of the book itself—not from book-related income. Those extra add-on monies, it states, should be the property of the author with no split to the publisher. Publishers argue that if it hadn't been for the publication of the book, there wouldn't have been any add-on sales. Both sides have a point. However, since this is your very first sale, don't be stubborn.

Again, with so many romances rubbing elbows in the racks, the prospects for you to make any big monies as a result of a subsidiary rights sale are pretty slim. That's not to say it can't happen, it's simply highly unlikely. After decades of writing romances, all of them huge successes, as far as I know only one flick has been made of Barbara Cartland's prolific output—and at that, it was made for TV, not as a feature film. Since she still reigns as the Queen of Romances, figure the odds for your own first, second (etc.) novel. Not very good. To date, only Danielle Steel has broken the romance barrier, and as noted before, she doesn't consider her books to be "just" romances. Okay. Her choice. Judith Krantz and Jackie Susanne never viewed their work as romances either—fair is fair.

And in truth, their plots were more intricate than the generic category of "romance" has usually provided.

So what's a fair subsidiary rights split? <u>Well, as I've told writers for decades, it's better to have fifty percent of something than one hundred percent of zero.</u> This is particularly true if you're unagented. If your publisher knows it will see half of the monies from such sales, it's an incentive to try to peddle subsidiary rights. If the publisher gets no percentage, or only a modest one, it becomes a matter of yawning indifference. So if you don't have an agent who's willing to strive for additional sales, this means your subsidiary rights sales are likely to be nowhere. Bear in mind that many agents only push for the original sale, but often don't concern themselves with lesser income-producing subsidiary rights sales. You could reasonably observe that this is not to the agent's benefit; but the fact is that more time is required for these lesser sales than to sell a new manuscript. The majority of agents have been at it for many, many years and have learned where to spend their time and efforts. And with romances, going for a subsidiary rights sale isn't worth it. Sad, but true.

Negotiating the subsidiary rights split isn't a cut-and-dry situation. Since it's extremely unlikely that a romance will be serialized in a newspaper, publishers are willing to give the author a larger cut on that. It's possible, though, that a magazine might be interested in excerpting a chapter or two, so perhaps you can drive home a 60-40 split in your favor. Condensations are another possibility, especially if a publisher wants to, say, condense three of your novels and publish them in one volume. Sort of, "The Best of . . . ." The publisher may hold out for a better split in its favor.

But you or your agent will sit down (or telephone) with Edna to discuss who gets what percentage on what kind of sale. Edna will then have to (in all likelihood) get an okay from her boss to draw up your contract with these splits. Dickering over these percentages when you're a first-time writer shouldn't take very long; at this point, it's far more important that you sell your novel than worry about subsidiary rights splits. But later, when you're becoming truly successful, it can be an arduous haggling. Let common sense be your guide.

Copyright

This clause is almost always clear-cut and easy to understand. Nice-guy publishers will file for copyright at its own expense (a modest sum); cheap publishers often expect the author to pay for it—but they're the exception and not the rule.

Under current copyright laws, a work is automatically copyrighted at the time of its creation. In order to file a formal copyright, forms must be obtained from the Copyright Office of the Library of Congress. They are completed and, along with a check for the fee and two bound copies of the published book, are returned to the Copyright Office. Some weeks or months later, the author is sent the official copyright number for that work.

If you claim your manuscript has been copyrighted already, you're telegraphing (1) that you're ignorant about copyright law, and (2) that you don't trust editors, fearing they'll steal your work. So claiming that you've copyrighted your manuscript is both a waste of money and a slap to the editor's face.

Under the Copyright Act of 1909, you couldn't get a formal copyright until the work had been published. The revised act, in 1978, permits a statutory copyright (prior to publication) only under certain specific conditions.

Another problem with copyrighting a book prior to its publication is that you limit its sales potential. Let's say you've written a truly remarkable romance and it really is good enough to be a hardcover first. Once you've copyrighted it, hardcover editors may assume that it's already been published and reject it. That leaves you only with paperback possibilities. Paperback editors, seeing that you've copyrighted the work, may assume you self-published it—what is called "vanity publishing." With both editors, hardcover and paperback, it may also mean your book could be considered "out of date." If it bears a 1996 copyright date and they can't publish it until 1998—remember how far in advance publishers work?—then they won't be interested.

If, out of ignorance, it's too late and you really have copyrighted your book...explain why to the editor. You would be wise to state how many copies of the book have been printed and distributed, and where. An example might be that you wrote a romance, had about 50 copies duplicated and spiral bound. These were then given to family and friends as gifts. The book was never on sale anywhere. An editor will want that information before glancing at the first chapter.

Or, you had 500 copies duplicated and bound, and managed to get several bookstores in your community to stock it. Local retailers sold, perhaps, 300 copies. Explain to the editor that it was sold only on the city-wide level; if statewide, say so.

But to copyright a manuscript is genuinely foolhardy. Too many complications arise. However, now that you know this, don't lie to an editor and pretend your novel was never copyrighted. This could really place you on an editor's black list. You can't copyright what's already copyrighted. Not knowing that you've already filed, Edna will apply for a copyright and subsequently be told that the novel's already protected. Now she thinks you're devious, if not an out and out liar.

It's rare that a publisher will want to copyright a work in its own name rather than the author's. Generally, this practice is restricted to "works for hire." A work for hire is material that was written for an employer while on the job. Or a work that was commissioned by someone, with topic provided (as opposed to an original idea on the part of the author). This might include, for instance, a ghostwriting job or being retained to perform a major rewrite.

By the way, the old copyright law in the USA was a real nuisance. It was only good for 28 years and had to be renewed for another 28. If you forgot to renew it, the book went into public domain (i.e., anyone could publish it and not owe you a dime). And after the full term of 56 years, it went into public domain anyway. Under the current copyright law, it conforms to what

England has had for generations. It's valid for the rest of your life plus fifty years. This allows you, then, to leave your copyright to your heirs so they can continue to see royalties—if any royalties are still due.

If you want more information about copyright laws, the address for the Library of Congress is provided toward the end of this book.

Termination

More frequently referred to as "Reversion of Rights." If the contract sent to you doesn't have such a clause, ask that it be included as a rider to the contract. Few editors will withhold this clause from you, if any. But it's a vitally important part of your contract.

Your romance novel is published in May—right? It sells rather well and then sales taper off and cease altogether. It will definitely be at the retail level for a month; longer than that is anyone's guess. If you hang around any store that sells paperbacks, you'll notice that only the Big Name authors, or topical paperbacks, remain on sale beyond a month or so. (The reason was explained earlier.) On occasion, small stores that don't bother to return books might keep your romance a bit longer; or sell them to a second-hand bookstore. Let's say the retailer is primarily a gift shop and not a bookstore. The shop keeps a few copies of certain titles just as a service to its customers. Returning the unsold copies at the end of a month is more bother than it's worth; the shop will probably just leave them out till they ultimately sell, or get rid of them in some simpler way than return-for-credit.

Up until the advent of malls, there were fewer than 2,000 "official" bookstores in the USA. The quotes are because I'm not counting supermarkets or drugstores that happen to sell books too; I'm talking about stores whose primary business is to sell books and book-related materials. The number of official bookstores probably hasn't changed dramatically since, with the chain bookstores, the mom-pop bookstores are not doing very well and many have folded.

Nonetheless, at least 40,000 new books are published every year in this country. Count 'em! Forty thousand. Now multiply that by how many copies of each title are published—called a "print run."

A print run of less than 25,000 copies of a single title means (in paperback terms) that the book probably shouldn't have been published in the first place. (Hardcover companies, though, can often break even with a sale of about 7,500 copies of a 200-page novel; after that, it's all profit.) But we're talking paperbacks here and publishers have to be confident they can sell in the multiple-thousands of copies to break even.

Paperback lead titles (see **Glossary**) can have print runs of 100,000 copies, or even a million copies. If you multiply the minimum paperback print run of, say, 30,000 times at least 40,000 new books . . . you begin to see that the availability of retail space is a very serious problem to paperback companies. Retailers want to stock books that will move off their shelves or racks in a hurry; they must make room for the next month's shipment of books.

Remember, most hardcover houses go by seasons and there is no set number of books they must publish at any given time. Paperback houses must publish x-number of titles every single month, month in and month out. It's a very different kind of business! What didn't sell at the retail level last month will be shipped back to the publisher even as the company is sending out the current month's list of books.

The new books have to be put somewhere if the retailer is going to make any money. As a publisher, what would you choose to do: Push the new books that stand a chance to sell quickly (fresh blood); or try to find new outlets for a book that has already had its crack at the market and didn't do too well? Obviously, as a good businessperson, you'd push the new books. It has nothing to do with the quality of the writing, but with the ability of the publisher to saturate the marketplace. Retail shelf space is at a premium and the competition makes encountering a killer shark look as dangerous as petting a kitten.

All right, let's pick it up at the beginning. Your book has been published and was on sale for a month. Weeks go by, then months, then years—your novel is totally forgotten by the publishing company. The corporate attitude (though not Edna's) toward you is pretty much the same as Casanova's feelings toward last week's fling. "It's over. Don't embarrass us both with pleading."

If you do not have a Reversion of Rights clause, you are really unable to do anything more about your novel. It slips with an inaudible whimper into limbo. If you have a Reversion of Rights clause, however, it's like getting a divorce. You may not still be a virgin, but at least you're free to wed again.

There are two other terms to remember with regard to this clause: "off sale" and "out of print." Off sale means that the book is no longer on any retailer's shelf. However, there may be thousands of copies in the publisher's warehouse. Out of print, though, means that there are no more copies available anywhere—not even in the warehouse. Watch for these terms carefully in the Reversion of Rights clause. They are very distinct from one another.

Knowing that it's highly impractical to redistribute a book after it's already been distributed, opt for a clause that permits you to request a reversion of rights when the book is off sale. You must be realistic, though, and allow sufficient time for all returns to come in so the publisher can accurately determine just how many copies were sold—not simply distributed. Suggest that the reversion be granted within six months of your written request. You may not get your way, but at least you've tried.

If the clause is phrased with an out of print status, it should also stipulate under what terms and conditions you're entitled to a reversion of rights. Usually, it's stated that you must submit a written "demand" (legalese for formal request) for all rights to your novel to be reverted to you within x-number of months (usually anywhere from thirty days to six months). Or, that the publisher must republish your novel, generally within six months to a year as of your written request, in order to conform with the contractual agreement.

Probably, the publisher will revert the rights to you—unless, in the interim, you've had yet another novel published that has done exceedingly well. If that's the case, the publisher may agree to republish your book to capitalize on the success of your current book.

With that reversion (and be sure you get it in writing, not just a verbal "Oh, sure"), you are then free to sell your book to some other publisher. However, let's be practical about this. Almost no paperback publisher is going to want your novel. It's already been in paperback before, and those readers who wanted it have already bought it. No hardcover house will be interested because it's already been in paperback (maximum exposure has taken place and a sale of paperback rights has already occurred, which lowers profits).

Another thing you ought to keep in mind when requesting a reversion of rights is the matter of subsidiary rights. Check your contract or ask Edna to explain your status with regard to foreign rights. Let's say your novel was sold to an English publisher, and it was sold to Germany and Denmark under foreign rights (published in British usage, and German and Danish translations, respectively). Just because you get the American rights back doesn't mean you're automatically getting the English, German, and Danish rights back.

If your novel continues to sell well in these other editions, and once you have your formal reversion of rights from the American publisher, you must be sure of your ground with regard to these other editions still in print. If your contract allows it, notify these other publishers that all future royalty reports be sent to you directly; that the American publisher is no longer involved. If your contract doesn't permit you to contact these foreign publishers for direct royalty payment, then request that the foreign publishers send you a duplicate of their royalty statements.

It's not really that the American publisher will knowingly keep these profits (generally quite small). It's more that accounting will overlook such tiny sums and forget to send a check along to you. Well, what's a "tiny sum" to one person is bread on the table to another.

But to reiterate, if you get the rights to your book back, you can wait a few years and then try to sell it again to a much smaller company, or a startup company. You'll get peanuts, but at least your book is back in print.

First refusal or option

This clause is standard publishing procedure. If you ask that it be struck from your contract, a goodly number of publishers will agree to do so. If they won't, then you can ask for more specific terminology in the clause.

The thinking behind the First Refusal or Option clause is that the publisher takes a chance when buying your book, and spends a considerable amount of money to get it out to retailers. Maybe your first book does just so-so. In order to recoup on the investment, the publisher would like to have the right to consider your next book for publication before anyone else sees it. That sounds straightforward and reasonable.

However, don't forget just how busy Edna Editor is. So you send her your next manuscript, and it takes her six months to get around to reading it. Maybe she buys it, and maybe she hates it. You've just lost six months by fulfilling your option clause terms . . . six months in which the manuscript might have already sold to someone else, or have been to three other publishers. Granted, that's a reach. As stated before, if your romance is written to specific guidelines, it's not likely it'll be of interest to anyone else. But still . . . . This clause can cost you a lot of time and possible income.

Or, let's say that you adored working with Edna, but she has since moved on to another company. You hate working with her replacement, but you're stuck with this new editor because of the option clause. Or (and this frequently happens) you decide to write a new book that isn't a romance. Instead, it's a how-to book on making your own stained-glass windows. It's obviously not for Raging Romances or anyone else's romance line. But you have to submit it anyhow because of the option clause. Again, lost time and possible income.

> **Any expense (inclusive of buying Edna Editor a drink, if she permits you to) related to your book is a bona fide deduction —if you sell your novel.**

So how do you avoid these pitfalls? If you can't get the clause struck from the contract, ask that it be reworded: (1) That the option apply only to your *next* manuscript in the *same* category. Your book on stained glass wouldn't have to be submitted to Raging Romances at all; (2) That the company must make its decision about your new book within thirty (or sixty) days of its receipt. While that makes it tough on Edna, still it's only fair that your work not be tied up for months and months; (3) Be sure it states that the option applies to only your next work, not *all* future works.

I've known several writers who have had their new manuscripts tied up with their publishers for as much as a year because the option clause was too vague.

And push come to shove, there's an old trick to worm your way out of an option clause even though you've agreed to it in the contract. Spend a few days writing thirty to fifty pages of an abominable, unpublishable manuscript, and send it in. The moment it's rejected, you're quit of any further responsibility. Ancient MacManus proverb: Play fair with me, and I shall play fair with you.

Delay of performance

This clause (it may have a different name from company to company, such as *"force majeure"*) is pretty standard with most publishing firms. If it isn't in your contract, ask that it be incorporated as a rider or addendum (legalese for rider).

What it does is assure you that if your publisher should fail to publish your work within a given period (frequently eighteen months to two years), the publisher forfeits all rights to your manuscript. You are then released from your contract. Most contracts will limit this "failure" to any reason *other* than those beyond the publisher's control: war, Act of God, fire, flood, etc.

The chances of an established publisher failing to publish your work are next to nil. However, if you are selling your novel to a small, new company, it's wise to be sure this clause is included.

Publishing books involves a considerable amount of money invested. You'll want to protect yourself in the event a smaller publisher goes out of business before your romance is published.

Miscellaneous

As long as we're talking about the dull side of being a romance writer, a few words about income taxes. <u>Save all your receipts from stationery stores for paper, typewriter (or printer) ribbons, pencils, or anything else you buy related to writing your romance.</u>

<u>Save all maintenance or repair slips for your typewriter or computer, too. Books that you buy for reference, the cost of film and developing for any snapshots you take with regard to locale for your novel (reference), are also tax deductible. Any expense (inclusive of buying Edna a drink, if she permits you to) related to your book is a bona fide deduction—if you sell your novel.</u>

Because this is your first book, the IRS and state tax laws will not allow you to make any such deductions unless you have sold your work. Once you've made that sale—even if it's on December 31st—you are then a "professional" writer.

Many of the tax laws for writers or other self-employed people are changing all the time. If you invite Edna to your home for lunch, for example. That used to be tax deductible: the cost of food, liquor, and a portion of the use of your dining and living rooms for business entertainment purposes. That's changed. Today's law requires that you take Edna to a restaurant before it can be deducted.

It used to be that a percentage of your rent or mortgage could be deducted, as well as a percentage of your utilities, telephone, and any business-related entertaining. This too has significantly altered and if you don't have an accountant, hie yourself over to the nearest IRS office. They are very helpful. Do your taxes in pencil and then ask an IRS auditor to double-check you. It's a free service, they know what you can and can't deduct, and are happy to advise you. But be sure to seek their advice well before April 15th when the IRS's offices are crowded. They'll be nicer to you and you won't have to stand in line for so long a time. Once armed with their input, then do your taxes in ink and send them in.

As a professional writer, you are self-employed and must file your income tax returns with the correct schedules to make that clear. It doesn't matter that you have a salaried job as well; that income is separate and apart from your self-employed income.

Agent's commissions, postage, paying someone to type your manuscript neatly, the cost of making a duplicate copy for submission, depreciating your new computer or word processor . . . if these expenses pertain to the writing of your romance, which has been contracted for by a publisher, they are legitimate tax deductions as a self-employed individual. At least at the time of this writing . . . .

And don't go to the expense of buying those hefty income tax guidebooks. The government publishes exactly the same thing and it's free at the offices of the IRS.

Accountants who are located in major cities, where there are likely to be many writers, are very familiar with what can be legitimately deducted and what can't. It's not so easy in smaller communities and you may find yourself explaining more to your accountant than your accountant can explain to you. Be patient.

And one more detail. I learned this the hard way and hope to spare you the same woeful fate. Be sure you pay enough taxes to cover your social security! If you use your deductions to get a full refund on what was withheld from your salaried job, the Social Security Administration (SSA) considers that you had no income whatsoever for that year. True.

While the IRS tells you that you only have to hold onto your 1040s and W2s or W3s for five years, that's not accurate. You can throw away your receipts after five years, but save your 1040s and W2s until it's time to file for social security. The Social Security Administration bases your benefits on how much you've paid in over the years. The IRS only cares that you filed your taxes and paid them. The two agencies don't discuss the matter betwixt them.

If you have any reason to dispute what the SSA states as your income over the previous years, and you haven't saved your 1040s and W2s, you will have no way to dispute the figures!

My own sad tale should serve to make your retirement years a bit more comfortable. When I disputed what the Social Security Administration stated as my income for various years, they recommended I write to the IRS to get copies of my tax forms. I did. The IRS sent me a printed form stating that all income tax returns prior to 1984 had been destroyed by authorization of the U.S. Congress; and that all W2 or W3 forms prior to 1978 had been destroyed under the same authorization. That's right. Destroyed. I had no way to prove that the Social Security Administration's figures were incorrect. (I have that notification from the IRS right in my file.)

So to conclude this section, most standard contractual clauses are rather easy to understand. There may be lots of legalese about remaindering your book, no royalties on copies published in Braille, etc., but don't worry about them. The important thing is to get that first contract.

I certainly wouldn't refuse a contract for my first novel simply because I didn't get my way with any of these clauses. They are mentioned here so you'll know what's involved, how they could affect you, and to make you knowledgeable about contractual matters. There's no harm in asking your editor if this or that might be changed (with a lilting tone and a smile in your voice) . . . but be prepared for the answer to be "No." Again, there's very little latitude with romances, and especially for beginning writers.

CHAPTER EIGHT

Fanfare and Hoopla

I know, I know . . . you've read in the paper how much Pocket Books spent on promoting Janet Dailey's last novel, or that another author was on Oprah's show; and you've read about a new romance writer "star" going on national tour, and so forth. Successful romance writers living in palatial homes, driving expensive cars. . . . "If there's so much money to be made out there, why isn't my publisher promoting my book?"

The truth is a matter of sheer economics.

Paperback publishers have what is known as lead titles. ("Lead," as in leading someone by the nose; not "lead" as in what's used to make pencils— English is a silly language.) Every month, there's a meeting of the key personnel to decide which will be the #1, #2, or #3 title for an upcoming list of books. The #4 title is treated like an unwanted stepchild, but Edna Editor must come up with four titles monthly and that's all there is to it.

Who will be present at these meetings will vary from company to company. I've worked with publishers where just about anyone could sit in on these meetings; and at others, where it was so closed-door that the editorial support staff was often the last to learn of the decisions made.

So let's go back to Raging Romances and set up a hypothetical situation. However, Raging Romances now has added an in-house department or two.

Okay. Edna Editor and her editorial assistant will definitely be in attendance; they're the only two who have read the books scheduled for publication. Their boss will be there too; probably a V.P. and an editorial director (if Raging Romances is an imprint of a larger company) are present. The publicity director, and the head of sales, plus whomever is in charge of subsidiary rights will also show up. This meeting takes place well before any salespeople go out into the field to solicit advance orders; and in all probability, even before the cover has been decided on. Why? Because the lead title might get a fancier cover than the other books for that month. Maybe it will have foil, or a raised surface, or a die-stamped cutaway to reveal a different cover underneath. That's expensive and <u>not all books will get the same treatment—only the lead title.</u>

If there's something about the novel or its author that is especially promotable, this too contributes to the decision as to which book becomes the lead title. It might be that the heroine is an Army nurse; that means the book would do well at military bases, adding sales beyond standard retailers. Or

141

that it has an Olympics background and could be released to coincide with the next Olympics whether in this country or abroad. And because more effort will be put forth to push sales of the lead title, it will have a larger print run. How large hasn't been determined yet; that's why there's a meeting, among other reasons.

So these key people get together to decide how much to spend on cover artwork and how large a print run each book should have. It's also to decide which of Edna's four books in that month will get whatever advertising budget Raging Romances is either willing to spend, or can afford.

As you can readily see, these decisions are all rooted in money: How much to spend for what.

Edna really thinks your first novel, *Romance of My Own*, is fabulous. It's fresh, free from clichés, moves smoothly, has a solid plot that hasn't been worked to death, and a very unusual career for the heroine—"unusual" in romances, not in real life. *Romance of My Own* has everything going for it: originality, pace, and it's like a brisk breeze in the smoke-filled arena of hundreds of overworked romances.

Whether Edna has taken a liking to you or not has nothing to do with anything. This is Big Business, not a social get-together. There are a few writers I've met whom I have come to love dearly as real, trusted, and respected friends. However, at a meeting of this kind, such considerations must be put aside. It is the book that counts—not Jim's adorable cleft chin or Marsha's caring support during one of my personal crises. (Sorry, Jim and Marsha, but you know it's true.) It's Edna's career at stake and it's put to the test on a monthly basis. If she plugs a book and that results in its becoming a lead title, then the book fails to sell even half of its print run . . . who do you think will be held responsible? Edna. It is the editor's responsibility to push the book that stands the very best chance of success in the marketplace.

In some ways, it's not fair (she said, wearing her writer's hat). After all, Tom Clancy or Danielle Steel do not need the push for success; their books sell no matter what and regardless of what the reviewers say. Logically speaking, it's the unknown author who should get the company's advertising budget. But it just doesn't work that way. It's just too risky. If an author is an unknown, publishers are loath to promote his or her first novel.

> **You will do yourself and your publisher a favor if you think like a businessperson**

There are exceptions, but very, very few. An example would be if a new writer is a "find," or has written a romance too marvelous to pass over as just another ho-hum paperback. (I would have loved to sit in when the meeting was taking place at Avon to decide how to promote Rosemary Rogers' first historical romance . . . . I'll bet there was a lot of Gelusil and Librium consumed till the campaign was proved a success!)

And too, albeit sadly, all too few first romance novels are worthy of a big expenditure. They're "good," or they're "okay," but not outstanding. It takes time to develop a solid writing muscle.

Advertising rates in two of the most important publications (to people in publishing) have doubled over the past decade. An ad in *The New York Times Book Review Section* costs over $11,000.00 for a one-time, half-page insertion. (This is a 1994 quote.) Think about that. Over eleven thousand dollars for a one-time half-page ad . . . that's probably considerably more than your advance! A publisher would have to be crazy to spend that kind of money to advertise your book! And at that, only for a one-time insertion? Far too expensive for the likes of Raging Romances!

As for *Publishers Weekly*, a one-time half-page ad rate (also 1994) is either $3,425.00 for an "island rate," or $2,140.00 for a horizontal ad. We're talking here about megabucks! Who do you know who routinely reads *Publishers Weekly?* Probably no one, unless you're on good terms with your local librarian.

An ad in *The New York Times Book Review Section* reaches millions of people—from average readers, librarians, retailers, to reviewers—on a nation-wide basis, not just The Big Apple. An ad in *Publishers Weekly* reaches retailers, librarians, and those directly involved with the publishing business. But look at the difference in cost. Who do you want to reach? Librarians (where nominal royalties or profits are involved) or retailers? Retailers or readers? If you had to pay for these ads, where would you put your advertising dollar? Hey, listen, it's one thing to be an author and quite another to be the publisher. Money talks.

Let's say it's not *Romance of My Own* but someone else's first novel, and you own the publishing company—where would you put your advertising budget?

Make note: In the paperback business, profits are measured in loose change, dimes per book—not dollars. The only reason paperback companies can survive is because of volume sales. Project your estimated sales by retail price and see what you've got left for advertising. If I'm spelling it correctly, it's *bupkiss* (Yiddish for animal droppings). The real world is harsh; yet dreams are hard to quench. You will do yourself and your publisher a favor if you think like a businessperson and not like a creative author—that is, once you've made that sale to qualify.

American paperback companies operate on the theory that it's best to overprint a book, allowing for returns, in order to reach the maximum number of retail outlets. The larger the print run, the lower the unit cost. Go for it.

English paperback companies, conversely, are infinitely more conservative. They only print what they are confident they can sell. If the book sells out, they go back to press. This is a more expensive way to go from a production standpoint, but then there are very few returns to contend with. So it's a moot point as to which is the better approach from a profit-and-loss perspective. And it's a gamble any way you look at it.

Now keep in mind that Raging Romances isn't one of the leading publishers of romances; it's now a medium-sized line. Its average print run for romances is around 40,000 copies (not the lead title, obviously). If they sell sixty percent of that, they're content; if they sell seventy percent, they are very happy; if they sell eighty percent, they're incredibly excited; and if they sell ninety percent, there's cause for jubilation. Needless to say, any sales beyond that, requiring a return to press, render editors catatonic from excessive euphoria. So before any decision can be reached on how much to spend on advertising, they must agree on which book is the most likely to succeed. Again, first novels rarely do. The reading public is more likely to spend its money on authors whom it's already read and enjoyed. Publishers know that. If Gertie Glutz is already an established seller for Raging Romances, in all probability her newest book will be targeted for The Big Push—even though yours may be a far better book.

Edna hasn't told any of her May authors where they might stand with regard to advertising or promotion. It would be cruel to get her authors' hopes up if Edna's preferences aren't realized. So she'll wait till there are final decisions before saying anything—if indeed, she tells them anything at all.

Everyone present has a synopsis of each book on the May schedule for ready reference. Sharpened pencils, notepads, or anything else that might be needed is within arm's reach. The jockeying for a book's position is no simple matter. And it isn't just because of the competition from other romance publishers. If you'll recall, I mentioned earlier that every department thinks its role is more important than any other department's. As often as not, there's a vying for control and power within the same company. This does nothing to improve sales; it has to do with egos. It also has to do with justifying the existence of a department in-house (as opposed to farming out the responsibilities), and therefore securing one's own job. There are very, very few job openings in publishing; one almost has to wait for someone to retire or die. Yes, publishing personnel do job-hop and that leaves an opening. But usually it's filled by someone with a proven track record from a different company. The old lament: You can't get hired without experience, but no one will hire you so you can get the experience.

Anyhow, Edna is really championing your romance. "All right," she concedes. "Gertie Glutz gets the Number One spot for the May list. *Romance of My Own* should be Number Two."

"Wait a sec," says the subsidiary rights director. "Is there something you're not telling me? Is her romance outstanding enough that I could lay it on magazines for excerpting or serialization?"

"Definitely," Edna says. "It should do very well with women's magazines . . . not to mention that it has a very strong dramatic rights potential. In the hands of the right director, it could be another 'Sleepless in Seattle.'"

"Really," drawls the publicity director skeptically. "What about the author? Is she presentable?"

Edna smiles tolerantly but pleasantly. "I haven't met her yet, but I've spoken to her on the phone. She's articulate, charming, and definitely not the sort to kick up her heels, giggling in girlish glee."

"Spare me," groans the publicity director, good-naturedly.

There's a round of: "Right," "Yeah," "Boy, you can say that again!"

"I don't know," the editorial director intervenes. "The other two romances for May are from authors we've published previously. Why the push for this one?"

Edna shakes her head. "The other two titles are so-so, nothing more. If

Romance of My Own doesn't outsell them, I'll unplug my computer and go home!"

"Very amusing," the editorial director replies, clearly not amused.

Edna glances at her furtively, trying to assess what mood she's in. She already knows that the editorial director is the type who runs hot and cold; she's either behind you one hundred percent, or she's wondering if it isn't time to consider replacing you. One mistake can tip the balance.

"Can I call her a rising star? Another Virginia Henley?"

"Sure," Edna responds to the publicity director. "Without exaggeration, too!"

"Well, I'm still not convinced," the editorial director states with deadly calm. "What do you think?" she asks the head of sales, who glances again at the synopsis of the book.

He strokes his chin thoughtfully. "There are a lot of women in the computer technology field—it might be worth a shot."

Silently, Edna senses the sales director is straddling the fence, not wanting to take a firm stand. But she's still in there pitching for your book to take the #2 position in May. "Well, the heroine isn't 'just' in the computer field. She's a computer genius, able to thwart the work of hackers trying to steal corporate secrets. The novel's both a romance and an insight into the dangers of the Information Highway." Edna's assistant smiles reassuringly but the others say nothing.

The meeting proceeds, rehashing cover decisions, sales potential, and so

> **Your romance goes on sale! You see two copies at the supermarket, but it's not at the drugstore, or the market on the other side of town. A frantic phone call to the editor will get you nowhere. The more hysterical you get, the less inclined she'll be to buy your next manuscript.**

forth. And for a while, it looks pretty certain that your romance will be the #2 for May. Edna is guardedly pleased because she has faith in your book. As the meeting is coming to a close, the editorial director says, "It's too risky."

The head of sales, being a yes-man, says, "You may be right. Why don't we wait to see how this first one does, and then maybe promote her next romance?"

And that's that. You and Edna have lost. *Romance of My Own* will be an also-ran, trailing at the bottom of the list. No advertising budget, no real promotional effort, less push from the salesforce, and subsidiary rights will do what it can—but not assertively. Hard as Edna tried, there's only room for one #1 or #2; there's no #1-A.

Naturally, you don't know that any of this has transpired. You're still regaling everyone at the office, or your neighbors, with what a huge success your novel will be—just you wait and see. (**A word of reality here. Every beginning author harbors the notion that his or her novel will top the bestseller lists. It's just human nature. However, the hard facts do not support this enthusiastic hope.**)

April rolls around and you receive the advance copies of your novel. All right, so the heroine on the cover isn't really a redhead, but sort of a strawberry blonde; why the hero is shown holding the heroine as if about to break her in half, you don't know—it wasn't in the story at all. The front cover blurb reads: "Her only hope of marriage to Bill shattered in the arms of another man." It did? That wasn't in the book either. Besides, that makes Bill sound gay. Oh, well. You've got the published book in your hands and, if you put on your glasses, you can clearly read your name on the cover. (An insider's tip: You can tell if an author is being promoted if her name appears at the top, before the title, and especially if the writer's name is the same size or even larger than the title.)

Or, maybe those things were in your novel; it's been so long since you finished writing it, maybe you've forgotten. The main thing is that it was published. You can hardly wait for *Romantic Times* to call you for an interview, or for the reviews that will appear in national magazines. And there's still a whole month to go before your romance is even on sale!

Then it's May. Yup. You saw two copies of *Romance of My Own* on sale at the supermarket. But it's not at the drugstore, or at the market on the other side of town. What's going on? You're a famous author—aren't you? Answer: No. And you mustn't personalize. A frantic phone call to Edna will get you nowhere; it's totally out of her hands. And the more hysterical you get, the less inclined she'll be to buy your next manuscript.

Why isn't your book on sale everywhere? Any number of reasons might be valid. Maybe that drugstore is notoriously slow to pay its bills; Raging Romances no longer bothers with them at all. They're more trouble than they're worth. Maybe the supermarket on this side of town buys from a different jobber from the one on the other side of town. Maybe the book buyer only had so much space in his racks, so took only two titles from the May list. Maybe the store is floorplanned, and the manager has no say in what titles are stocked. Maybe a lot of things. It is not the "fault" of your publisher; the company needs to make as many sales as possible to stay in business.

You are bitterly disappointed and a whole lot dejected. All your work, your hopes . . . shot down. Your neighbors look at you pityingly; your husband tries to buoy up your spirits, but to no avail. Friends in Los Angeles or Tulsa write to ask where they can find your romance; it's not on sale in their area. Why did you fill out the publicity questionnaire if no one at Raging Romances was going to use the fact that you belong to several women's clubs or that your spouse is a big shot with the Knights of Columbus?

The answer is that *Romance of My Own* wasn't #1 or #2 on Raging Romances' list for May. To borrow from the Peggy Lee song: "Is that all there is?" Yes and no.

Try to find out as early as you can what Raging Romances plans for your book. This might be decided at an editorial meeting, a promotion meeting, or even at the salesforce meeting. Do this sleuthing shortly after the contract has been executed and returned to you for filing. With a friendly letter or phone call to Edna, ask: "At what stage does Raging Romances determine which will be its lead title for the month? When does that meeting take place?"

Armed with that information, make a note to yourself on the calendar to contact Edna again about a week after the meeting was supposed to take place. (Note: "Supposed." Meetings do get postponed or even cancelled.) Graciously inquire if you were lucky enough to make the #1 or #2 slot with your romance. If yes—smile a lot for the rest of the day and take your husband out to some romantic restaurant for dinner.

If the answer is no, *all is not lost!*

Ask Edna when she expects to receive advance covers, the ones that are issued to the salesforce in their kits. Mention that you're aware this isn't usually done (letting an author see the cover before the book's published), but might she make an exception in your case. And remember to ask only for only a few covers, not a hundred. Having developed a good working rapport with you, Edna decides to cooperate with you. As busy as Edna is, though, she may well forget to send it to you. But you've noted when they're expected, so drop her a postcard as a gentle reminder. You are going to do your own hype for your romance.

To accomplish this, *first* find out from Edna if it will be okay; that you won't be stepping on publicity's toes. She'll probably give you the name of the person in charge of publicity so you can clear your plans with him or her first. Do nothing, absolutely zilch, till you have an okay! Once you have that, then also ask for the person who's in charge of direct sales (the importance of this was discussed previously, but this will broaden your understanding). And get a copy of the retailer discount schedule. Sometimes that's a sliding discount scale, increasing as the number of copies is increased; sometimes it's a flat discount. Check with the person in charge of direct sales if the discount is given to non-bookstore retailers as well as bookstore. That's important.

If Raging Romances has an 800 number, find that out too. Many publishers don't (unless just for sales orders) due to the interruptive nature of phone calls; but they will sometimes accept collect calls. Verify this with Edna.

Okay. You have received an advance cover of your book. (There's a hole punched at the upper right-hand corner of the cover; this will not be present when your book is bound. The reason for it is to avert anyone using that cover illegally, sending it back to the publisher for a credit when it didn't come from the bound book itself.)

With a piece of plain typing paper, type on it who's in charge of direct sales, and what number to telephone or where to write. Also type who's in charge of publicity or promotion, and how to contact that person. Then type in the book's publication date. If there's any specific information you feel would be of interest to retailers, type that on too. Then paste this on the back of the cover and trim to size. The additional information on the back of that cover might look like the sample on page 148.

Include anything else that's **relevant** to a retailer about your book and the book's sales potential—and don't restrict yourself only to bookstores. If the book might be of interest to a non-book retailer, or could be of interest as a special item to a business, indicate this.

Information Sample:

```
TITLE:   Romance of My Own
AUTHOR:  Jane Doe

PUBLICATION DATE:  May 1996
Raging Romances, Inc.
123 Madison Avenue
New York, NY 10003.
Telephone: 212/_____.

DIRECT SALES:  Anthony Anthony  212/555-0743

PUBLICITY:     Mary Mary 212/555-0765

DISCOUNT SCHEDULE:  (Type in what it is.)

AUTHOR INFORMATION:  Jane Doe is a native of (your
community) and has been an employee at _____ since _____.
She is active in the following local organizations:
    To contact Ms. Doe directly, please telephone: _____
```

Now, take a clipboard and curl up with your telephone directory. You are going to make a list of all the independent bookstores you can contact; but not the major chains such as Waldenbooks. The publisher will cover the big retailers. Then list all the other places that sell paperbacks (drugstores, discount stores, etc.) in your area. Ask to speak to the store manager and inquire if their paperbacks are ordered by a store buyer, or if they're floorplanned. Either way, you've introduced yourself and that may lead to additional copies being sold. You're a local, after all.

And also get a list of local newspapers, throwaways, regional magazines; and every other possible source for review of your romance, or free publicity. Your local PBS station, for instance, might interview you on TV; or some of your local radio talk show stations. Reminder: If you're on a talk show, be sure to mention who your publisher is.

Once you have tallied all these places, march directly to your local quick-print store and run off as many copies of the original cover as you will require. Modern technology permits these places to print both sides simultaneously, so it's only one sheet of paper to mail and that saves on postage.

Don't overlook sales potential due to the setting or theme of your book! Is your story about an Italian family that's been in this country for two generations? Contact your local pizza chain and ask the regional manager if s/he will sell your book next to the cash register; or, buy up a quantity (at discount) and use it as a promotional item with every pizza delivery over, say,

148

$20.00. It doesn't cost to ask, and if the pizza chain agrees, that's a lot more copies sold.

Try to think like a resourceful salesperson. Who, besides readers of romances who browse at major bookstores, would be interested in your novel? Is your hero the owner of a new car dealership? That's right. Contact a new car dealership—especially if your novel has a lot of insightful information about this business. If it's just a casual mention, then it's not going to be of interest to a dealership. Yet again, while you're formulating your plot, think of careers for your heroine and hero that are not commonly used in romances. Then be sure it's the type of career where you can get some real information; interview people in that business for the lowdown to make it believable. Many women, for instance, are entering the automobile salesforce . . . why not for your heroine? Then find an auto saleswoman in your area and interview her. Why not? It's just good foresight and planning to increase the sale of your novel.

I used to be extremely shy about tooting my own horn. It was after all, poor manners to brag or pitch my own work (especially for a woman of my generation). It's false modesty. You wrote the novel. You want it to be on sale, available, and read. <u>More importantly, you want the sales to be impressive—not just for the royalties, but to show Raging Romances that you are a profitable author for them. If your book doesn't sell very well, why should they consider the acquisition of your next one?</u> Again, at this point, you're not "the creative artiste" but a businessperson. You have a product to sell; sell it.

Everyone knows that Jackie Susann's *Valley of the Dolls* was a bestseller, and continues to this day to enjoy very good sales. What few people outside the industry realize is how this came to be. For decades, *The New York Times Book Review Section* has carried a list of bestsellers based on sales reported by selected book retailers. This list of retailers was Top Secret and sacrosanct; a lot more so than which households are hooked up to the Nielsen monitor for TV ratings. As it is told in publishing circles, Ms. Susann somehow managed to acquire that list of stores that reported to the *NYT*. Then, as soon as her novel was published, she spent a mini-fortune going to each and every one of those retailers and bought up copies of *Valley of the Dolls*. She even had to rent a garage to store them all, it's said. Result? The stores reported that they couldn't keep her book in stock, that it was selling like the proverbial hotcakes.

Well, of course, the novel climbed to #1 on the bestseller list in very short order. And Americans being what we are, we all rushed out to buy the latest bestseller . . . which in turn really legitimatized the status. By the way, the *NYT* has since changed its *modus operandi*—you couldn't pull that trick today.

Another example was that of an unknown writer from whom I had bought a romance. It was probably one of the worst books I ever saw to press. I put it into schedule with gritted teeth, my eyes clamped shut, and a fresh string of worry beads. I simply had to have one more title for that month's list and it was all that was available to me. I could only hope that the cover art, the sell copy (blurb), and the category would carry the day—and that I didn't receive dozens of poison-pen letters from irate readers.

Shortly after this romance was published, I was informed that it was doing very well—was I planning to buy another romance from this writer? To say I was shocked is to put it mildly. I mean, it was *really* a terrible novel, and I knew we hadn't spent a dime to advertise or promote it. How had this happened? Assuming the tone and attitude of ever-the-gracious-editor, I telephoned my author to share the good news with her. In truth, my motive was sheer curiosity; she was not only a poor writer, but also a pain in the neck.

Naturally, she was pleased with the news. She then proceeded to tell me that she had personally hounded book retailers, local newspapers, and so on, about her book. On her own, this writer had turned a probable dud into a profitable surprise. She'd contacted her old schools and talked them into running reviews of her book for the school papers; since she worked with a major corporation that had its own newsletter, they raved about her romance. By sheer dogged determination, she saw to it that her book was on sale and reviewed—publisher be damned. So it can be done.

And you can accomplish this too. Bear in mind, though, that if Raging Romances is going to put some teeth into the promotion of your novel . . . *stay out of the way!* Do not step on the publicity director's lines. Render unto Caesar what is Caesar's, and unto publicity what is publicity's. If they're going to do a job for you, the last thing in the world they want from you is intervention, or worse, what's known as "double planting" (two people plugging the same thing with the same source).

But if they're not going to give your romance a push, then—after obtaining permission—swing away. Local cablevision needs all the material it can get; offer yourself as a guest for interview. If you're too shy to do it, then ask a friend to make the suggestion. Offer to be a guest speaker at the local high school, or if there's a creative writing class at a nearby college, contact the instructor and volunteer your services. Set up a card table with copies of your book on sale. You can buy them at author's discount (usually 50%) and the rest is pure profit for you.

Or if you cringe at such crass commercialism, contact the local chapter of your favorite charity and suggest they do a promotion featuring your book. All profits to be donated to that charity. With a romance, why not the American Heart Association? It's a logical tie-in.

Whatever you can think of that might help to sell your book is fair play— provided you've been given the Green Light to do so.

If you are among the Chosen, wonderful. Do not expect it to happen with your very first romance; that would be unrealistic. But at least you now know there are many ways you can promote your own romance—push come to shove.

Do not—as happened some years ago—rent an airplane and buzz your publisher's offices out of frustration that nothing's been done to promote your book. I don't really blame that person who did it, mind you. Publishing can be very frustrating. But if that author had read this book first, he could have saved the cost of renting a plane and avoided the subsequent arrest. Publishers often work in mysterious ways, but they generally do have valid reasons for their actions . . . or lack of action.

CHAPTER NINE
The Denouement

As you can see for yourself, you're rapidly reaching the end of this how-to book. Are your palms growing moist? Fear not. You—nor the book—will not self-destruct. If you need to refer back to it frequently, don't be embarrassed about it. There's an awful lot of information on these pages; you can't be expected to memorize it all in one sitting.

So let's recap:

1) You know your characters and the plot are the most important aspects of writing a romance. The story must be vivid, colorful, believable, and flow with ease.

2) You have read dozens and dozens of romances and already know which kind you enjoy the most.

3) You've written to the publisher and have requested its latest set of guidelines (see **Guidelines**). These will change with market needs; in fact, at press time, Kensington Books—Zebra, Pinnacle—changed its guidelines. They will no longer accept any unsolicited manuscripts—only agented ones. To my knowledge, they're the only company to institute this policy. Moreover, they've dumped hard-and-fast "rules" about what they want in their romances. Instead they offer parameters (again, see the **Guidelines**) but aren't sticking to them as unswervable rules. So things do change. Most publishers will tell you just how far they want you to go with love scenes; some will even help you out by stating what's been overdone within their own lists of romances. Do they expect the locales to be exotic or not; is the hero always about ten years older than the heroine; does the heroine have to have a distinctive career or doesn't it matter; and so forth.

4) You then block out the plot lines for at least six romances of the type you enjoy; and then sit down with family or friends to work out your own plot. By now you have learned how to avoid static, dull writing; how important action verbs can be and visual descriptions. Additionally, you now know enough about writing techniques to be able to write any kind of fiction—romance or other. One day, the popularity of romances—as we see it now—will begin to taper off. But from this day forward you will never have to worry about that.

There will be new popular categories of fiction, and you are now prepared to tackle any subject of your choice.

5) And you know how to prepare a manuscript as well as how to write a query letter. <u>You, intrepid reader, are about to embark on a whole new career.</u> You may not earn a great deal of money with your first romance but, as you improve and your name is seen more frequently at paperback stands, you will earn more and more.

6) The decision of whether or not to seek an agent has been made simple for you.

7) You now know the editorial process your romance will go through.

8) You also know what to expect when your romance is published.

You are better prepared at this very moment than any beginning writer I have ever met. There are only two things you have left to fear: A double chin and a thickening waistline. People who sit at desks for a living ultimately develop both. Exercise regularly! I don't. My reward is a double chin and a thickened waistline. I wish I'd read this book when I first started out, and I hope that it will answer all your questions.

In essence, gentle reader, when you are accepted by an editor, you are being paid to do what you enjoy doing. How bad is that?

<u>Good luck to you all, and welcome to the insane world of publishing!</u>

(Hum a few bars from "The Hallelujah Chorus.")

APPENDIX

Glossary of Terms

Publishers' Guidelines

Important Names and Addresses

Glossary of Terms _____

Advance against royalties: Those monies paid to the author of a book prior to the work's publication. It is usually paid half and half; half the total amount upon execution of the contract, and half upon completion of an *acceptable* manuscript; or in some instances, half on publication of the book.

The kicker here is the waiting period. Don't expect the first half a few days after you've signed the contract. It's after the publisher has signed it, or an authorized executive. If it's summer holiday time, or peak flu season, that can take awhile. Then, once it's signed, it has to be vouchered for payment and sent to accounting. Allow two to ten weeks after you've signed the contract before expecting your first check.

Ditto the second half. The editor must read the completed novel, with or without revisions, to be sure it doesn't need any additional work. That's what "acceptable" refers to. If everything's okay, then the second payment will be vouchered; again, allow for the accounting department's delays.

Advance orders: The publisher's salesforce, armed with covers of that month's books and any other materials they are provided, go out to the retailers in their territory to solicit orders for the books in advance of publication.

Some publishers offer retailers a special price if books are ordered prior to publication (or even to the general public). Most paperback houses do not.

Advertising: Advertising is paid for; publicity and public relations are not. Advertising encompasses ads in newspapers, magazines, television, or other media. Do not expect your first romance to receive the benefit of any advertising; it might, however, be included in an overall ad for the entire month's list. This is not, though, very likely.

Author's alterations (AAs): Any changes you may make in your romance after the book has already been set in type that veer from what appeared on the original manuscript.

Back matter: Any printed material that appears at the end of your romance. This could be ads for forthcoming romances; a listing of romances already available; or even quotes from happy readers of romances from your publisher.

Blurbs: (See **jacket copy**.) Technically, blurbs are quotes from well-known people who are willing to "endorse" your romance with a short comment about its merits.

Brownline/blueline: More commonly used with computer typesetting systems. They are, in essence, the same as signatures.

Ca.: Means "circa," approximately. Used in many books on manuscript submission because it's supposed to appear on the title page.

Certificate of registration of trade name: (See **Doing business as**.)

Cliff-hanger: Any device at the end of a chapter to pique the reader's curiosity so that she or he will want to turn the page and continue reading.

Copyeditor: (See **Editors**.)

Copyright: Protection under the law, filed at the Library of Congress, that you own all rights to the romance you've written. However, in signing your contract, what you are doing is temporarily (provided your contract has a Reversion of Rights clause) agreeing to give those rights to your publisher in exchange for a sum of money to be applied against royalties.

Cover artwork: Anything that pertains to how the front and back cover of your romance is presented. The size and style of your romance's title and your name; the positioning of both; how it's to be illustrated; the positioning of the publisher's logo, the book number, its retail price and where the front cover blurb goes, plus any information that goes on the spine.

Wraparound cover: Where the illustration is carried over so it's continuous from back cover to spine to front cover.

Foil cover: A process whereby the title or other aspects of the cover are done in "shimmering" foil to catch the buyer's eye; ideally, away from other books on display to focus on yours .

Die-stamped cut-out cover: Where a portion of the front cover is mechanically cut out to reveal another illustration beneath.

Cover information: The typewritten information supplied by the editors to the art department. This will include the book's ISBN, retail price, month of publication title, author, category, front and back cover blurbs, synopsis of the story; and suggested concepts for illustration, inclusive of descriptions of the main characters, and significant dramatic moments from the story itself that lend themselves to illustration.

Delay of performance: A contractual clause wherein the publisher agrees to publish your romance within a specified time, unless prohibited from doing so by extreme outside influence such as war, strikes, Acts of God, and so on.

Direct sales: Any sale of your romance that is not through the publisher's regular distributor or jobber. It may be a book retailer who prefers to deal directly with the publisher; an individual who is having difficulty finding your romance on sale locally; or a women's group wanting to buy a quantity of your romance and is seeking a discount.

Doing business as (d/b/a): A notification to the general public via your town clerk or local newspaper—usually a neighborhood paper—that states you intend to do business under a name different from your own. This enables you to legally sign all documents and contracts under the name you have chosen to conduct business in. Also known as: Certificate of Registration of Trade Name.

Double planting: Most often heard among publicists and public relations personnel. If the publicist at your publishing company sends out a release about your romance to a magazine or reviewer, and you have also contacted the same people, it's known as "double planting." It makes everyone very angry and upset, and is to be avoided.

Editors: Titles will vary depending on the size of the company, and peculiarities of top management (I have worked at companies where there is no editor-in-chief because the owners of the firm didn't want anyone to have such a lofty title). The pecking order is usually as follows:

Executive editor or Editorial director: No one knows for sure which title is higher up than the other unless one works for that particular company. If it's important for you to know, ask.

Editor-in-Chief: Generally, the buck stops with this person; especially if there is no executive editor or editorial director. The ed-in-chf (a little abbreviation humor in the industry) is responsible for the total work flow, often for the future editorial direction of the company, and not only for the quality of the books published by the firm, but also that they are profitable. In some companies, the ed-in-chf is more of an administrator than an editor; at other companies, you'll see the light on in this individual's office long after everyone else has toddled off for a relaxing martini at the end of the day.

Acquisitions editor: Some publishers woo them; others couldn't care less. An acquisitions editor is a publishing talent scout. Usually she or he has a strong rapport with agents, and has been around long enough to have a list of writers who are willing to switch alliances to wherever the acquisitions editor is working at the time. That, or someone who has such persuasive selling powers that she or he can entice better writers away from their current publishers.

Senior editor: There is usually more than one senior editor. It does not have anything (necessarily) to do with longevity with the company so much as on-the-job expertise.

Editor: This can mean anything, depending on which company is involved. If there is only one editor (and none of the above), then that person is the top banana. If, though, there are people at the firm with the above-mentioned titles, then the editor (in all probability) can do the job of the senior editor, but simply hasn't received the promotion as yet.

Associate editor: Might be interchangeable with editor, or someone who is very capable, but not quite ready to fully accept the responsibility of seeing a book through all its stages.

Managing editor: More often than not, the managing editor is responsible for the other editors meeting their deadlines, a smooth flow between editors and the production department, and overseeing that schedules are adhered to. In some companies, however, the managing editor also edits, and is ranked directly beneath the editor-in-chief.

Copyeditor: The person responsible for catching and correcting all your misspellings, typographical errors, incorrect grammar, or unclear sentence structure. This person will also bring to the attention of the editor any questionable areas of your romance such as your writing that it was a Georgian home on page 10, then referring to it as a raised ranch later on; or jarring information such as your stating that the heroine paid $25,000.00 for a VW Beetle. The copyeditor can question the arrangement of your material, or even the content, but is not authorized to make any editorial changes without consulting the editor.

Assistant editor: Higher up than a secretary, but still quite new to the business of editing. Doubtlessly quite young, and forced to live at home due to imposed poverty level via low salary.

Ellipsis(es): The formation of three consecutive dots, or periods, to indicate that one or more words have been deleted from the original material; or to indicate hesitancy or a suspended thought in dialogue or narrative.

Excerpting: The sale to a magazine or periodical of the right to publish a single chapter or portions of your book.

First-person narrative: Books or stories (fiction and nonfiction) told with the viewpoint of "I."

First refusal: (See **Option**.)

Foil cover: (See **Cover artwork**.)

Font: (See **Typeface**.)

Frontispiece: Originally and correctly, this is the illustration that appears before the book actually begins; traditionally, facing the title page. It could be an illustration from the book itself, or a picture of the author. However, it was borrowed into paperback language to refer to a short version of a scene from the book (in fiction) to hook a buyer's interest. It can also be used to describe how important (or funny or what-have-you) the book is, or to list quotes of the reviews the book has received.

Front matter: All that goes before the body of the book itself (known as "text"). It will include: Frontispiece; a list of other books you've written; the title page; the copyright page; dedication; and possibly a preface or foreword. It can also include a half-title page. Anything prior to the preface or foreword is not paginated; hence, many books begin on page five. If there is a preface or foreword, those pages are numbered in lower-case roman numerals; in which case, your romance might not begin until page 7 or 10, etc.

Galleys: Long, narrow strips of cheap paper on which the body of your book is printed. They are the first stage of physically reproducing your book. The typeset material is as wide as it will be in the bound book, but there is no pagination; just line after line of what has been set into type from your manuscript.

Grant of rights: (See **Territory**.)

Guaranty: (See **Advance against royalties**.)

Half title: Seldom seen in paperbacks, but it is a page that has nothing more on it than the title of your romance; your name will not appear, nor the name of the publishing firm. If used at all in mass-market publishing, it's generally because the manuscript ran too short of words and the publisher can't think of any other way to use up an extra two blank pages.

Impulse buyer: Those people who leave their homes to do anything other than buy a book . . . yet end up buying one on the spur of the moment. Illustrators of book jackets are very fond of taking the lion's share of the credit for impulse-buyer sales—they may well be right.

ISBN: Abbreviation for International Standard Book Number. Due to the overwhelming number of books published, or imported, and with the advent of computer technology, retailers, librarians and schools can track down any given title by its ISBN far more quickly than with the old system. In this way, every publisher is assigned an ISBN prefix that no one else in the world has, or can use. It's like, in a way, a Social Security number; only one publisher can have that prefix. After the prefix, the publisher can use any additional numbering system it may choose; but to the computer, only the ISBN counts.

Italics: Represented on your typewriter by underscoring the word or number you select; the printer will know to automatically set any underscored word in italics—letters, numbers, or words that slant to the right.

Jacket copy: "Soon to be a major motion picture," or "Six months on the bestseller lists," or quotes from reviews, or one or more lines to capture the flavor of the book to convince the browser to buy it. Whatever appears on the front or back cover that is written to sell your book is jacket copy, despite the fact that paperbacks do not have jackets. (This, too, was borrowed from hardcover terminology. However, hardcover books seldom have any sell copy on the front cover; instead, it appears on the flyleaf.)

Lead title: Generally, both in hardcover and paperback, one book is selected out of the entire season's or month's list of books to really receive the biggest push with advertising, promotion and so on. It is referred to as the lead title. There may be lesser ones, and they will receive proportionately less of the budget.

Log in: A running register of manuscripts received (as well as hardcover books for reprint possibilities, or works from other nations for publication in this country in paperback format). Date of receipt, author's name and title are shown; if agented, this is often included.

Lower case: Not capitalized.

Mass-market: Paperbacks that fit into traditional pockets or shelves for display. They are about 4-3/8" wide by about 7-1/4" high. As the term implies, these paperbacks are intended to be read by the masses rather than more scholarly types. (See **Trade paperback**.)

Mechanical: A pasteup of the cover; front, back and spine, precisely as it is to be printed, except in black and white. The illustration has been scaled to size and positioned perfectly. Overlays of tissues will give all the necessary instructions as to which colors are to appear, where, and a color transparency has been made of the artist's illustration for use by the printer. Some editors (very few) will send trusted authors a Xerox copy of the mechanical so they can get an idea of what their books will look like. Too often, authors—especially novices—panic and want changes, demand different blurbs or another illo (short for illustration). It is best not to send copies of the mechanical unless the editor knows the author very, very well.

Merchandising: This encompasses any variety of things from selling your romance as a premium or giveaway by a manufacturer, to arm bands with the title of your book and your name, to figurines being made based on your characters. (Remember *Love Story* and the dolls, plates, and dozens of other non-book products? That's merchandising.) It is the process of capitalizing/profiting on "spin-off" merchandise, gleaned from your book, but not the book itself.

Multiple viewpoint: A novel told from the point of view of two or more characters. A one-line break is required to indicate that we are switching from one character's viewpoint to another's. With each change of viewpoint, it is treated as if it were a first- or third-person narrative; each character can only know what she or he witnesses, is told and so on.

Off sale: When the book has been published and distributed, but is no longer available at the retail level. Usually, some copies would still be available from the publisher directly.

Omniscient viewpoint: The actual definition for omniscient is "having infinite awareness, understanding, and insight; possessed of universal or complete knowledge." It is the form of writing wherein the author knows everything, and reveals it to the reader through several main characters, or by projecting the author's perspective into the book. The characters can't know anything beyond the rules already explained, but the author may interject knowledge beyond what the characters know. A very tricky viewpoint to handle, best left to highly experienced, professional writers (who are, one expects, fearless).

On sale: The book has been published, distributed, and is currently available at the retail level.

One-line break: A lineal space between paragraphs, in the same chapter, that denotes a change of viewpoint; or, more likely in romances, to alert the reader that we are jumping ahead in time, flashing back, changing locale without a transition, or in any other way indicates a "break" in the sequence of events that precede it.

Option: A clause in a contract that gives the publisher the exclusive right to be the very first company to consider your next book for publication (unless otherwise modified). Also known as First Refusal.

Orphan: The last line of print on a page that falls short of halfway across.

Out of print: When a book has been published, distributed, was on sale, then went through a period of off sale. There are no more copies in stock, and there are no plans to go back to press with the book. The contract may still be in force and binding, but your romance is moribund.

Over the transom: A publishing phrase to indicate that a manuscript was submitted without benefit of a query letter or any other form of advance notification to the editor, or permission to submit.

Pageproofs: The stage following corrected galleys. At this point, the typeset lines have been measured off so they are even at top and bottom, and the pages are numbered. Called repros in computer typesetting.

Paginate: The act of numbering the pages, either of a manuscript or the typeset book.

Partial manuscript: A work in progress, incomplete. Should consist of the opening three chapters, minimum.

Printer: The individual, or company, that literally prints your romance. Typesetting and binding might be done by the printer, or independent companies that specialize in either.

Printing: It is used in one of two ways: Either to indicate how many times your romance has gone to press ("It's had five printings"); or occasionally used to specify how many copies of your book were published ("It had a 300,000-copy first printing").

Print run: More frequently used exclusively for how many copies were printed at one time ("It had an initial print run of 300,000 copies").

Production: The central control of all the mechanical processes involved between turning over the copyedited manuscript to the bound book, ready for shipment to the distributor.

Proofreader: The person(s) who reads the galleys or proofs of your romance immediately following the manuscript being set into type. (See pages 117 - 118)

Promotion: The act of giving your book added sales boosts with, for instance, special displays, banners, posters that retailers may place on their windows or inside the store, etc. It can also refer to retailer incentives such as one book free if ten are ordered, or even a prize of a free vacation to the Bahamas.

Public domain: When a work is no longer protected by copyright, either because the term of copyright has expired, or some legality has been trespassed upon. A case in point (older readers might recall) was the publication of the novel *Candy* in the early 1960s. The authors were Americans living in France; the novel was published by a French publisher, but in English. The work was not simultaneously copyrighted in the USA, and according to the laws at that time, this was a violation of copyright protection. While *Candy* was well on its way to becoming a bestseller in this country, several somewhat less than integrity-filled publishers took advantage of this violation, and there were three or four different editions of the same novel on sale concurrently—with no royalties paid to the authors, and no recourse.

Publicity: The generating and disseminating of "news" about your romance. It could be (Oh happy day!) an unexpected snapshot of the First Lady reading your novel on an airplane—which the publicist would instantly have reproduced and sent to every newspaper, TV network and magazine—or a "plant" in *The National Enquirer* that your life would be complete if only you could have a date with Brad Pitt. Anything that a publicist can do to promote you and your novel, that obtains media attention, is publicity . . . and it's free.

Publisher: You will soon learn, after your romance is contracted for or published, that few people can tell the difference between a publisher and a printer. A printer is a tradesperson (often an artiste, but still . . .); he or she might also be publishers. A publisher, however, is a person, or persons, or a corporate entity that underwrites all the expenses for the publication of books, and attendant costs such as advertising, overhead, and so forth. A publisher and the salaried or freelance staff, are responsible for the acquisition of books, readying them for press, and seeing them through to bound books. The publisher is the top executive (unless you start to get into chairpersons of the board, and all that).

Reader: Larger companies employ readers. These are usually young people eager to become a part of the publishing industry. The sole responsibility of a reader is to read the manuscripts that are submitted, then type up a book report—with a recommendation for acceptance or rejection. Your romance may have one or three readings before it is sent up to a higher editorial authority for final decision.

Reader Identification: As the term implies, the ability of whomever is reading your romance to "identify" with the heroine or other main characters. Even though the reader may be a brawny male, as author you should be able to make him understand, and empathize with, your characters—male and female, young or old, etc. Charles Dickens was a master of reader identification; even when his characters were hateful, we still had sympathy for them because we could put ourselves in those characters' places. He made us transcend our own selves and "be" his characters.

Release: A printed page with special information (or an update) about you or your book that is sent to the media in hopes they will want to use it.

Remainder or remaindering: As it implies, it refers to what's left of the print run—unsold and not likely to be. If there are enough copies left, a publisher may elect to remainder them. That is, sell them at a highly discounted price to retailers who will offer them at a marginal markup.

Repros: (See **Galleys**.)

Retail price: The price on the cover of a book.

Returns: Any unsold copies that the retailer returns to the distributor, jobber, or the publisher, for credit.

Reversion of rights: A contractual clause that grants the author the opportunity to reacquire all rights to her or his book, contingent upon the book being no longer in print, and subject to written demand ("demand" shouldn't be taken literally—a cordial request will do).

Roman type: Straight type, not italic—what you're reading now.

Royalties: A percentage of the cover price of a book, payable to the author based on copies sold—not copies printed. The book is generally required to be on sale for at least six months before a royalty report is due. However, depending upon when the book is contracted for, and actually published, this can far exceed six months. A novel might be contracted for in May of this year, yet not be published until July of the following year. It will not have been on sale for a full six months when the next royalty report would be sent to other authors (usually semiannually); consequently, though a July book, no royalty report, or any monies, will be sent until May of the following year. This is not uncommon at all.

Royalty report: Incomprehensible to anyone other than that touted breed known as "any child can do it." Even CPAs don't understand them; I doubt that the royalty departments understand them. They should tell you how many books were printed, how many were distributed and how many are (tentatively) sold—tentatively only because not all the returns are in. Based on your royalty rate, it should say how much you are due, and how much they are withholding against returns. If you can figure out a royalty report, please explain it to me at your earliest opportunity.

Running heads: You've seen them a hundred times and simply didn't know what they were called. It's the line of type at the top of the page, on either left- or right-hand (or both), that carries the name of your book, or your name, or the title of the chapter—or all of it. Seldom done in mass-market paperbacks unless the manuscript runs short and the publisher needs to pad it out by taking up extra space at the top of the pages.

Secondary retail outlets: What it sounds like—not the really big book stores, or chain bookstores. That is not a slur on the smaller stores; only an indication that they do not buy in sufficient volume to warrant the added shipping expense, warehousing, invoicing, and (sadly) too frequently, delays in paying for the books received. There is a running argument about the plight of small, independently owned bookstores . . . but it would take too much space to cover in this book. Both sides have a valid case.

Sell copy: A catchall term for just about anything that is designed to convince others to buy—whether your efforts to give the editor a sales pitch, promotional materials, or jacket copy.

Serialization: Sometimes a condensed (though usually not) version of the entire book run in consecutive issues of magazines or newspapers.

Signature: A single sheet of paper that, when folded, provides thirty-two pages of consecutive, typeset pages; the last stage prior to going to press for the printing and binding of the book.

Slushpile: The stacks and stacks of manuscripts and partial manuscripts awaiting a first reading. Usually unrequested manuscripts.

Style: The decisions required regarding the appearance and format of the body (or text) of the romance.

Subsidiary rights: The sale to others to in some manner use your romance for their own advantage or profit. This can include—but is not limited to—movies, TV, book clubs, condensations, magazines, foreign translation, and so forth.

Syntax: The way in which words or phrases are put together. For example, it is considered incorrect to end a sentence with a preposition or prepositional phrase. I believe it was Winston Churchill who, irked at the absurdity of this rule, declared: "I will no longer up with it put."

Termination: (See **Reversion of rights**.)

Territory: A contractual definition specifying where the publisher has the right to sell your book in the English language.

Text: The work as a whole, minus front or back matter.

Third-person narrative: A book written from the viewpoint of "she," or "he."

Trade paperback: A larger format but still with paper covers. Usually no smaller than 5" wide by 8" long, but this varies. Originally trade paperbacks were reserved for more "important" books such as the classics or noted nonfiction. This no longer applies.

Typeface: (Also known as font.) The size and appearance of a given kind of type; there are dozens to choose from, distinctive from one another in varying degrees. Each comes in several sizes, from the kind that your arms aren't long enough to read, to headline size.

Typeset: For centuries, this process was done by hand. A person hand selected the letters necessary to complete a line of text, and added leading slugs before commencing to set the next line. It became automated in this century, and of late, is giving way to computerized systems. One "sets your manuscript into type," but "the manuscript has been typeset."

Upper case: Capitalized; either a letter or an entire word.

Unsolicited manuscript: Succinctly, it's "Who asked you!"

Widow: Infrequently found nowadays, but it is the top line of a page that has so few words that it doesn't even go halfway across. To the eye, it appears all alone and abandoned—a widow.

Word count: An estimate of how many words are contained in a manuscript; or a projection of how many words are to be typeset.

Wraparound cover: (See **Cover artwork**.)

Publishers' Guidelines ─────────

In their own words─

Bantam Books
1540 Broadway
New York, NY 10036
(212) 354-6500
Editors: Wendy McCurdy, Beverly Lewis, Shauna Summers, Leslie Meredith

Current Guidlines:

At Bantam Books there are no guidelines for Women's Fiction because the stories and styles of our books cover the entire spectrum of the genre. If you wish to submit your work for consideration by Bantam and are unagented, send us a query letter. The query letter should be no more than three pages, covering the basics of who your characters are, what the conflict is that they face, and how your plot develops. It usually takes eight weeks to receive a response from us. Please don't submit sample chapters or a complete manuscript until we request them. Unfortunately, we can not give comments on any submissions. Be sure to include a self addressed, stamped envelope; we can not respond to queries which are not accompanied by return postage.

We advise you to review the titles we have published during the past several years by such bestselling authors as Sandra Brown, Amanda Quick, Iris Johansen, Deborah Smith, Tami Hoag, Teresa Medeiros, Rosanne Bittner, Susan Johnson, Kay Hooper, Lynda Robinson, and Jessica Bryan.

For further assistance in preparing your work, we suggest you consult *The Literary Market Place* or *The Writer's Market* which can be found in your local library.

We're constantly searching for the stars of tomorrow, the new authors who are the genre's life blood. If you write a great book, we'll buy it!

Bantam Doubleday Dell
Loveswept
1540 Broadway,
New York, NY 10036
Telephone: (212) 345-6500 • Fax. (212) 302-7985

Original Guidelines:

Thanks for your interest in our LOVESWEPT line. Here are some pertinent facts about our romances:

LOVESWEPTs run about 60,000 words and are set in the present. The books are wonderfully written and feature sparkling dialogue rather than long narrative. Quickly paced, our LOVESWEPTs are page turners!

The characters are deftly crafted, well-rounded people whom readers care about and root for. They should meet as close to page one as possible and never be apart for more than 8 to 10 manuscript pages. The sexual tension and attraction between the hero and heroine should be apparent from their first encounter on, but their love for each other should be based on emotions and feelings, not simply on sexual attraction.

We expect mystery/intrigue/adventure/paranormal and other elements to be kept to a minimum and that the romance remain the focus of the story at all times. Secondary characters should also be limited in number and in importance. More valuable than any "tip sheet" or "guideline," the books themselves are your best tools for learning what we're looking for in a LOVESWEPT. Read as many as possible before you submit to us.

Send us a query letter if you don't have an agent. The query should be no more than two or three pages, but it should cover the basics of who your characters are, what the conflict is that they face, and how your plot develops. It usually takes eight weeks to receive a response from us. Please don't submit sample chapters or a complete manuscript until we request them. Unfortunately, we cannot give comments on any submissions. Be sure to include a self-addressed, stamped envelope; we can not respond to queries which are not accompanied by return postage.

For further assistance in preparing your work, we suggest you consult *The Literary Market Place* or *The Writer's Market* which can be found in your local library.

We're constantly searching for the stars of tomorrow, the new authors who are the genre's life blood. We're willing to take chances with new ideas and new authors—if you write a great book, we'll buy it!

Sincerely,
The LOVESWEPT Editors

Dorchester Publishing Co., Inc.
Leisure Books
276 Fifth Ave. Suite 1008
New York, N.Y. 10001
Telephone (212) 725-8811 - FAX (212) 532-105
Editor: Alicia Condon

Editorial Guidelines for Leisure Books and Love Spell—

Historical Romance—Sensual romances with strong plots and carefully thought out characterizations. Spunky heroine whose love for the hero never wavers; he's the only one she makes love with and she's as passionate as he, although he may have to instruct her in the ways of love, since she's almost invariably untouched before she falls in love with the hero. Hero is often arrogant, overbearing; heroine often can't stand him at first, but discovers that beneath the surface lies a tender, virile, and experienced lover. It helps if both the heroine and hero have a sense of humor—a certain amount of wit leavens the heavy-breathing passion. Hero and heroine are separated by emotional conflict or the twists and turns of the plot, but in the end they overcome the barriers between them and live happily ever after.

We don't want a heroine who sleeps around, or a hero who's sadistic, although if there's a villain or villainess, he or she can be as nasty as possible.

Historical background, details of costume, etc., should be accurate; however, we don't want endless descriptions of battles, the political climate of the period, or a treatise on contemporary social history. Our readers are much more interested in the trials, tribulations, and love life of the heroine than in how many men Napoleon lost at the Battle of Waterloo.

Historical Romances should be approximately 120,000 words.

Futuristic Romance—Futuristic Romances contain all the elements of Historical Romances—beautiful heroine, dashing hero, some conflict that separates them, a happy ending, etc.—but they are set in lavish lands on distant worlds.

Avoid science-fiction-type hardware, technology, etc.

Finished manuscripts should be 120,000 words.

Time-Travel Romance—A modern-day hero or heroine goes back in time and falls in love. Traditional guidelines for Historical Romances apply. The challenge here is to maintain credibility during the transition between the present and the past. The fun is seeing history and another way of life through the eyes of someone from our own time. The conflict and resolution of the romance arise from the fact that the hero and heroine are from different eras.

Beware of a lot of philosophizing about fate, the meaning of time, and how the past affects the present. No time machines please.

Finished manuscripts should be 120,000 words.

Paranormal Romance—Either historical or contemporary romance with magic, witches, ghosts, vampires, etc., as a subsidiary element. Must have a happy ending.

Finished manuscripts should be 120,000 words.

Angel Romance—Historical, time-travel or contemporary romance in which a guardian angel lends a hand in bringing the lovers together.

Finished manuscripts should be 120,000 words.

Guidelines for submitting material to Leisure Books and Love Spell—

Please query or submit synopsis and first three chapters only—no complete manuscripts unless specifically requested. Include a stamped, self-addressed envelope (of sufficient size) for possible return of proposal or manuscript. No material will be returned without SASE.

Synopsis, sample chapters (and manuscript if requested) must be typed, double-spaced. Word processors are okay, but letter quality only. Please retain a copy of all material sent in case the original gets lost in the mail.

For a free catalogue of Leisure Books, please send a self-addressed, stamped envelope (#10) to the above address.

The best way to learn to write a Leisure or a Love Spell romance is to read a Leisure or a Love Spell romance.

Harlequin Enterprises Limited
Located in: New York; Don Mills, Canada; Richmond, Surry, England

To the romance author:

Enclosed are editorial guidelines for Harlequin's various romance lines. Please keep in mind that they will give you some tips but no easy answers. There is no "formula" to writing a publishable romance novel.

Remember that if you hope to write romance fiction, it's important to enjoy reading it. If you are already a fan, your appreciation will be apparent in your writing. If you have not done so already, we encourage you to read many books in each series available on the market. The line that emerges as your favorite is probably where you should submit your manuscript.

Remember, too, that reading is an emotional experience. We hope you will write from the heart, that you will let us feel touched by what you have to say. When you put pen to paper, do so because you indeed have something to share with other readers.

On the other side of this page you will find answers to some frequently asked questions. Should you wish further information, don't hesitate to get in touch with me.

Sincerely,
Karin Stoecker
Editorial Director

General Information
•Submission Format: Query letter—state the length of your manuscript and enclose a brief synopsis as well as any pertinent information about yourself, including publishing credits and professional affiliations.

•Agents: We give equal consideration to manuscripts sent by authors and agents. We do not give recommendations.

•Return Postage: Please include sufficient return postage, preferably a money order or international reply coupons.

•Customs Value: The declared value of a manuscript copy should be a maximum of $10.00 to expedite processing through Canadian customs. This does not apply to manuscripts mailed in the U.S. to our New York office.

•Simultaneous Submissions: We will not consider any submission that has been sent simultaneously to another publisher.

•Financial Arrangements: We enter into discussions about payments only when we are going to contract. This information is confidential.

•Copyright: Under the United States copyright law, copyright for any work is secured automatically when the work is created; i.e., an author has copyright protection the moment the work is put on paper and can be visually perceived. When a manuscript is published by Harlequin, every copy bears a copyright notice that entitles the copyright holder to certain additional rights. Harlequin registers all copyrights with the United States Copyright Office; this registration, although not a requirement for protection, establishes a public record of the copyright claim. For more information regarding copyright, write to: Copyright Office, Library of Congress, Washington, DC 20559.

Here are tips on the professional presentation of any manuscript:
• The title page should include the author's real name and address, the title and the approximate number of words should be stated. Also indicate pseudonym if applicable.
• Manuscripts must be typewritten, error-free, double-spaced and on one side of the paper only. Leave a one and one quarter (1 1/4) inch margin around the entire page, and be sure to use a good grade of white bond.
• In the upper right-hand corner of each manuscript page, include the author's last name, and the page number, e.g., Smith - 12, Smith 13, etc.
• If you use a computer printer, the print must be letter-quality.
• Be sure to make a complete copy for your files.
• Do not bind or staple your manuscript. Use an envelope or box large enough to contain your manuscript flat.

Harlequin Guidelines

INTRIGUE 70,000-75,000 words
Senior Editor and Editorial Coordinator: Debra Matteucci
300 East 42nd Street, 6th Floor
New York, NY 10017 U.S.A.
Query

Taut, edge-of-the-seat contemporary romantic suspense tales of intrigue and desire. Kidnappings, the stalking of personal-ad applicants, and fiances wrongly accused of murdering their brides-to-be are examples of story lines we love most. Whether a murder mystery, psychological suspense, thriller, espionage tale, or an account of a woman in jeopardy, the love story must be inextricably bound to the mystery at the level of the novel's premise. Gripping plots twist, turn and thicken, ever leading toward a final resolution where all loose ends are tied up neatly ... and shared dangers lead right to shared passions. As long as they're in jeopardy and falling in love, our mature heroes and heroines may traverse a landscape as wide as the world itself. Their lives are on the line ... and so are their hearts!

AMERICAN ROMANCE 70,000-75,000 words
Senior Editor and Editorial Coordinator: Debra Matteucci
300 East 42nd Street 6th Floor
New York, NY 10017 U.S.A.
Query

In this fun, fast-paced, well-plotted page-turner, a dynamic premise hooks the reader instantly, sweeping her into a contemporary fairy tale where anything's possible and all dreams come true. Whether the themes are innovative, or romantic staples such as marriages of convenience and brides on the run that suddenly take daring, imaginative new twists, our lusty, adventurous heroes always meet their greatest challenge in a sassy, headstrong heroine. Sizzling repartee and spirited one-upmanship barely masks the attraction that underlies their every moment together, and they're bound to encounter the unexpected in their situation, in each other, and in a world where everything comes out right in the end.

SUPER ROMANCE 85,000 words
Senior Editor: Paula Eykelhof
225 Duncan Mill Road
Don Mills, Ontario M38 3K9
Canada
Submit first two chapters and synopsis

These books are Harlequin's biggest romance novels—in scope as well as length. They're complex, compelling stories about complex, compelling people. The key to writing a Superromance novel is characterization: it's essential that your hero and heroine be well-developed, fully explored people whose lives and loves will involve the reader completely. Take advantage of the longer format to create characters whose personalities are formed not only by the events and circumstances in their past, but by their expectations for the future and the networks of relationships and responsibilities that surround them. These are characters who define and drive the plot not vice versa. We're looking for a wide range of story types and tones (including highly dramatic, humorous, heart-warming, suspenseful and adventurous stories). Above all, we want exciting, innovative, emotionally genuine, page-turning stories and we want you to write your story your way.

ROMANCE 50,000-55.000 words
Editorial Department. Mills & Boon Ltd., Eton House
18 - 24 Paradise Road,
Richmond, Surrey, TW9 1S4
United Kingdom
Query

Written in third person, from the heroine's point of view, each book should focus almost exclusively on the developing relationship between the main protagonists. The emphasis should be on warm and tender emotions, with no sexual explicitness; lovemaking should only take place when the emotional commitment between the characters justifies it. These heartwarming stories must be written with freshness and sincerity, featuring spirited, engaging heroines portrayed with depth and affection—as well as heroes who are charismatic enough to fulfill every woman's dreams! Readers should be thrilled by the tenderness of their developing relationship, and gripped by romantic suspense as the couple strive to overcome the emotional barriers between them and find true happiness in the romance of a lifetime!

PRESENTS 50,000-50,000 words
Editorial Department, Mills & Boon Ltd., Eton House
18 - 24 Paradise Road,
Richmond, Surrey. TW9 1S4
United Kingdom
Query

Pick up a Harlequin Presents novel, and you enter a world full of spine-tingling passion and provocative, tantalizing romantic excitement! Although grounded in reality, these stories offer compelling modern fantasies to readers all around the world, and there is scope within this line to develop relevant, contemporary issues which touch the lives of today's women. Each novel is written in the third person and features spirited, independent heroines—who aren't afraid to take the initiative!— and breathtakingly attractive, larger-than-life heroes. The conflict between these characters should be lively and evenly matched, but always balanced by a developing romance which may include explicit lovemaking. Presents novels capture the drama and intensity of a powerful, sensual love affair.

TEMPTATION 60,000 words
Senior Editor: Birgit Davis-Todd
225 Duncan Mill Road
Don Mills, Ontario M3E3 3K9
Canada
Submit first two chapters and synopsis

This is Harlequlin's boldest, most sensuous series, focusing on men and women living—and loving—in the 1990s! Almost anything goes in Temptation: the stories may be humorous, topical, adventurous or glitzy, but at heart, they are pure romantic fantasy. Think fast-paced, use the desires and language of women today, add a high level of sexual tension, along with strong conflicts and then throw in a good dash of "what if. . . ." The results should sizzle!

Heartsong Presents
P.O. Box 719
1810 Barbour Drive
Uhrichsville, Ohio 44683

Guidelines for Writers and Editors

Our readers are primarily women who consider themselves born-again Christians. One of the reasons they choose Heartsong Presents books over other reading material is because our books confirm their values and beliefs. As a writer/editor, you must take this into consideration.

The Basics: All manuscripts in the Heartsong Presents inspirational line should present a conservative, evangelical Christian world view. Manuscripts that do not reflect this position will be returned to the author(s).

Specifics: Heartsong Presents will consider contemporary and historical manuscripts between 50,000-55,000 words. A historical manuscript for our purposes, is any time period covering the years prior to and during World War II. A contemporary manuscript would be any time period after or post-World War II, although, strictly speaking, we would probably not consider a manuscript set in the 1950s as contemporary. Since all of the contemporaries we have published thus far have been set in the 1990s, your best bet for acceptance is the present time period.

Things to Consider: The underlying theme in all of our romances is the belief that a true and honest faith in God is the foundation for any romantic relationship. Although we are not looking for "sermons in novel form," the importance and need for a personal relationship with Jesus Christ should be important.

Things to Avoid: Avoid the truly controversial. Although conflict is important for any storyline, certain matters should be avoided at all costs. Stay away from any language that could be considered foul. Avoid euphemisms like "heck" or "darn." To many of our readers these words are substitutes for curses, and in their minds as bad, or worse. Main characters should be Christians (or Christians by the end of the book) and should act accordingly. They need not be "saints," but their actions should be consistent with Christian teaching.

The hero and heroine should not be divorced. This is acceptable for secondary and non-Christian characters. The idea of divorce and remarriage for a Christian is a problem for most of our readers.

Most of our readers also find a woman as a pastor, or even an assistant pastor unbiblical. If your heroine is a woman who is a pastor or youth pastor, etc., we will not consider your manuscript.

The use of alcohol is offensive and incompatible with Christian teaching according to many of our readers. While drinking is unacceptable for the Christian characters, however, for non-Christians this conflict can be explored. In handling drinking in your novel, it is important that the reader understand that this behavior is not acceptable. Exceptions such as may be found in historical novels will be evaluated individually. The same is true for dancing, another activity that is offensive to most of our readers. Dancing in historical novels, however, is not as offensive as it might be in a contemporary novel. In contemporaries it is usually the setting that is more offensive than the dancing, for example a bar/club.

Avoid controversial doctrinal issues. We will not list these (there are too many), however, if you keep in mind that we are appealing to a broad range of Christian evangelical readers, we believe you will be on the right track.

Physical tension between characters should not be overdone. Do not be overly descriptive when describing how characters feel in a particular romantic moment, for example, kissing, embracing, and so on.

Characters, especially women characters, should be modestly dressed. They should never appear outside their bedrooms in nightgowns, underwear, and other private garments. No matter how innocent some of this may seem to you, we will edit questionable scenes out of the manuscript.

Summary: One particular biblical message should be threaded throughout if possible. This can be presented from many different characters, through symbols, and so on. The main element of books is the romance and to that end, characters must be perceived as appealing and capable of finding each other attractive. Conflict within the relationship will draw hero and heroine closer and involve the readers more personally.

Few would doubt the breathless appeal of a love story. But a Christian love story combines the elements of enchantment and inspiration to produce a tale that is unforgettable—

Hot Topics: Controversial Items to Steer Clear of—
1. Spirit baptism. 2. Water baptism (meaning of). 3. Time of Spirit baptism (at conversion vs. second experience of grace). 4. Time of water baptism (children or adults). 5. Gifts of the Spirit (e.g., are tongues still around?) 6. End times (setting dates). 7. Lord's Supper (ordinance vs. sacrament). 8. Women's ordination. 9. Christian perfection. 10. Transferring qualities of Jesus—or passages in the Bible that refer to Jesus—to heroes in the books. This also applies to Mary, Jesus' earthly mother.

To Submit: If you believe you have an inspirational romance that would fit Heartsong Presents guidelines, please send a summary of the story along with three to four randomly selected chapters to:
Heartsong Presents
Editorial Department
P.O. Box 719
Uhrichsville, OH 44683

Computer Preparation of Manuscripts
If you will be typing your manuscript on a computer, it would save us a great deal of time if you send us the manuscript on disks along with a printout. This simplifies production and prevents errors in typesetting. This can only be done if you have an IBM or IBM-compatible computer using a MS-DOS operating system (no Apples). The word processing program you use

174

generally doesn't matter.

If your manuscript has already been typed into your computer, do the following:

1. Print out the manuscript (double spaced).

2. Label your disks with your name and indicate the correct order of disks (1, 2, 3, etc.) on each disk.

3. Enclose in your cover letter the brand of computer you used and the name and version of your word processing program.

4. Package everything carefully. There are disk mailers you can buy to protect the disks, or you can protect them with heavy cardboard. Mail the disks in the same package as the manuscript to avoid mixups.

If you haven't typed in the manuscript yet and work with ASCII files do the following:

1. As you type, only hit RETURN at the end of a paragraph, never at the end of a line. Let the computer wrap the text itself until you reach the end of a paragraph, then use one RETURN to indicate a new paragraph.

2. Use no centering, no flush right, no boldface, no italics. Instead, indicate these with a note within parentheses.

3. It is very important to use uniform tabs and/or indents.

4. You may use underlines to indicate italics.

5. Double space the manuscript.

6. Use Arabic numbers (2) instead of Roman numerals (II).

7. Be sure to include dedications and/or acknowledgments on disk.

8. Print out the manuscript, then follow the directions listed above for labeling and mailing. If you want, you can indicate on the manuscript such things as subheads, extracts, etc.

*To avoid loss of disks, please wait to send disks until the publisher requests them.

Thanks for Your Help

New American Library
1633 Broadway
New York, NY 10019
Telephone: (212) 397-8000
Editors: Regency - Hilary Ross, Mainstream Hardcover - Michaela Hamilton

VISTA
Dear Authors:

Romance is and always will be a special concern of the young adult market. Although Signet Vista has refocussed its requirements in this area, we will continue to seriously consider single romance titles.

Our needs have changed along with the needs of the young adult reader. A few general remarks should clarify how we see the change. We feel that books dealing with problematic situations and experiences should approach the subject in a humorous manner, since kids often feel uncomfortable dealing with problems directly and use humor as a means of coping with serious and poignant situations. We are particularly interested in seeing romances in which the protagonist and love interest form a strong basis for interaction. Dialogue should be used often and accurately to reflect the characters' personalities as well as the needs of the immediate situation. The settings and scenarios for the stories should be authentic to contemporary teenage experience, contributing to the reader's identification with the story. Because the conclusion to the novel is so important, we feel very strongly that there should be an emotionally satisfying resolution to the various relationships depicted in the story. For example, the protagonist should come to terms with his/her feelings about a relationship along with the other characters; or the protagonist could realize within herself an important judgement about her problems and relationships and come to an understanding about what really constitutes love and caring.

The best advice we can give anyone who wants to write for this market is to read the new titles coming from Vista each month like *Seaside Heights, Meet Super Duper Rick Martin* and the eagerly awaited *The Princess Routine.*

Our guidelines for submissions are as follows: published authors may submit three chapters and a complete outline, unpublished authors may submit complete manuscripts. Naturally we want to see your work, so our tips end here. Good luck, we look forward to hearing from you.

REGENCY ROMANCES
Dear Authors:

Your heart thumps and your pulse quickens. You are lost in a glittering world where beautiful heroines and dashing heroes, combined with just the right amount of innocence, intrigue and derring-do, find love in a time long gone—in a time where dreams come true. You have been swept away by a Signet Regency romance.

Regencies are lively, witty, love stories of ca. 75,000 words set in England between 1795 and 1821 and told in third person, largely from the heroine's point of view. There are two types of Regencies—the traditional one by such authors as Barbara Hazard and Sheila Walsh in which the heroine experiences her first romance; the more sexually explicit type by such authors as Sandra Heath and newcomers Mary Balogh and Barbara Allister in which the hero and heroine's relationship is more sensuous and intimate. Each book should contain the following elements: a feisty, young (18-32) woman of the British gentry who becomes romantically involved with an experienced, slightly older hero from the aristocracy; a credible central conflict that keeps the hero and heroine at odds throughout much of the book, and descriptions of the social world of the time (i.e. dress, architecture, gambling, duels, coming out seasons, etc.). Sex may be shared between husband and wife, and hugging and kissing between unmarried characters, but as with all Regencies, the romantic relationship must develop through witty dialogue and ingenious plot twists rather than through steamy encounters, and must always remain within the bounds of believable behavior for a woman of the period.

Nobody publishes Regencies better than Signet. We first launched Regencies in 1979 and as a result of its success, the line has rapidly grown and we are presently seeking new talent. We currently publish three Regencies per month and one favorite Signet Regency reissue. The best preparation for writing a Signet Regency is to read the books in the line and see what type best suits you as a writer. And remember, as in all Regency romances, dreams do come true.

Sincerely,
Hilary Ross
Associate Executive Editor

SIGNET REGENCY ROMANCE GUIDELINES
Length 75,000 words
Definition:
Regencies are lively, witty love stories set in England between 1795 and 1821. Each book should feature an intelligent, appealing, and spirited heroine, usually of the British gentry, who becomes involved with an experienced and slightly older hero from the aristocracy.

Types:
There are two types of Regencies: (1) the traditional romance in which the naive heroine experiences her first romance with the hero; and (2) the more realistic, more explicit romance in which the hero and heroine's relationship is more sensuous and intimate. However, no matter what the level of sensuality, the focus should remain on the developing romance between the hero and heroine, and the story must unfold through clever, humorous dialogue and ingenious plot twists. The relationship must remain in the bounds of believable

behavior for a woman of the period. For example, the fact that divorce was rare and contraception practically unknown should be taken into account.

The Regency should contain descriptions of the social world of the period. Authors should draw upon such standard Regency elements as modes of dress, architecture, fashionable carriages, social customs, balls, Almacks, gambling, curricle races, duels, coming-out seasons in London, etc. to provide a proper background for the story.

Point of View:

The story is told in the third person, largely from the heroine's point of view, although some scenes may be written from the hero's point of view.

Sex:

In the Regency, sex can be shared between husband and wife. To satisfy today's more liberated readers, we prefer there be scenes involving some lovemaking—kissing, caressing, etc.—between the hero and heroine, whether they be married or not. Also, since the heroine is more sexually aware, there is greater opportunity to develop sexual tension between the two characters. But as with all Regencies, the romantic relationship should develop through clever situations rather than through passionate encounters.

How to Submit:

Submissions are welcome from unagented and novice writers as well as from published authors. We prefer complete manuscript but will accept three sample chapters and an outline, including a full plot synopsis and thorough descriptions of the main characters and setting. Published writers should send a resume of their works. Payment depends on the author's track record and past experience.

Manuscript Preparation:

Please leave one-inch margins on both sides of the page. The manuscript should be neat, well-typed, double spaced on standard-sized plain white bond paper. DO NOT use onion-skin, color, erasable, or odd-sized paper. Polish your work, proofread it carefully, and send us your best.

Please enclose a stamped, self-addressed manilla envelope with your submission. Be sure to keep a file copy of everything you submit, including the manuscript. Study our guidelines and other Signet Regency Romances. And please make sure the work you submit meets with the requirements outlined above.

HISTORICAL ROMANCES

Signet historical romances are the bodice-rippers of the '80s: adventurous, sensual stories featuring intelligent, feisty characters. They are not stories of rape and pillage, nor are they graphically distasteful. Our historical romances are in the tradition of such bestselling authors as Bertrice Small, Rosemary Rogers, Rebecca Brandewyne and Johanna Lindsay.

Signet is not launching a new line of historical romances. What we are is even more exciting. We are launching authors. We actively seek storytellers who can combine adventure, sexuality, and the most fascinating hero and heroine set against a background of historic time and place that will sweep the reader into a fantasy of page-turning enchantment.

Signet historical romances are between 125-150,000 words in length, and the emphasis is on the adventure, both in the plot and particularly in the romance. Sensual scenes follow a natural progression and are never gratuitous. When submitting historical romances for publication, we prefer at least half the manuscript from non-published authors accompanied by a detailed synopsis of the rest of the plot (8-15 pages). Published authors should submit three chapters and a detailed synopsis of the rest of the book along with their published work. Three months is the average review period you should give our editorial department for responding to your work.

We do not distribute specific guidelines for these novels because we do emphasize unique books, and because we want to develop authors rather than a "type" of the genre. We believe that each author creates her own special story, told only as she can write it! So the best advice I can give to an aspiring Signet author is to read the historical romances we publish, re-read your favorite historical authors, and then stretch your imagination for a truly unique novel!

HISTORICAL SEXY GOTHICS

Gothic romances have been an important part of the mass market list throughout publishing history. Only a few years ago, gothics consumed most of the romance market before a glut resulted, leaving only the most successful authors' books on the shelves. I believe the time is right for historical gothic romances to return. Historical romance sales have increased, and intrigue has become a significant element in all areas of romance publishing. It seems natural that in such an environment the gothic will return with renewed enthusiasm.

Signet will launch a new series of sexy historical gothic romances with an added twist: sensuality! We are currently seeking well-written historical romances of 80-110,000 words which capture the suspense, romance and adventure of the bestselling novels of Victoria Holt and Phyllis Whitney. Keep the following in mind when writing for this genre

Sexual descriptions should be evocative rather than brutal or graphic. Describe the sensational with all five senses responding. How does the wind feel when it grazes the heroine's neck. What fragrances are in the summer air?

Update the gothic genre by making the hero a bit more accessible to the heroine and the relationship. He can still be mysterious without being a recluse. And by making him more visible in the plot, he and the heroine will develop a sexual relationship naturally.

Retain the elements of the gothic genre through bleak settings, suspenseful atmospheres, and a questioning tone. The reader must get the sense that something is very wrong in the situation presented from the very first chapter.

Remember to use history as a backdrop and emphasize the mystery and romance.

I don't want to be any more specific than the above because it's really up to you to create your own story. I don't encourage formula writing; I am seeking talented writers with a unique ability to translate their imagination into fiction. Think of your favorite authors, re-read their novels, add your own special touch to an innovative plot, and you'll have what I'm looking for!

SCARLET RIBBONS GUIDELINES
Signet Historical Romance Line

Length: 125,000 - 150,000 words
Setting: No specific guidelines
Time Period: 1066 - World War I

Point of View:
The story is told in the third person, largely from the heroine's point of view, although some scenes may be written from the hero's point of view.

Hero and Heroine:
The heroine should be young and, if not American, partly or wholly of a nationality with which the reader can identify—such as Scottish, English, or Irish. She should also be intelligent, strong willed, and independent, a character not easily discouraged.
The hero should be slightly older and also of a similar nationality.

Plot:
The story must focus on a strong central romance. We do not want the hero and heroine to be separated for the bulk of the book, the heroine should not sleep with numerous other men and violence should be kept to a minimum. Rape, except in certain very special circumstances of the heroine by the hero, is to be avoided. Definitely NO gang rapes.

How to Submit:
Submissions are welcome from unagented and novice writers as well as from published authors. We prefer complete manuscripts, but will accept three sample chapters and an outline, including a full plot synopsis and thorough descriptions of the main characters and setting. Published writers should send a resume of their works. Payment depends on the author's track record and past experience.

Manuscript Preparation:
Please leave one-inch margins on both sides of the page. The manuscript should be neat, well-typed, double-spaced on standard sized white bond paper. DO NOT use onion-skin, color, erasable, or odd-sized paper. Polish your work, proofread it carefully, and send us your best.
Please enclose a stamped, self-addressed manilla envelope with your submission. Be sure to keep a file copy of everything you submit, including the manuscript. Study our guidelines and other Signet historical romances. And please make sure the work you submit meets with the requirements outlined above.

Palisades Romances
c/o Questar Publishers
P.O. Box 1720
Sisters, OR 97759

WRITERS' GUIDLINES for PALISADES ROMANCES
Formerly "Harbor Romances"

The word "palisades" means the stakes that form fortress walls. Truly, we want readers to feel safe in our own little "fortress" of fiction; reading a Palisade Romance should be equated with finding refuge escaping into a safe place. We want to tell an entertaining, uplifting story while ennobling our faith and marriage. Authors published under this imprint should keep these values in mind as they write.

Length; 64,000 - 68,000 words

Plot: Story lines may be relatively simple, though there must be enough complexity to maintain interest for the required 64,000 plus words. Subplots that add elements of mystery, suspense or adventure are fine, as long as the emphasis remains on the central romance. The plot should not be too harsh; readers pick up a romance to be uplifted, not depressed. Keep your reader in mind. She wants to be swept away into an intriguing, delightful story! The story should uplift true love, ennobling marriage—there may be times of trouble—but the relationship always survives. Your heroine may be single or a widow; tread lightly if she's a divorcee her new romance should show her that true love is possible and that this is a relationship that will last until death. Successful storylines are entertaining and portray Christian values.

Style: Generally light and natural; humorous only if it fits naturally into a story. There should be active dialogue, reflecting the way people actually speak, but keep swearing out and provocative language in check.

Sensuality: We want passionate, yet chaste relationships. Even married couples' most intimate scenes are to be left to the reader's imagination. Readers want to understand the incredible draw of our heroes and heroines, but characters must know where to draw the line to maintain their high moral standards. Obviously, stay away from anything that smells of erotica. Think of emotional response over physical response in intimate scenes. Editor will have final say as to what goes in or stays out.

Hero, heroine and setting: We do not want to "formulize" our romances into a dull, run-of-the-mill lot. We want to see innovative plots, intriguing characters, and interesting settings. Please think beyond teaching professions and do not write about women who cannot cook. We like strong characters. The rest is up to you! Send us a story about people we cannot refuse. NOTE: WE

HAVE A SPECIAL NEED FOR AFRICAN-AMERICAN, ASIAN-AMERICAN, AND HISPANIC CHARACTERS

Gospel message: Foremost, we want believable characters! In real life, everyone doesn't come to salvation and people express their faith in unique ways. We want characters that echo life: Christian characters that help show the way but aren't perfect; non-Christians who glimpse the wonders of Christ but don't always grasp the importance all at once. Obviously, there can be salvation, but make it work naturally. Beware of platforming or preaching to your reader. You should also clearly depict biblical principles, values and morals somewhere in your novel.

Submission guidelines: Include a cover letter with the following information, as well as a 2-page outline and 3 chapters:
- word count
- pertinent information about yourself, such as whether you have ever been published (if so, what, when and where) and why you want to write a Christian romance.
- how long you've been writing
- how familiar you are with romance novels, and why you think your book is right for Palisade Romances

If you send sample chapters with your letter, please include an SASE with proper return postage. We cannot be accountable for returning those manuscripts unaccompanied by an SASE.

Send your submission to: Lisa T. Bergren

Some suggested reading to give you an idea of what we admire: *Silk, Under Eastern Stars*, and *Kingskote* by Linda Chaikin.*Wings of the Morning*, by Lori Wick, *Voice in the Wind* and *Echoes in the Darkness* by Francine Rivers.

Please read at least one Palisades novel before submission.
Available Palisades Titles (at your local Christian bookstore):
Refuge, Torchlight, and Treasure (0-88070-725-9) by Lisa Tawn Bergren
Secrets (0-88070-721-6) by Robin Jones Gunn
Sierra (0-88070-726-7) by Shari MacDonald
Westward (0-88070-751-8) by Amanda MacLean
Glory (0-88070-754-2) by Marilyn Kok
Love Song (0-88070-747-X) by Sharon Gillenwater

Reference: *How to Write Romances* by Phyllis Taylor Pianka 5/95

Silhouette Books
300 East 42nd Street - Sixth Floor
New York, NY 10017
Telephone: (212) 682-6080
FAX: (212) 682 4539
Isabel Swift—Editorial Director

Silhoutte Submission Guidlines

Thank you for your interest in Silhouette Books. We do not accept unsolicited complete or partial manuscripts, but ask instead that you submit a query letter. Please indicate what Silhouette series you think your project is appropriate for, if it is completed, what you think makes it special, and previous publishing experience (if any). Also include a synopsis of your story that gives a clear idea of both your plot and characters and is no more than two single-spaced pages. A self-addressed stamped envelope (SASE) will ensure a reply. Should your manuscript be requested, please note the following information:

We publish only category romances! Please do not submit any other type of fiction or non-fiction. Your manuscript should take place in the present and be told in the third person, primarily from the heroine's point of view. However, the hero's perspective may be used to enhance tension, plot or character development.

All material should be the author's own original work. Stories that contain scenes or plot lines that bear a striking resemblance to previously published work are in breach of copyright law and are not acceptable.

All material must be typewritten, double-spaced and on 8-1/2" x 11" paper. No disk submissions. Computer-generated material is acceptable, but must be letter quality, and pages must be separated. Any material received on computer reams will be returned without evaluation.

Do not submit your material bound in binders, boxes or containers of any kind. Secure material by rubber bands. Cover sheets must have your complete name, address and phone number. Each page should be numbered sequentially thereafter. Please type your name and title in the upper left-hand corner of each page. If we ask to see your manuscript, please include a complete synopsis. Enclose a self-addressed, stamped postcard if you wish acknowledgement of receipt.

All material will be evaluated in as timely a fashion as volume allows. Please do not call regarding the status of your manuscript. You will be notified by mail as soon as your work has been reviewed.

Do not send any material that is being considered by another publisher. "Multiple submissions" are not acceptable. A literary agent is not required in order to submit.

You must enclose a SASE with all material you send in. This will ensure the return of your material. Please send an envelope large enough to accommodate your work and adequate postage.

This sheet is designed as a guide to aid you in understanding our requirements and standards. However, there is no better way to determine what we are looking for than reading our books.

SILHOUETTE ROMANCE
53,000-58,000 words
Senior Editor: Anne Canadeo

Silhouette Romance requires talented authors able to portray modern relationships in the context of romantic love. Although the hero and heroine don't actually make love unless married, sexual tension is a vitally important element. Writers are encouraged to try new twists and creative approaches to this winning formula. Our ultimate goal is to give readers a romance with heightened emotional impact—books that make them laugh or cry, books that touch their hearts.

SILHOUETTE DESIRE
55,000-60,000 words
Senior Editor: Lucia Macro

Sensual, believable, compelling, these books are written for today's woman. Innocent or experienced, the heroine is someone we identify with; the hero irresistible. The conflict should be an emotional one, springing naturally from the unique characters you've chosen. The focus is on the developing relationship, set in a believable plot. The characters don't have to be married to make love, but lovemaking is never taken lightly. Secondary characters and subplots must blend with the core story. Innovative new directions in storytelling and fresh approaches to classic romantic plots are welcome.

SILHOUETTE SPECIAL EDITION
75,000-80,000 words
Senior Editor: Tara Gavin

Sophisticated, substantial, and packed with emotion, Special Edition demands writers eager to probe characters deeply, to explore issues that heighten the drama of living and loving, to create compelling romantic plots. Whether the sensuality is sizzling or subtle, whether the plot is wildly innovative or satisfyingly traditional, the novel's emotional vividness, its depth and dimension, should clearly label it a very special contemporary romance. Subplots are welcome, but must further or parallel the developing romantic relationship in a meaningful way.

SILHOUETTE INTIMATE MOMENTS
80,000-85,000 words
Senior Editor & Editorial Coordinator: Leslie Wainger

Believable characters swept into a world of larger-than-life romance, such is the magic of Silhouette Intimate Moments. These books offer you the freedom to combine the universally appealing elements of a category romance with the flash and excitement of mainstream fiction. Adventure, suspense, melodrama, glamour—let your imagination be your guide as you blend old and new to create a novel with emotional depth and tantalizing complexity, a novel that explores new directions in romantic fiction, a novel that is quintessentially Intimate Moments.

Characters:
The Heroine

Silhouette Romances are always written in the third person but the point of view is exclusively the heroine's. The heroine is young (19-29). She is not beautiful in the high fashion sense, is basically an ingenue, and wears modest make-up and clothing. Frequently she does not consider herself to be a beauty, and this attitude is used to play off against the other woman (women). She has a good figure, and is often petite and slight of build. Naturally, when she dresses up she is stunning. Her outfits are described in detail, as is her physical appearance. In spite of her fragile appearance, she is independent, high-spirited and not too subservient. She should not be mousey or weepy. Often she is starting a career, leaving college, unhappy with her present job, or too caught up in her work. The book then opens with an unexpected change, challenge, or adventure in her life which she accepts eagerly, though with some trepidation. Her reactions to the amorous advances of the hero mirror the conflict between her desire for him and her strong belief in romantic love. She never truly believes that the hero loves her until the final chapter of the novel. She is usually without parents or a "protective" relationship. Sometimes she has lived with an elderly female relative but breaks away to lead a life of her own. A brother is permissible, but she is often in the position of caring for him, rather than vice-versa; he may be weak, handicapped or uncertain as to his morals or future. He can in no way suggest the type of character that is our hero's prerogative.

The Hero

The hero is 8 to 12 years older than the heroine. He is self-assured, masterful, hot-tempered, capable of violence, passion and tenderness. He is often mysteriously moody. Heathcliff (in *Wuthering Heights*) is a rougher version; Darcy (*Pride and Prejudice*) a more refined one. Always older than the heroine, he is rich and successful in the location of his choice. Or he can be independently wealthy with some interest to which he devotes his time. He is always tall, muscular (but not muscle-bound). He is not necessarily handsome, but is above all, virile. He is usually dark, although we have seen some great Nordic types, and recently, a gorgeous redhead. Here, as with the heroine, physical descriptions and clothes are important. He is never married to anyone but our heroine, but may be widowed, and even divorced.

Plot

A Silhouette romance is not a Gothic, or a novel of suspense or adventure. Murder, gunplay, abductions, beatings, drugs, spies, and nurse-hospital novels, the occult, are out. The action should explore the relationship between the lovers. The author should get to their initial meeting, or the events that lead up to that meeting, in the first chapter. In the beginning of the book, the background material the author wishes to convey about the heroine should as much as possible be in the form of memories or flashbacks. We do not want extended initial chapters on the heroine's life before she meets our hero. After the lovers meet (as soon as possible in the story) the narrative should be sequential and straightforward.

The story usually begins with a clash between the hero and the heroine. Often this has to do with misapprehensions each has about the other. Sometimes the heroine has heard a great deal about the hero and has some reason to resent him before they actually meet, or they meet under inauspicious circumstances and the heroine is put off by the hero's ruthless, domineering and arrogant manner or the hero has formed an opinion of the heroine before he meets her.

The Other Woman:

Usually mean, over-sophisticated, well-groomed. She often catches the heroine in embarrassing situations—in a tender scene with the hero, dressed in old clothes, etc. She NEVER gets our hero.

The Other Man:

Appealing, but not assertive, egotistical in some cases. Occasionally (very seldom) a bad type. He cannot ever take the limelight from the hero. He is not as well-rounded as the hero and is often offstage throughout most of the book.

Love Scenes:

It is all right for the hero and heroine to go to bed together, although they should not make love before they are married. Bringing them to the brink of consummation and then forcing them to retreat either because of an interruption or because one or both of the lovers suffer from doubt or shame is an appropriate Silhouette device. Descriptions of lovemaking should be sensuous with some details. They cannot be limited to "he kissed her passionately." However, there are some limits to what and how it can be described. Nudity is permissible depending upon context, but it should not be too graphic. Of course, references to pain and blood are out. The only pain permitted is the sweet pain of fulfilled (or unfulfilled) desire. Above all, Silhouette love scenes should be romantic—our readers should be as in love with the hero as is the heroine.

Setting:

It is always contemporary, and preferably exotic or lush. In certain circumstances, a familiar setting works, depending on the author's ability to romanticize it. The setting should transport the reader.

Writing:

No long-winded descriptions—rather, extremely sensuous details (sense, taste, and touch are all important). Dialogue should be natural. The style, while colloquial and contemporary, should neither be slangy, obscene nor profane. Racial and religious slurs are out. Local idioms should be used sparingly and explained. We prefer a minimum of dialect. Foreign words and phrases should be used with extreme discretion.

Length:

We are asking for approximately 53-56,000 words, divided into no less than ten chapters, and no more than twelve.

Send only completed manuscripts please.

SILHOUETTE SPECIAL EDITIONS
Silhouette Special Editions are longer, more sophisticated romances, featuring realistic plots and well-developed characters. As with Silhouette Romances, these books are built around romantic tension.

The Heroine: A Special Edition is always written in the third person, but it is the heroine's point-of-view which shapes the novel. The heroine is generally 23-32 and she is intelligent and mature. Independent and accomplished, she supports herself successfully in her chosen profession and is never clinging or weepy. The heroine need not be a virgin. She accepts sex as a natural part of any loving relationship. She should be single when the book opens, but she may have been married in the past. If she is divorced, it must be clear the divorce was not her fault.

The Hero: The hero, older than the heroine, is a dynamic virile, supremely masculine man, one any woman could imagine herself falling in love with. Though he is self-confident, he also has a gentler, more vulnerable side, and may even admit to an occasional human weakness. He is never brutal or gratuitously cruel. Like the heroine, he may be a widower or divorced but he is usually single when they meet. The narrative may sometimes include the hero's point-of view in order to more fully develop his character and the plot.

Subsidiary Characters: Subsidiary characters never overshadow the hero and the heroine. They must be realistic, not stereotypical, and they often bring out the aspects of the hero and heroine that aren't evident in their relationship with each other.

The Plot: In keeping with the sophistication of these books, the plots must be complex and believable. The plot centers on the developing relationship between the hero and heroine and the problems they must overcome on their way to a happy ending. The tension comes from a real problem that has to be solved and not merely from misunderstandings. This problem should be a realistic one, and deep enough to sustain the length of the book. It's crucial that the reader feel she is being presented with real people solving real problems, yet the story should never slip from the romantic to the mundane.

These books incorporate subplots that either complement the action or play against it in some way. The subplots are an integral part of the book, should hold the reader's attention without overwhelming the romance. Silhouette Special editions are contemporary romances. Elements of mystery, suspense and the occult are inappropriate. These are not Gothics, not nurse-doctor romances or thrillers.

Love Scenes: The hero and heroine may enjoy premarital lovemaking, although the heroine should not be in any way promiscuous. The only man we see her go to bed with in the hero, and her feelings for him are always deep, even when she is unsure whether they are returned. The emphasis in the descriptions of their lovemaking is always on the sensuous and the emotional, not the graphically physical. The tone of the entire book should be romantic and sensuous, and this simply takes on increased importance in their love scenes.

Setting: American or foreign, the locale must always be interesting and appropriate setting for romance.

Length: 75,000-80,000 words

SILHOUETTE INTIMATE MOMENTS

The Intimate Moments line is designed to appeal to readers looking for a heightened feeling of romance and fantasy in a category novel. The Intimate Moments novel ought to sweep the reader away into a special world where everyday cares are forgotten in the thrill of passions which are frankly larger than life.

Heroine: The romantic heroine is the reader's entree to the story. The events of a Silhouette Intimate Moments are seen primarily through her eyes, so it is essential that she be a sympathetic character. Independent, intelligent and strong-willed, she should also be emotionally vulnerable. Though she may find herself in circumstances unfamiliar to most readers, she reacts to them in a familiar and believable way. The reader should experience her fears and joys as though at first hand.

Hero: The Intimate Moments hero is not the average boy next door. He should be a uniquely charismatic character, a man who has unusual presence and emotional strength. He may have overcome tremendous obstacles to rise to his present position; he has lived life to the fullest. He feels at home in situations, professions and life styles which the average person rarely experiences. In short, he is the man every woman dreams about in her most exciting fantasies.

Setting: The setting of a Silhouette Intimate Moments may be foreign or American, but it should seem exotic and different. The story should introduce the reader to a new world. This may be accomplished by using a glamorous, high society background, an unusual locale, or by giving the hero and/or heroine offbeat jobs.

Love Scenes: The level of sensuality should be high throughout the story. Sexual tension between hero and heroine will build until they actually make love—probably about halfway through the book. Several detailed love scenes— between the hero and the heroine only—should be included. There must be evidence of emotional commitment before they actually go to bed together.

Plot: The Intimate Moments plot centers on the romance between hero and heroine, but it may incorporate elements of adventure, suspense or melodrama. These elements must never overshadow the romance; instead, they should be used to heighten the emotional highs and lows of the developing relationship between hero and heroine. The Intimate Moments will be more action-oriented than the average romance, often dealing with life and death situations and always featuring an emotionally moving, dramatic climax. Ideally, it will elicit a few tears along the way, as well as a buoyant feeling when we learn that the two lovers will, indeed, live happily ever after.

Length: 80,000 words.

SILHOUETTE DESIRE

The Heroine: The Desire heroine is a mature, capable woman of 25-32 who has a strong sense of her own individuality and an unshakable resolve to be happy no matter what obstacles she encounters. She need not be a virgin and is definitely not a naive young girl. Rather, she is a vulnerable, sensitive woman looking for a partner to share to the fullest the joys and challenges of life

The Hero: The hero must be a realistic, believable modern man, one any woman could image herself falling ln love with. He should be strong, caring, sexy and warm. He will tend to be in his mid- to late thirties.

The Setting: Both international and American locales are encouraged, providing the setting is presented in a romantic and appealing way.

Writing Style: The writing should be extremely sensuous, providing vivid, evocative descriptions of lovemaking and concentrating on the characters' reactions to each other and the sexual tension between them.

The Plot: A Desire book centers on the developing relationship between the hero and heroine. The book should open with their meeting or the events leading up to it and end with their decision to make a lifetime commitment to one another. The tension and excitement in the book stem from the fact that neither protagonist is certain of the other's love until the end. Each scene must contribute to the process of discovery they are going through. The plot should not consist of a series of chance encounters, coincidences or filler scenes in which nothing substantial happens.

Emphasis: Desire books will emphasize innovative, unique plots, exploring realistic relationships which have been ignored up to now in other romance lines. They should depict the fears, doubts and problems, as well as the exhilarating wonder, of falling in love. Because Desire intends to mirror the real lives of modern women, marriages of convenience and similarly contrived situations are inappropriate for this line. For the same reason, realistic and detailed love scenes will be possible, providing they are tastefully handled. Sexual encounters—which may include nudity and lovemaking even when the protagonists are not married—should concentrate on the highly erotic sensations aroused by the hero's kisses and caresses rather than the mechanics of sex. A celebration of the physical pleasures of love, as well as its emotional side, should be an important part of these books.

Length: 53-56,000 words

Contemporary Gothic Tip Sheet

A Silhouette Contemporary Gothic is a romance, with elements of mystery, and an overall Gothic tone. We are not interested in historical Gothics, murder mysteries, horror or occult stories, or romantic suspense. The primary focus should be on the romance, the story centering on hero and heroine. Their meeting, or the events leading up to it, should begin in the first chapter. The tensions of their relationship should be as, if not more, important than the tensions of the intrigue and suspense, and there must always be a happy ending. The story should be told in the third person, but from the heroine's point of view. First-person narratives should be cleared with the editor.

One thing that is vitally important to Gothics—that sets them apart more than any plot device—is the quality and tone of the writing. They are written in a more elaborate fashion than the usual contemporary romances. They are more descriptive and evocative, creating mood, atmosphere, tension and oppression. The writing is extremely important and must be of the highest quality. Go to the library or second-hand bookstore and read some Gothics. The tone is similar in both contemporary and historical Gothics. This quality is essential, but don't overdo it!

The Gothic heroine need not be beautiful, though she must be presented attractively. She should be mature, perceptive—humorous, even witty if you can do it well—and should be an individual. She is not a naive Silhouette Romance heroine, but more like the heroine in a Silhouette Special Edition— accomplished and intelligent. She can be anywhere from 22-35 and can have interesting and endearing quirks.

The heroine's uncertainty as to the true nature of the hero (wondering whether he is hero or villain) and her uncertainty about her own desirability (questioning whether the hero really loves her or is just using her, thinking that there is some ulterior or sinister motive for his attentions) contribute to the suspense of the story and the romantic tension. Often the heroine's mere presence—or the fact that she is asking questions, attracting the hero, seeing something she shouldn't—poses a threat, and is enough to set the wheels of the plot in motion.

The Gothic hero is usually slightly older, enigmatic, brooding, strong. He often views life with a world-weary gaze. He sometimes seems all-seeing, knowing things about the heroine before she is even aware of them, though he has his blind spots and vulnerabilities. He has frightening elements; there may be moments when the heroine believes the hero to be the villain. There may be times when the reader isn't sure—but we shouldn't doubt whom we want to be the hero—his rugged attractiveness his occasional charm used to devastating effect, his sadness, his mystery, his wit, his appreciation of the heroine's more singular and unique features all insure that we are interested, intrigued and attracted.

The villain and/or villainess can be the "other" man or woman. There may be moments when the roles of hero/villain/other man seem interchangeable, creating doubts and tensions within the heroine's and the reader's mind—but only enough to intrigue, not so much as to distract or really confuse.

If there is a ghost or supernatural presence, it should be explained logically, or the reader should be left uncertain as to whether it existed only in a character's imagination or not.

The setting can be either American or foreign, and is usually isolated. It is either physically isolated, or because of the way the setting is presented by the author or because of the circumstances of the plot it seems isolated. Gothics tend to have a certain closed-in quality.

Jane Eyre and *Wuthering Heights* are the original Gothics—Daphne DuMaurier's *Rebecca*, the novels of Victoria Holt, Phyllis Whitney, and many others are more modern interpretations. While the Gothic genre has qualities and elements in it that must be sustained, do try for originality. Don't be trite and clichéd—no governesses, brooding houses with windows like eyes, etc.—strive for a certain freshness and imagination within the bounds of a good Gothic tale.

The intrigue is an important aspect of the story, and must be viable and believable, as well as interesting and complex. Drug smuggling, spies, cops and robbers are not appropriate plot devices for a Gothic. Gothics tend to be interior stories in which the difference between what appears to the heroine to be true and the reality of the situation is explored. The character's hidden motives, desires, dreams, fears and preconceptions are also an integral element of the plot. The heroine of *Rebecca* combats the power of her husband's past wife; many Victoria Holt heroines explore a past death or murder whose present solution not only threatens her, but alters her and the reader's conceptions of the characters. The Gothic heroine faces the tensions of both interior and exterior challenges. She resolves the conflicts between her sense of self, her sexuality, her place in the world, and her relationship with the hero.

An important difference between these Gothics and past Gothics will be the level of sensuality; these heroines can be older and should be more sexually aware. The sexual tension between hero and heroine must be intense. It is often repressed in the beginning, but when it breaks out it can be explosive. Premarital lovemaking is acceptable, though the heroine should in no way be promiscuous. Whether or not they know it, the hero and heroine's passion is a declaration of commitment, and they both hold traditional values.

The power of the emotions, the uncertainties and fears between hero and heroine, should be great. The descriptions must be sensuous and in good taste. The sensuality should be a natural expression and logical outcome of the story, given the intense emotions generated between the hero and heroine—it should not be tacked on.

70-75,000 words. Completed manuscripts please.

SILHOUETTE SHADOWS
Editorial Guidelines

In an empty house, the air thick with darkness, a woman waits alone. Her heart beats faster as she hears the creaking of the front door, and then a man's voice, soft with menace, calls out, asking if anyone is there. Is the threat in his voice for her? Or will danger turn to passion when he finds her waiting for him? Her heart begins to pound, and the blood runs hot through her veins as she prepares to confront her fate . . .

And now we at Silhouette Books invite you to join us as we embark on an exciting new publishing venture, the creation of Silhouette Shadows. These are tales from the dark side of love, designed to keep the reader on the edge of her seat as she, like the heroine, steps into the unknown, risking everything in a search that can lead to the fulfillment of love or the edge of madness, even the possibility of death. Behind every door lies danger, down every curving corridor the embodiment of fear, and even the heart of the man she loves may hide a fatal passion in place of the enduring romance she craves. The possibilities, like your imagination, are limitless.

The heroine is a strong, contemporary woman, capable of confronting and conquering the dangers that threaten her, whether physical or psychological, of the world as we know it or from beyond. She is always a match for the hero as they play out a compelling romance in the midst of a plot that may range from Gothic in tone to a woman in jeopardy story, even incorporating elements of the paranormal and moving into soft horror. The hero may represent—even personify—the danger she faces, or he may provide support and comfort in the midst of a dark and menacing world. Always, though, their ending must be a happy one, with lasting romance her reward for triumphing over darkness.

Silhouette Shadows novels are contemporary romances that explore the dark side of love, that send shivers up the spine and make the heart beat faster—from passion and from fear. These novels are atmospheric, dark, sensuous in the fullest sense of the word and always frightening. Black humor and occasional comic relief may play a role, but these are not ghostly romps or spoofs of the genre.

Classic examples that capture the tone and types of stories we envision, even if not the contemporary setting, include Mary Stewart's *Nine Coaches Waiting*. Victoria Holt's *Menfreya in the Morning* and Daphne DuMaurier's *Rebecca*

When complete, these contemporary romance manuscripts should be 70,000-75,000 words in length, and will generally be written in the third person, though first person is acceptable.

We are accepting submissions of query letters, partial manuscripts and complete manuscripts. Enclose a self-addressed, stamped postcard if you wish acknowledgment of receipt.

Leslie Wainger:
Senior Editor and Editorial Coordinator and the staff of Silhouette Books

192

St.Martin's Press Incorporated
175 Fifth Avenue
New York, N. Y., 10010-7848 .
Telephone: (212) 674-5151
Cable Address: SAlNTMART
FAX: (212) 420-9314
Editors: Hope Dellon, Barbara Anderson, Jennifer Weis, Sandra McCormack

Submission of Manuscripts to Publishers

Trade Books
Trade books, in the jargon of publishers, are books of the type that one might normally expect to find in a general bookstore. Thus, textbooks, highly technical books and manuals, and certain classes of specialized academic books would usually be excluded from the definition. The observations that follow refer primarily to trade books.

Manuscript Format
Manuscripts should be typewritten, double-spaced, with a 1 to 1.5 inch margin on 8.5 x 11, opaque white paper. The original copy, marked with author's name and address, is sent to the publisher, and a carbon copy or Xerox is retained by the author. If the manuscript is illustrated, photostats of the illustrations may be included. Original art work is retained by the author until requested by the publisher.

Selecting a Publisher
The book, *Literary Market Place*, published annually by R.R. Bowker Company, contains the names and addresses of publishers, notes on the type of material they publish and much other information useful to authors. It is available in bookstores and libraries. Librarians and bookstore clerks are familiar with the types of books put out by major publishers and may suggest appropriate publishers for particular works. A quick survey of your local bookstore or library will reveal which publishers are currently interested in cookbooks, poetry, fiction etc. Please note that St. Martin's Press does not publish juvenile books, poetry, or "formula" romance series, nor do we have any guidelines for the writing of romance or crime fiction novels.

Letter of Inquiry
After a list of "sympathetic" publishers has been compiled, a brief letter (not more than a page) is written to each, describing the manuscript, giving the author's qualifications for writing such a book, and asking if the publisher is interested. If the publisher asks to see the manuscript, he is in no way obligated to offer a contract for its publication.

Submission of Manuscript
Manuscripts of a hundred pages or so may be sent registered mail, but larger ones are more economically shipped at the special book rate. Unsolicited manuscripts (those submitted to a publisher who has not asked to see them)

should be accompanied by stamps, a money order or check to cover return postage and insurance, in case of rejection. St. Martin's will accept unsolicited manuscripts (not all publishers do), but strongly recommends that a query letter be sent first.

Waiting Period
Publishers vary in the amount of time they require to consider a manuscript. At least eight weeks should be allowed. After this period it is appropriate to write and ask if a final decision has been made.

Rejection
Of the tremendous number of manuscripts that are submitted to publishers each year, relatively few are accepted for publication. Reasons for the rejection are varied, and do not necessarily reflect the literary or practical value of the work. For instance, a publisher may reject a fine manuscript on the American Civil War because she is about to bring out another book on this subject and she prefers not to have competing books on her list. Some firms publish no poetry, others no fiction, etc. Another consideration is the sales potential of the work. Many excellent manuscripts are rejected because the demand for such books is very small. The more specialized the book, the smaller the demand for it. A long series of rejections can be very discouraging, but much time can be saved if the publishers to whom the manuscript is submitted are chosen with care.

Individual criticism of a manuscript is seldom given unless a publisher is considering offering a contract. A writer desiring professional assistance is advised to enroll in a writers' workshop at a university, or to contact an instructor in writing who may be willing to criticize the manuscript for a fee or recommend another qualified critic.

Acceptance
An editor may be very enthusiastic about a manuscript, but before a contract can be offered, the manuscript must have three or four (or often more) readings by various persons within the firm, and a specialized manuscript may be sent out to an expert in the field for evaluation. This process is a slow one, as is the entire process of publishing. Years may be spent getting a manuscript accepted by a publisher and it is advisable to count on at least another year after acceptance before the book is available in the bookstores. Contract terms vary.

Literary Agents
Most authors market their works through literary agents. Thus they are relieved of the time-consuming business of dealing with the publisher. It is sometimes as difficult for an unknown writer to engage a reputable literary agent as it is for him/her to find a publisher, since agents work on a percentage of the monies earned by the actual published book, and make nothing on a manuscript which they can not place for publication. Names of reputable literary agents may be obtained from **The Authors Guild, Inc.**, 234 West 44th Street, New York, NY 10036 or **The Society of Author's Representatives**, 40 East 49th Street, New York, NY 10017.

Thomas Bouregy & Company Inc.
Avalon Books
401 Lafayette Street
New York, NY 10003
Telephone: (212) 598-0222 • (800) 223-5251
FAX: (212) 979-1862
AVALON BOOKS/AIRMONT CLASSICS
Barbara J. Brett
Vice President/Publisher
Editor: Suzanne Rose, Avalon Books

Writers Guidelines

Under its AVALON BOOKS imprint, Thomas Bouregy & Co., Inc., publishes hardcover secular romances and westerns for the library market. Our books are wholesome adult fiction, suitable for family reading. There is no graphic or premarital sex or sexual tension in any of our novels; kisses and embraces are as far as our characters go. It is the author's responsibility to heighten the romantic atmosphere by developing love scenes with tenderness, emotion, and perception. The heroines of the romances and the heroes of the westerns should be looking forward to marriage at the end of the book. There is never any profanity in any of our books.

We publish sixty books a year in bimonthly cycles of ten. A cycle consists of two career romances, two mystery romances, four general romances, and two westerns. All the romances are contemporary; all the westerns are historical. The important action in all the books takes place over a relatively short period of time, ranging from days to no longer than a year. Books range in length from a minimum of 40,000 words to a maximum of 50,000 words (usually about 160 to 210 manuscript pages).

ROMANCES
General Information: We do not want old-fashioned, predictable, formulaic books. We are looking for contemporary characters and fresh, contemporary plots and storylines. Supporting characters and subplots should be interesting and realistic, and they should add an extra and interesting dimension to the book.

Heroines: Every AVALON heroine should be an independent young woman with an interesting profession or career. She is equal to the stresses of today's world and can take care of herself, yet she remains feminine and loyal to traditional values; when he comes along, the man she loves will take priority in her life, just as she will take priority in his. She is American, in her mid-twenties, and has never been married (no widows or divorcees, please!).

Heroes: AVALON heroes should be warm, likable, realistic, sympathetic, understanding men who treat the heroine as an equal, with respect for her intelligence and individuality, and with courtesy. The rude, overbearing, patronizing, egotistical, brooding, macho men and Heathcliff types are not welcome in AVALON romances; they make very poor models for husbands—and men—in today's world. AVALON heroes are in their late twenties to early thirties (the age gap between the hero and the heroine should be no more than three to six years), and though it is preferable that they have never been married, they may be widowed or divorced (but, of course, in the case of divorce, the ex-wife must be the party who was at fault).

MYSTERY ROMANCES: The heroine is always the protagonist in a mystery romance, and though she and the hero should work together to solve the mystery, she should be the major force in unraveling it. The element of suspense is very important, but it is equally important to avoid contrived, predictable, and mechanical plots and the old cliches. Murder, of course, is often a necessary part of a mystery, but avoid long, gory descriptions. Remember that these are mystery romances; pay careful attention to the development of the love interest.

CAREER ROMANCES: The only difference between a romance and a career romance is that the plot of the career romance is centered around the heroine's job. We want these novels to explore the many exciting professions open to women today. They must be carefully researched so that all background information is authentic. It is all right for a career romance to straddle categories and have a mystery plot.

WESTERNS

General Information: All westerns are historical novels, and it is important that they be placed in that time and that the background be carefully researched. Avoid using words and phrases that were not part of the language at the time your western is set. Plots should be suspenseful and action packed, but vivid descriptions of the gory details of violence are to be avoided. Suitable, believable euphemisms for profane words (including "hell" and "damn") must be used. Though it is important for flavor and authenticity to use some westernisms in dialogue ("pardner" and the dropping of the final "g" in present participles, for example), overuse of dialect is to be avoided; it slows down the reader's pace and, as a result, the narrative pace too. During the course of the story the hero must find himself drawn to, and ultimately fall in love with, a virtuous, but independent, young woman who will add a new and fine dimension to his life; at the end he will propose marriage to her and she will accept.

Heroes: The hero must be a strong individual with sound values: He's excellent with his fists and a gun, but not overeager to resort to either. He is unmarried and in his late twenties to early thirties.

General Tips For All AVALON Books
Substitute suitable, believable euphemisms in all instances where profanity (including "damn" and "hell") might be used. Make similar substitutions for

"Oh, God!", "My God!", etc.

Be sure the story and the characters sound contemporary in all details: For example, today's young women do not use handkerchiefs and they open their own car doors.

Be sure dialogue sounds realistic and contemporary: Avoid using old-fashioned words and phrases (When was the last time you actually heard someone in real life say, "Very well," unless he was referring to his health?) and old-fashioned mannerisms. For example, all young people these days address each other by first names after introduction; they do not call each other "Miss Jones" and "Mr. Smith" until granted permission to do otherwise.

Avoid all use of dialect. It is sufficient to note that someone speaks with an accent or twang.

Avoid long descriptions and repetitive descriptions: If you have told us a character has blue eyes once, there is no need repeat that detail every time his or her eyes are mentioned.

Avoid stereotypes in both major and minor characters. Pay attention to transitions and keep them smooth. Check all facts carefully; research is extremely important. Pay strict attention to spelling and grammar.

In attributing dialogue, always place the noun before the verb ("Mary said," not "said Mary"). Also, use varied and interesting verbs that denote speaking; no one can nod, smile, laugh, sigh, snort, grunt, or grin dialogue, and no one can hiss a sentence or word that doesn't have S sounds.

Remember that editors must read thousands of manuscripts and proposals a year. Please facilitate this for us by using a dark typewriter ribbon and by making all corrections clear and easy to understand. All submissions, whether proposals or complete manuscripts, must be typed with double spaces between the lines.

Submissions: We prefer to see the first chapter and a brief summary of the rest of the book; however, if you have a complete manuscript that you are positive fits all our requirements, you may send it in. If you are submitting a complete manuscript, please include a one-page summary of the story with it. Please be sure to include a stamped, self-addressed envelope for the return of your material if it is not suited to our needs. Because of the vast number of manuscripts and proposals we receive, it takes at least three months to report. We do not accept simultaneous submissions.

Payment: We pay an advance of $600 for the first book, $800 for the second, and $1,000 for subsequent books. The advance is paid against the first 3,500 copies sold. (Our initial run is 2,100 copies.) A royalty of ten percent is paid on any additional sales. The first half of the advance is paid within two weeks after signing of the contract, the rest within thirty days after publication.

See **Suggested Reading** list on following page—

Suggested Reading

Romances
YESTERDAY'S DREAMS- Alice Sharpe
IN LOVE'S OWN SWEET TIME- Audery Lazier
THE RUNAWAY HEART- Anne Ladley
THIS TIME, FOR ALWAYS- Holly S. McClure

Career Romances
PRESCRIPTION FOR LOVE- Anne Ladley
LOVE ON TRIAL- Wendy Martin
PROGRAMMED FOR DANGER- Karen G. McCullough
HARVEST OF LOVE- Nancy Sheehan
WHERE THE HEART SEEKS SHELTER- Anne Ladley
A STORYBOOK LOVE- Alice Sharp

Mystery Romances
DANGEROUS ODYSSEY- Jane Edwards
THE NIGHT PROWLERS- Karen G. McCullough
THE VANISHING BRIDEGROOM- Alice Sharp
THE DARK SIDE OF PARADISE- Alma Blair
SECRETS OF ECHO MOON- Jill Gienke

Westerns
DEAD MAN'S WALK- Lee Martin
DEVIL'S RAIDERS- Clifford Blair
TRAIL OF THE LONG RIDERS- Lee Martin
RAID AT BLACK PERSIMMON BLUFF- Howard Pelham
THE RUINATION OF DAN BECKER- Robin Gibson

Warner Books
Time & Life Building
1271 Avenue of the Amencas
New York, NY 10020
(212) 522-7200
Editors: Karen Kelly, Jeanne Tiedge, Joann Davis, Jamie Rabb, Susan Suffes

Thank you for your interest in Warner Books. Since our historical and contemporary romances are not written to any formula, we do not have a tip sheet. We look for well-plotted sensual love stories between likable characters in a realistic and interesting setting.

The best way to familiarize yourself with the sorts of books various publishers prefer is to read their recent releases, so you may want to look at some of our books to see if your work is similar to them in tone and theme.

If you decide to submit your work to Warner, please send a query letter describing your novel and any writing experience you might have. Our editors can thus decide if the novel sounds suitable for our list before they ask to see any of the manuscript. Please address your query letter to the particular editor you believe best suited to review your work.

Although we in no way wish to discourage you from submitting your work, we believe you should know we have not recently acquired any women's fiction from unpublished authors. Our desire to discover fresh talent remains firm, but, unfortunately, the current market and our own full inventory limit our ability to aggressively promote new authors.

For your information, the Popular Library imprint has been dissolved; we are no longer accepting submissions for that line.

Good luck with your writing!

Zebra Books/Kensington Publishing Corp.
475 Park Avenue south
New York, NY 10016
Telephone: (212) 889-2299 • FAX (212) 779-8073
Editors: Ann La Farge, Beth Lieberman, Monica Harris, Jennifer Sawyer,
Tracy Bernstein, Elise Donner, Denise Little

TO LOVE AGAIN
Tip Sheet: For a new series of novels about women in the prime of life

We are actively seeking and acquiring manuscripts for this new series of
books about women forty-five and older. Initially, we'd like to look at a short (2-
4 pages) synopsis of your plot line; then, as quickly as possible, we'll let you know
if we'd like to see more—a fuller synopsis, chapters, or the whole manuscript if
it's already written.

In order to clarify what it is that we're looking for, we've prepared the
following general guidelines to let you know what we want—and what we don't
want. Manuscripts should be 110,000 words in length.

What We Want:
First and foremost, a strong, interesting woman who has recently lost the
man to whom she's been married for all of her adult life, either through death,
divorce, or "the other woman." Now, she has to rebuild that life. It will be hard,
but she never falters in her passage forward. . . and she never gives in to
discouragement, though the obstacles in her path are many.

An inspirational, upbeat tone that says, from the very beginning and
throughout all the struggles, that a woman's life doesn't end when she loses her
spouse, and that it is possible to make room in her life for another man.
Essentially, the heroine of our novels is experiencing not only a loss, but also
a new beginning—a spiritual, sexual, and personal rebirth.

A progression, throughout the novel, of the heroine's hopeful struggle for
independence, confidence, and reborn sexuality. We want to see our heroine
take over the reins herself in many areas:

Financial: Perhaps she has never had to handle money before; her husband
always did it. At first she is baffled, but in the course of the story, she learns how
—and finds that she's good at it!

Social: Her friends were "his" or "ours"—rarely hers. Now, as a single woman, she
finds (perhaps after some initial trepidation) that there are lots of ways to meet new
people—especially new men. Traveling (especially cruises), reunions, visits to
friends,community interests, the gym, sports (how about that silver-haired tennis
partner?) a new job . . . maybe she even meets a man through her adult children—
perhaps the widowed or divorced father of one of their new love interests.

Professional: Our heroine is a woman of intellectual resources, though
perhaps she's never had to use them to earn a living or to fulfill a life of her own.

Now—on her own again—she can go back to school and get that degree; take that course at the local college (also a great place to meet men!), polish up that resume . . . and give those Baby Boomers some stiff competition in the workplace.

We've saved the most important for last. SEX. There are exceptions, of course, but our heroine has, most likely, had sex with only one man in her life: her husband. Maybe it was glorious, maybe only cozy, but now she's faced with the challenge of going to bed with another man. She's scared, maybe; certainly, she's apprehensive; and she's a bit confused: the rules have changed drastically since she was a girl. Our heroine will handle this challenge gracefully and with great panache. She may have to weave a few fantasies first, and it may take a bit of courage the first time but . . . she makes it.

And remember: the new man in her life doesn't have to become her second husband. Maybe he's not Mr. Right. By now, she's confident of her powers. She knows there'll be lots of chances, lots of men. She reached an age that is not a marker that means "this way to the end," as Gail Sheehy recently pointed out, "but a gateway to a second adulthood."

What We Don't Want:

Recycled stories of contemporary romance with a couple of decades tacked on to the heroine's age.

Stories about women who are depressed, downbeat, or pessimistic about their ability to forge a new life.

Hastily-written, category-type stories that trivialize the very real experience of starting all over again at midlife.

Stories that emphasize the physical ills of midlife: menopause (please, no hot flashes!), thickening middles, wrinkles.

You don't have to be young to fall in love, and you don't have to be middle-aged to write a book for this series. We look forward to hearing from you.

Send synopsis, with a SASE, to:

Ann La Farge, Senior Editor

Romantic Times Magazine
55 Bergen Street
Brooklyn, NY 11201
Telephone: (718) 237-1097
FAX: (718) 624-4231

Romantic Times Presents a New Line That's a First!
Lady Barrow's Secret Library
A Collection of Novels Based on Women's Romantic and Sensual Fantasies
An imprint to launch in the Fall of 1996

Guidelines
Style: Sexual fantasies for women written by women.

Word Count: Circa 90-100,000 words. Approximately 12-15 chapters.

Setting: Historical and Contemporary.

Tip: Concentrate on the "upscale." Women like to dream about being rich and affording luxuries, therefore their sexual fantasies are in exotic or beautiful places. Passion and love in a leaky cold hovel is not necessarily dreamy unless there's a darn good reason, i.e. plot point! American settings such as Aspen or Santa Fe are two of the few places in the USA that seem to evoke an erotic setting. Otherwise, distant places and time settings work best.

Sub-Genre Categories: Four categories are being sought:
Historical—Contemporary—Mystery/Thriller—Paranormal/New Reality (No science fiction)

Tone: Cheerful, exciting, adventurous, sexual, frank, unforgettable. (After all, sexual liberation is fun and oh so healthy!)

Story Content: The exploration of human sexual activity centered on emotions and mechanics. Although primary relationship should be monogamous (once they bond), prior to that and during an agreed upon separation, multi-experimental relations are acceptable. Readers want strong emotions, i.e. solid story, to accompany sexual build up and climaxes.

Characters: Hero can be the perfect lover because this is a work of fiction. He is trustworthy, therefore she will happily and willingly go all the way sexually, experiencing eroticism to the fullest. Female is always in control, working on/or living out sexual fantasies. Even when not, she could be! Villainy, a *frisson* of terror, is acceptable as an aphrodisiac, depending on the plot. Reader must care about the characters and American readers, particularly, enjoy commitment.

Storyline: Along with exploring authentic sexual fantasies, these books are also "info-fiction." Reader should be given some background on a career, hobby, or special interest. (Example: Opening a bed and breakfast, running an established business, starting a specialty food line, learning about antiques or dealing with mental, sexual, or health problems.)

Characters and Sexuality: Good wholesome main characters and sex, with plenty of reasons and opportunities to indulge. All of which leads to happy people! Detailed descriptions of sexual activity. Stress long, teasing build-ups with increasingly exciting passages that lead to a climactic moment. Readers must become aroused. Only tasteful acts and vocabulary, befitting female fantasy.

Action: Story should be adaptable to film so think TV/video as you write. (Tip: A long walk in the woods while daydreaming is boring film!)

Submission (of Manuscript!!): First 15 pages and a synopsis (no more than 5 pages) plus SASE. Include a self-addressed postcard to confirm the MS was received. You will receive an answer and a check-sheet that will rate your work within 6 weeks.

Will a Written Evaluation Help You Understand Your Rating Sheet Results? We do not have the woman-power handling this contest to suggest lengthy changes or give you counsel for your sensual "partial." The rating sheet that will be returned with your submission within six weeks is just that; something that our editors check off to let you know how you stand for the contest.

If you want more direction, we do have an editor as part of our manuscript evaluation service who will return a written personal critique of your submission, if you would like detailed information on how your manuscript can be developed, improved and/or polished for this sub-genre.

Send a check for $20 (or charge it to your credit card) and include it with your submission. Payable to Romantic Times.

Editor's Note: Marketing research shows an existing niche for a new women's sensual fiction line.

1) Men have had erotic literature to feed and flame their fantasies, now it's the women's time. Except for very sexy historicals, women do not.

2) Many women still feel sexually repressed and are beginning to realize it's healthy to be sexually liberated.

3) Many women have an embarrassment about liking men's bodies. They need to feel it's permissible to be aroused by a virile male.

4) The danger of AIDS helps make the idea of "just fantasizing" significantly more attractive to everyone. (Safe sex.)

5) Certain deeds and "obscene" words will spoil the fantasy for female readers unless carefully orchestrated. Most women know which ones they are.

Important Names and Addresses

(NOTE: Companies do move, so be sure to verify that any of the following are still at the same address.)

Writers' Organizations:

The Authors Guild, Inc.
330 West 42nd Street
New York, NY 10036-6902
212-563-5904   FAX 212-564-5363

The Authors Guild is the the oldest and largest of the authors organizations. You must be a published author (or have a book contract in hand) to join the Authors Guild. The book must be published by an established publisher within the last seven years. For short fiction or non-fiction, you must have been published by a periodical of general circulation in the past eighteen months. First year dues are $90 but after that the dues are based on annual writing income:

Writing Income	Dues
under $25,000	$90
$25,000 - $49,999	$150
$50,000 - $100,000	$300
over $100,000	$500

In exchange for your dues, you get:

1. A legal review of your publishing contract *before* it's signed, including tips on negotiation strategies.
2. Seminars and information on the latest developments in publishing.
3. Business advice.
4. Information on publishing mergers and bankruptcies and how they affect writers.
5. Professional, legal and accounting advice.
6. A sample of a recommended trade book contract along with a guide explaining each clause.
7. Opportunities to attend social and professional events.
8. Choice of health, hospitalization, dental and life insurance plans.
9. Their quarterly bulletin.
10. On-line services.

The Guild will intervene in publishing disputes. They lobby on behalf of authors at the local and national levels when it comes to copyright, taxation and freedom of expression. The Guild currently has over 6,700 members who write in all genres.

National Writers Union
873 Broadway
Suite 203
New York, NY 10003-1209
Phone 212-254-0279
FAX 212-254-0673

337 17th Street, #101
Oakland, CA 94612
Phone 510-839-0110
FAX 510-839-6097

This is a labor union for freelance writers—dues are based on writing income—and other publishing professionals and unpublished writers as well. There are over 4,000 members. To be eligible to join, you must have published a book, play, three articles, five poems, one short story (pick one) or an equivalent amount of newsletter, publicity, technical, commercial, government or institutional copy. You are also eligible for membership if you have written an equal amount of unpublished material and you are actively writing and attempting to publish your work.

The NWU provides members with resource materials such as: "preferred" literary agent agreements; guides to book contracts, electronic rights, small claims court, journalism contracts; using the Internet, etc. They hold special events, seminars and workshops. They can issue press credentials, file grievances on your behalf, have a database about agents, have group health insurance and discounts on such things as car rentals and delivery services. They also publish a quarterly journal, *The American Writer.*

Novelists, Inc.
P. O. Box 1166
Mission, KS 66222

This is an organization for writers of popular fiction. To join you must have published at least two novels, one of them within the last five years prior to your application for membership. Membership gives you instant access to other member writers—most of whom are full-time writers and who are willing to share their expertise and experience. They also produce a monthly newsletter, *Novelists' INK,* for the professional writer (no how-to articles). And they have a rotating annual conference (a different location each time) that is four days of casual networking and roundtable discussions with members, editors and agents. This conference is open to members only.

If you join, then you must also agree to have your name and a mailing address published in the membership roster, which remains confidential. Annual dues are $50.00 with a one-time application fee of $25.00. The actual number of members is not known, but probably under five hundred. The organization also works to better the status of popular fiction writers as a whole, networks with other writers' organizations, and provides support and information.

Romance Writers of America (RWA)
Suite 315
13700 Veterans Memorial Drive
Houston, TX 77014
713-440-6885
FAX 713-440-7510

Joining this organization is a must! And you do not have to be a published author to join! RWA has 7,800 members worldwide, with 150+ chapters in the United States and Canada. <u>"If you're seriously pursuing a writing career in romance or romantic fiction, this is the place for you."</u> Annual membership fee is $60 plus a $10 processing fee. If you live too far from a chapter, for an additional $20, they have an Outreach chapter, for networking by mail.

The RWA publishes a monthly *Romance Writers' Report*, full of in-depth articles, market news, notices of members, forthcoming books, upcoming contests, conferences, etc.

If you are a published author, there is a subgroup called Published Authors Network (PAN); joining is no extra charge. Any RWA member can receive the PAN bimonthly newsletter for an additional $20. The newsletter, *PANdora's Box*, has hard-hitting issue-oriented news and opinions by PAN members.

There are also chapters for specific fields of interest: The Beau Monde (Regency); Mystery/Suspense; Young Adult; Futuristic, Fantasy and Paranormal; On-Line CompuServe forum; Published Authors' Special Interest.

The RWA annual conference is something a writer definitely should attend. They offer five days of workshops for writers of all levels, and opportunities to meet and network with agents, editors, and other writers. They have an awards ceremony where the Golden Heart award is presented to *unpublished* writers, the RITA award to those romance/romantic novels judged the best in their field, and the Favorite Book of the Year award, voted on by the membership.

Here's a listing of the upcoming RWA annual conferences:

July 10-14, 1996
The Wyndham-Anatole Hotel
2201 Stemmons Freeway
Dallas, Texas

July 30-August 3, 1997
Marriott's Orlando World Center Resort
8701 World Center Drive
Orlando, Florida 32821

July 29 - August 2, 1998
Anaheim Hilton and Towers
Anaheim, California

July 28-August 1, 1999
Sheraton Harbor Island Resort
San Diego, California

July 26-30, 2000
Sheraton Washington Hotel
Washington, D.C.

July 18-22, 2001
Sheraton New Orleans Hotel
New Orleans, Lousiana

Large blocks of rooms are reserved for conference attendees: you must register with the RWA and receive special paperwork to get the lower conference room rates.

Other RWA benefits include a Professional Relations Committee, sort of a Better Business Bureau for members to check out agents and editors. They also send a team each year to meet with publishing industry officials to discuss issues of vital concern to authors, such as poor availability of print run, reserve against returns, sellthrough information, forced use of pseud-onyms, erosion of author royalties, and other detrimental business practices.

Members gather in local chapters for networking and for critiquing—RWA members will read and comment on each other's work and offer advice, discuss the latest in romance publishing, what the editors have to say, etc. Chapters are often a mix of published and unpublished writers. The RWA allows you to attend two chapter meetings for free, to sample how the organization works, before you are required to join. The over 130 chapters are spread throughout North America and Canada, according to regions. The lists and maps below will let you figure out what region you live in. The RWA main headquarters can provide you with the name, address and phone of the person in charge of the closest chapter to your location.

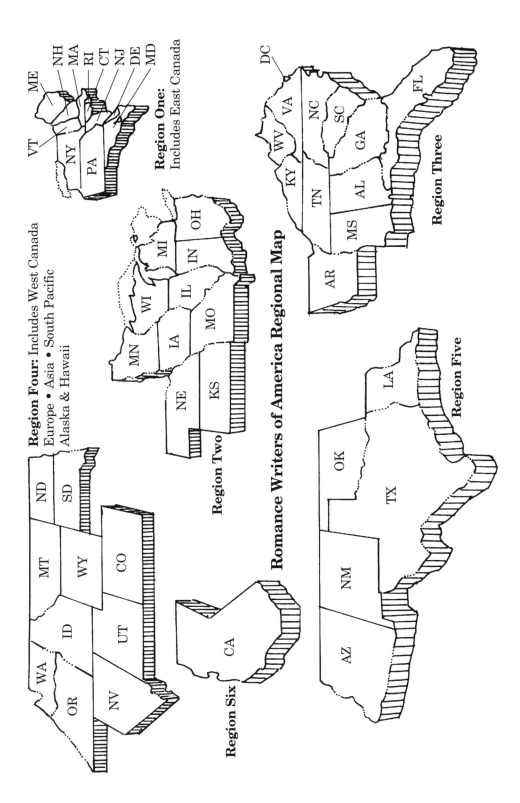

Region One:
Includes East Canada

Region Four: Includes West Canada
Europe • Asia • South Pacific
Alaska & Hawaii

Region Two

Region Three

Region Six

Region Five

Romance Writers of America Regional Map

Sisters in Crime
P. O. Box 442124
Lawrence, KA 66044

Founded in 1986, Sisters in Crime is open to "all persons worldwide who have a special interest in mystery writing." They have approximately 2,600 members comprised of writers, readers, editors, agents, booksellers and librarians. There is a quarterly newsletter, a membership directory, regional chapters, networking, a speakers bureau, and annual gatherings. A biannual catalogue of members' works is sent to over 4,400 wholesalers, distributors, bookstore chains, mystery bookstores, libraries, and periodicals. Annual dues are $25.

Western Writers of America
Box 29, Star Route
Encampment, WY 82325

This is an association of professional writers involved in preserving and celebrating the heritage of the American West, past and present. There are over 550 members throughout the United States and in several foreign countries, including writers of books, periodicals, newspapers, screenplays, and other media, as well as historians. Non-writers can also join if a substantial portion of their work concerns the West (publishers, booksellers, artists, film producers, etc.). There's an annual convention with awards (held in June each year), the *Roundup* Magazine, a membership directory, etc. Annual dues are $60.

Writers Guild of America, East, Inc.
555 West 57th St.
New York, NY 10119
212-767-7800

Writers Guild of America, West
8955 Beverly Boulevard
Los Angeles, California 90048
310-550-1000
Registration office
310-205-2540

The WGA is for screenwriters. You can't join unless you have sold a screenplay to an accredited motion picture union member. However, the WGA does provide a valuable service: they will formally register your screenplay or teleplay within its own records and thereby give it a measure of protection (in addition to your copyrighting it). You can register a complete script or a treatment. Contact the WGA first and they will send you the proper form to fill out, along with instructions. You can then send a copy of the material to be registered, along with a check for $20.00, to either location.

Scripters don't sell their work to the WGA but to producers, directors, et. al., who are (with rare exception) union members of different guilds.

Magazines, Newsletters:

Publishers Weekly
249 West 17th Street
New York, NY 10011

This is a weekly magazine to the publishing trade. Currently the subscription is something like $150, so subscribers are usually professionals in the field. It covers all the latest trends and what publishers are doing, through articles and ads, lists all the current bestsellers in fiction, non-fiction, audio, etc. It also has an extensive book review section but is choosy when it comes to reviewing romances, though it periodically does a detailed examination of the romance genre. With any luck, your local library will carry it.

Romantic Times Magazine
55 Bergen Street
Brooklyn, NY 11201
718-237-1097
FAX 718-624-4231

This is the bible of the romance industry and a <u>must</u> subscription. *RT* is monthly: $30 for six months or $60 for one year of 1st-Class delivery, or $21 and $42 respectively for 4th-Class. Canadian rates are $33 for six months, $66 for one year, delivery in approximately one week. Single issues are $4.00, $5 for Canada.

The magazine covers all aspects of romance publishing: historical, mainstream, mystery, science fiction/fantasy, Regency, and series lines such as all those published by Harlequin, Silhouette, etc. There are numerous articles about: writers; books; profiles of editors, agents, and publishers; information, reference material, writing tips; networking among readers, on-line, bookstores, etc. Also extensive reviews, with ratings, which are very informative.

RT holds an annual convention, which everyone interested in getting published should go to. This convention is well attended by writers, agents, and editors. Workshops, seminars, a book fair, an awards ceremony, parties, etc., go on all day and evening. In addition, you can make appointments to meet directly with agents and editors. Publishers, booksellers, and readers all have their own hospitality suites. There, current books are on display, and you can meet editors and well-known writers as well as get all sorts of information "from the horse's mouth." Every night there is an open house as well as publishers' parties; these are free.

October 31- November 3, 1996

The *RT* convention will be held in Baton Rouge, LA.. The convention cost is $350, which covers all seminars, the book fair, meals and all social events. The hotel rooms are $75 a night for a single and only $10 for each additional person in the room up to a total of four people. You can't get a room unless you are first registered for the convention.

There are all-day workshops and seminars for aspiring writers, readers, and booksellers. An all-day Romance Summit is planned for published authors. VIPs from every aspect of the industry will assemble to discuss the state of the romance industry. Although it is designed for published authors, it is open to anyone who wants to learn about the business of publishing.

For entertainment, there is a costume competition, a masquerade dinner party, a cover model pageant, and a dinner and dance party.

RT also sponsors local workshops, seminars and lectures. And they have a separate evaluation service that reads and analyzes romance manuscripts.

Agents' Organizations:

The Association of Authors' Representatives, Inc.
10 Astor Place
3rd Floor
New York, NY 10030
212-353-3709

The AAR is an organization for literary agents. If you send them a check for $5.00, along with a self-addressed stamped (currently 55 cents) legal-size envelope, you will receive a list of their member agents, a copy of the Canon of Ethics, and a brochure describing the role of agents and how to obtain an agent. The AAR will also answer letters on a variety of topics, if you include a self-addressed stamped envelope. However, they will not answer any questions about which agents handle what kinds of manuscripts (they recommend looking at *Literary Market Place* instead), nor will they tell you what agency handles a specific author. If you call their phone number, you will get a recording with this same information, so writing is recommended.

The Corporate Society of Authors' Representatives, Inc. (COSAR)
1627 Geneva Street, # 102
Aurora, CO 80010
303-367-0875
Reynauld Cinocco, Director
Zo Anderson, Vice President
Gwen Foss

This is *not* an agents' organization but a *referral* service for writers looking for agents. Its purpose is to "find proper, competent and reliable representation for talented individuals." Writers pay COSAR a fee, listed below, and in return receive information about which agencies are looking for the writer's type of book. COSAR stays in contact with many literary agencies, large and small, and updates their information on agency preferences on a quarterly basis. Therefore they are in an excellent position to steer authors toward those agencies that are most likely to be interested in their work.

COSAR also offers advice on an author's proposal format and what peripheral information might be included that will help get an author noticed. For the one-time fee, clients receive a list of agencies looking for their category of work, usually from two to ten. COSAR claims a very good success rate: approximately half of their clients find agents with their help.

<u>COSAR Referral Fees</u> *
Beginners	$20 - $50
Experienced	$50 - $250
Professionals	$250 - $500
Celebrities	$500 - $1500

*Placing scriptwriters (or actors, musicians, etc.) with WGA (Writers Guild of America) or SAG (Screen Actor's Guild) franchised agents may involve more expense, so the above literary fees may not apply.

Other Important Addresses:

Library of Congress
Office of Copyrights
Washington, DC 20559

Your publisher probably will copyright your published book, so you won't have to worry about that. But keep this address handy for any questions that might arise.

Social Security Administration
Department of Health and Human Services
Baltimore, Maryland 21235

The Society for Creative Anachronism
P. O. Box 360789
Milpitas, CA 95036-0789
FAX 408-263-0641

If you are interested in historical or fantasy romances, this is the group to join (many science fiction and fantasy writers turn out to be members of the SCA as well). The SCA is a non-profit educational organization dedicated to recreating the Middle Ages. They have an extensive list of small and inexpensive publications on a wide variety of subjects—tapestry, calligraphy, chain mail, brewing, clothing, customs, and all aspects of Medieval life in various countries—which are essential for research. Members can attend innumerable events, but you must be in appropriate costume. There is an SCA gathering held just about every weekend throughout the U.S. and Canada. A bimonthly newsletter lists all the events. In addition, members are divided into kingdoms and shires, depending on where they live, and local shires meet periodically to arrange their own events, put on demonstrations, practice for tournaments, and learn about various arts and sciences appropriate to the period.

Every August, there is a huge convention/gathering known as "Pensic," held in western Pennsylvania. Somewhere between five and twenty thousand members pitch tents or build small buildings to either display their wares or just make merry.

Membership is $30 annually.

Writers!

Do You Want More Info About Publishers And Editors?

The *Out-To-Lunch Market Report* is a bimonthly newsletter that tells you what's selling now!

• What's happening today in the publishing industry • What is selling in bookstores • What the editors are looking for now • Hard facts about contracts • The impact of literary legal cases • Which publishers are doing what kinds of books • The magazine markets • What movie and television producers want • Trends in Publishing • Inside gossip • Tips on submitting and selling your work • Genres • Conventions • Commentary and opinion

The *Out-To-Lunch Market Report* is compiled by Sharon Jarvis, a literary agent, editor, packager, publisher, and author with 26 years experience—and a former acquistions editor at Doubleday, Ballantine, Ace, Playboy and Popular Library. She is the author of 9 published books, fiction and non-fiction. As an agent she sold hundreds of books of all types, both here and abroad. Her multimedia corporation, Toad Hall, Inc., also publishes fiction and non-fiction under numerous imprints.

Acknowledgments: Cover design and interior pages by Steven Dale. This book was designed on a Macintosh™ Quadra 630, using a UMAX™ Vista S8 scanner and a DELTIS™ Olympus external optical drive. All graphics were manipulated in ADOBE™ Photoshop, Text and page layout was done in Page Maker™. Body copy is 10pt New Century Schoolbook, chapter titles and boxed copy is Avant Garde. Display fonts are Arquitectura, Laser, and Corvinus Skyline.

Steven's print media services can be reached at:
dale1dr@aol.com or by writing to:
Steven Dale
23420 Happy Valley Dr.
Newhall CA 91321